CHRISTIAN ENGLAND

Born in 1929, David L. Edwards was educated at the King's School, Canterbury, and after reading history at Oxford was elected a Fellow of All Souls College. He later taught in the Divinity Faculty at Cambridge, where he was Dean of King's College.

He is the author of more than a dozen books but has, however, been chiefly occupied with his work as a clergyman of the Church of England. For eight years he was Editor and Managing Director of the SCM Press, and later he returned to London for another eight years to serve as Sub-Dean of Westminster Abbey, Rector of St Margaret's, the Speaker's Chaplain in the House of Commons, and Chairman of Christian Aid. He became Dean of Norwich in 1978. Married, David Edwards has a son and three daughters.

David L. Edwards

CHRISTIAN ENGLAND

ITS STORY TO THE REFORMATION

Collins
FOUNT PAPERBACKS

. Durham Cathedral from the river Wear .

First published in 1981 by
William Collins Sons & Co Ltd, London
Published, with corrections, by
Fount Paperbacks, London in 1982

Printed in Great Britain by
Richard Clay (The Chaucer Press) Ltd,
Bungay, Suffolk

To the people who are now
the cathedral and diocese
of Norwich

Contents

Preface

This book which ends with the Reformation in the 1540s tells the story of almost a thousand years of English Christianity, with its Roman and Celtic prelude, and so far as I know no other book covers the same field in the same way. Although I have tried to base myself on scholarship as it stands in 1982 I am writing for readers who are not professional historians. I have paid more attention to people, to literature, architecture, art, and prayer, and to the Church's setting in the social and political life of the age, than to ecclesiastical administration or theological controversy. I realize how incomplete my presentation is, but I believe that it matters that we should appreciate the impact which the Christian religion has made on the lives and imaginations of the English people.

The reason is not only that history can be enjoyable. Those who live in countries where the English language is spoken but the English culture is distant (and perhaps becoming more distant each year) still need to assess the significance of the English element in their heritage. Those who find it impossible to accept Christianity's doctrinal claims, and find much that is dubious in its traditional ethics, can still be enriched by entry into the experience of the very long period when to be English (or European) automatically meant to be a member of the Christian Church. Those who are preoccupied by the many challenges to Christianity arising within the modern world can still be inspired by a more thorough familiarity with Christians of the past – and by a more honest recognition that these men and women lived in a world of struggles and often gross imperfections, not in stained glass windows. And those who are members of Churches divided from others at the Reformation or later can still find a unity in acknowledging a common background: the years which passed between the arrival of Christianity in Roman Britain and the arrival of Protestantism. We can all make discoveries in trying to do justice to the people of those centuries, instead of staying trapped in prejudice and propaganda. There is surely something impressive in the courage of these long-dead people in serving the vision which they had seen and surely we can grant this without sharing their vision to the full. I hope that I have at least succeeded in showing how false it is to say, with the author of a recent history of England, that 'the truth is that the English are not, and never have been, a religious people' (Paul Johnson, *The Offshore Islanders*, London, 1972, p.164).

I have explained technical terms as I have gone along, and my main purpose in mentioning recent books and articles has been to recommend some which contain abundant clues for further work. I am deeply grateful to the scholars whose laborious researches and reflections form the basis of this simple story, and am specially conscious of my debt to those who taught me history at Magdalen College, Oxford, some thirty years ago. I want to thank some institutions as well as books and teachers – Canterbury Cathedral and its King's School, where I was a boy; All Souls College, Oxford, and King's College, Cambridge, where I had the honour and stimulus of being a Fellow; Westminster Abbey, which I served for seven and a half privileged years; and Norwich Cathedral, which has welcomed my family and me with such friendship and has given its Dean some time for his own work. I have not used my life in full-time historical work, as I once thought I would; rightly or wrongly I have felt the present and the future to be too important, and anyone who is curious to know why may consult my book *A Reason to Hope* (1978). But I could never feel myself completely cut off from the centuries which created these colleges and churches where I have lived. Although incapable of poetry I have shared T. S. Eliot's experience:

> while the light fails
> On a winter's afternoon, in a secluded chapel
> History is now and England.

I must also thank my always encouraging publisher, Lady Collins, the Oxford University Press, New York, which honours me by publishing the American edition, and my secretary, Miss Jean Cooper, who patiently typed successive drafts.

The Deanery, Norwich   D. L. E.

Part One

THE FIRST ENGLAND

CHAPTER ONE

PRELUDE: ROMANS AND CELTS

An impression of the Roman church at Silchester.

ENGLAND BEFORE THE ENGLISH

The Anglo-Saxon tribesmen who started to occupy England less than four hundred years after the birth of Christ retained the values which had given some dignity to their lives on the coastal plains on the other side of the North Sea.

They believed in hard work on the land. Many of the fields, roads and villages of the English countryside were made by them, and there were also settlements by 'Saxons' in Gaul (now France) and across Germany. Theirs was 'the saga of man against the forest' – or the epic of the heavy plough against the

heavy soil.[1] In peace or war, they believed in loyalty. 'The
chiefs fight for victory, the companions for the chiefs', Tacitus
had observed about the first-century barbarians in the area
which the Romans called Germania; it was a tribute they
would have loved. Above all they believed in courage – in
that, rather than in success. Their ships were taken without
fear across seas or up rivers, and a fifth-century bishop
marvelled that the Saxons seemed to regard shipwreck as a
form of training; but for all their courage, they had no great
hopes of what lay at the end. They were very conscious that
the fields, roads and villages which they or their oxen made
would not be their personal memorials, since others would
soon live there and would not remember them. Even their
most heroic leaders were among the subjects of fate, whose
destiny lay in the darkness. Over all the Anglo-Saxon mind
hangs the shadow of failure – failure which can be redeemed
by the defiance of fate in work and in courage.

The most famous of Old English poems, *Beowulf*, opens
with a picture of the royal barge of old King Scyld, shining
with ice and all ready to sail. On it they place a cargo of
treasure, a mass of weapons and armour, a heap of jewels; a
golden standard is high overhead. Then they push the ship out
to sea and it disappears bearing the body of the king. Such
death-defying loyalty to the dead, even to the defeated dead,
was much praised and much practised by these Anglo-Saxons.
The two most famous lines in their poetry are spoken by a
warrior who is about to lay down his life when his lord ('the
man so dear') has already been killed. Byrthwold cries out
towards the end of the battle fought at Maldon in Essex one
August day in 991:

Mind must be stronger, heart must be bolder,
Courage must be greater, as our power grows less.

When these heroic values received the seed of the Christian

[1] H. R. Loyn, *Anglo-Saxon England and the Norman Conquest* (London, 1962), p.36. There is a fine chapter on 'The Making of the Landscape' in P. H. Sawyer, *From Roman Britain to Norman England* (London, 1978).

religion, a fascinating society was the harvest. These people made *Englaland* – a word which came into general use in the century before the Norman conquest. Their England became a country more deeply Christian than most 'Christian' societies have managed to be; and its religion, now defying fate with faith, was a creed fit for heroes and their admirers. The Anglo-Saxons were loyal to the men and women who were now the enduring and conquering soldiers of Christ. As their surviving biographies or letters prove, within their Church the strongest link between leaders and led was often a loyalty of love. In their monasteries they read the lives and deaths of their heroic saints to each other, as in their banqueting halls a *scop* (minstrel) would sing of the lives and deaths of their fighting heroes. They worked heroically to cover England with stone crosses, timber churches and stone churches. These, at least, might escape the doom of death. One timber church (at Greenstead in Essex) and parts of more than three hundred stone churches are still standing, and there is evidence that there were once more than four hundred Anglo-Saxon churches in Kent alone. They filled these churches with the superb work of their craftsmen, although almost all such treasures were to be looted by Vikings or Normans. And their courage spread the faith they had adopted to Germany and to Scandinavia. Eventually English was virtually to replace Latin as the international language of Christianity, as English forms of the religion spread to continents far beyond the knowledge or imagination of these Anglo-Saxons.

But there is a very strange prelude to the story of Christian England. For centuries before the arrival of the Anglo-Saxon invaders the Christian Church had been present in the island, although the invaders seem to have made very little contact with it. The Britons who were now enslaved or kept as slaves did not communicate their religion to their new masters. Those who remained free in the west of the island became Welsh (the English word *wealas* meant 'foreigners') and produced great saints during these years. St David, for example, although of royal blood, was so austere that he forbade his monks to use oxen when they could draw their ploughs themselves. Under such leadership the Welsh accepted the gentle

yoke of Christ with enthusiasm. But the forgiveness of those
enemies who had stolen most of their island they evidently
found too difficult. There is no record of a single Welshman
becoming a missionary among the English.

Archaeology – particularly the investigation of buried
pottery – has shown that the English arrived in successive
waves from about 375. Sometimes they were invited as
mercenaries by the Romans or the British. More often they
arrived uninvited. These settlers – Angles, Saxons, Jutes,
Frisians and others – mostly resumed the life they had lived on
the mainland, despising the towns, villas and churches of
Roman Britain. They had little of the humility which in Gaul
led the invading barbarians to adopt the town life, language
and religion of the Roman empire. Only occasionally, it
seems, did they marvel at the higher civilization they now
encountered.

A fragment of a poem is preserved in the library of Exeter
Cathedral; it is usually called *The Ruin*. It is probably a
description of the Roman spa, Aquae Sulis, which the English
renamed Bath. At the time the poem was written this was a
ghost town. The poet meditated on buildings which seemed
the work of giants, completed a hundred generations ago and
now being pulled down by fate. Tiles lay smashed on the
ground and frost was eating the plaster. A wall stained red
and grey with lichen had survived the rise and fall of
kingdoms – but now was crumbling. Skilled master-masons
had raised the city – and now were in the earth's hard embrace. This hall had been filled with cheerful noise in the days
of pleasure before the massacre and the plague – but now the
scene of banquets was becoming rubble. Heroes had been
merry and proud here, flushed with wine, glittering in their
armour or splashing in the hot springs – but now the city was
bright no more.

In general, it seems, the Anglo-Saxons found the Roman
towns and villas already decayed or abandoned, and had few
sensitive feelings about the ruins or about the way of life they
represented. In some cities – London or York, Canterbury or
Winchester, Rochester or Lincoln, Gloucester or Chichester,
Dorchester-on-Thames or Carlisle – there was some continuity

of occupation. A life of St Cuthbert written some fifteen years later shows us the saint as a marvelling tourist in Carlisle in 685; he was taken round the city wall and saw the fountain 'wondrously built by the Romans'. But a different story is told by traces of squatters' fires on the mosaic floor of the great Ditchley Park villa or in the nave of the abandoned little church at Silchester. It seems that it did not usually occur to the Anglo-Saxons to make proper use of Roman buildings. The villas – country mansions spread over the south, where life for the gentry would not be as gracious again until the eighteenth century – held no attraction to the settlers. They made their peasants' huts, their farmers' more comfortable homes, and even their royal halls, of wood. When in 674 Benedict Biscop, fresh from one of his visits to Rome, built a stone church for his monks at Wearmouth, he could obtain the stones locally, for Hadrian's Wall, the fortified northern frontier of the Roman empire, was only three miles away. But he had to send to Gaul for men who understood how to mix mortar, lay stones and make glass, some of which still survives.

Where almost all the buildings were reduced to ruins, other forms of human self-expression did not survive even in fragments. The literature of Roman Britain, written on papyrus or in a few cases on parchment, was entirely rotted by damp or consumed by fire. Thousands of letters or memoranda must have been written every year, but not one has been found – unless the monk Gildas, writing on *The Ruin and Conquest of Britain* about 550, is quoting from a genuine letter of 446 when he gives us the futile plea of the British to the consul Aetius: 'the barbarians drive us into the sea, and the sea drives us back to the barbarians. The two kinds of death give us the choice of being drowned or slaughtered.'

How complete was the break with the Roman past may be seen in the naming of the days of the week in English. All the names but one (Saturn's day) honour Anglo-Saxon divinities. The day of the sun is followed by the day of the moon; the day of Tiu by the day of Woden (these were two gods of war); the day of Thor, the god of thunder, rain and fertility, by the day of Woden's wife, Frig. The chief Christian festival is still called in English by the name of the Anglo-Saxon spring goddess,

Eostre. In the long run the invaders settling in an island on the
edge of the Roman world could not escape coming to terms
with that world if they wished to trade and prosper; thus the
English took names for the months from the Romans. But in
day-to-day reality for many years, life in England owed very
little to the centuries in which Rome had conquered the
known world and had been conquered by the religion of
Christ.

THE CHURCH IN BRITAIN

What, then, remains of the Christianity which was the religion
of a minority in the Romans' Britannia?

There are some relics of temples of the old British tribal
religion, which the Romans tolerated although they broke the
power of the Druid priests and stopped their human sacrifices.
One such temple, to the god Nodens, was built at Lydney in
Gloucestershire on a considerable scale as late as the closing
years of the fourth century. There are also many relics of un-
official cults such as Mithraism (supremely the soldier's
creed) — and of the official Roman religion. A column has survived in Cirencester which the governor of that part of Britain
re-erected to Jupiter during the fourth-century reaction
against Christianity led by the emperor, Julian the Apostate.
And other archaeological finds bring before our eyes relics of
Christianity, a religion which for a time the Roman empire
treated as it had treated the barbaric superstition of the
Druids.

The most dramatic find (in the 1940s) has been the Milden-
hall Treasure. This consists of silver goods which were buried,
presumably in the 360s during the disturbances caused by the
'barbarian conspiracy' which brought invaders from west,
north and east simultaneously. It is a mainly pagan collection,
and as a work of art the great dish is the equal of any other
Roman object now in the British Museum. The name of
Eutherios, a highly placed minister under Julian, is scratched
on the bottom of two of the pieces. The treasure includes three

spoons marked with the Greek letters *Chi Rho* for Christ (not with a cross, still to Roman eyes the instrument of a low-born criminal's execution). Those spoons begin the story of Christian art in the island.

Less artistic but still impressive is the earliest known collection of Christian silver in the Roman empire, found at Water Newton in Huntingdonshire in 1975. It seems that it, too, was hidden in the fourth century, perhaps during a time of persecution. From many places in Roman Britain come spoons, rings, bowls, tombstones or lead tanks (presumably for baptisms) marked with Christian symbols. In Cirencester and Manchester there survive cryptograms scratched on plaster, containing A and O to represent the first and last letters of the Greek alphabet and PATER NOSTER, 'Our Father'. Thus Christ and his teaching were defiantly made public at a time when it was dangerous either to display his cross or to name him.

Traces of buildings which probably were small Christian churches have been found at Silchester (built about 360) and Caerwent, although no building known to have been used as a cathedral or major parish church has yet been discovered. Several Roman villas which have been excavated seem to have had Christian owners. The most remarkable evidence of this kind so far unearthed has been brought together in the British Museum. From Hinton St Mary in Somerset comes a large mosaic floor excavated in 1963 and including a portrait of a clean-shaven Christ with *Chi Rho* behind him. Beside him are two pomegranates symbolizing eternal life. In the same mosaic floor is a scene from pagan mythology (Bellephoron slaying the Chimaera) which seems to hint, like the pomegranates, at Christ's victory over death. From Lullingstone in Kent, where four rooms in a villa seem to have been set apart as a 'house church', comes a wall-painting of six well-dressed people, three at least of them *orantes*, worshippers who pray standing with outstretched arms. These may be portraits of the family that owned the villa. Three times *Chi Rho* is encircled with the laurel wreath of victory. Both the floor and the wall-painting seem to date from the middle, or second half, of the fourth century. Like many passages in the New Testament, they are

reminders that during its early centuries the Church was based
largely on Christian homes.

When we try to get at the life behind these scanty remains of
Christianity in Roman Britain, we are in difficulties.

A story was preserved by Nennius when he compiled his
History of the Britons in the first half of the ninth century. It
was to the effect that a British king, Lucius, had accepted
baptism from missionaries sent by the pope in 167. That is
clearly a legend. But a book *Against the Jews* by Tertullian of
Carthage (a rhetorical writer) boasts that 'parts of Britain in-
accessible to the Romans were indeed conquered by Christ'.
That was written about two hundred years after the birth of
Christ. If the boast is accurate, it shows that the Church was
then present in south-west Britain, an area not yet reached by
the Roman conquest which had begun in AD 43. Presumably
the religion had been carried there by traders across the
Channel from a prosperous and heavily Romanized Gaul, but
students of history are unable to say who was the first Christian
whose feet walked on this land.

Much later legends told of the establishment of the
monastery at Glastonbury in this dim period; even of the
coming of Joseph of Arimathea with the Holy Grail, the cup
used at the Last Supper – or with the Christ child himself in
the hidden years about which the gospels are silent.

Archaeology establishes that Glastonbury was inhabited in
the first century AD, and that there was in this period considerable traffic across the Channel. We also know that the
British kept control of this area long after the south-east had
fallen to the Saxons. When Ine, King of the West Saxons
688-722, arrived in Glastonbury as its conqueror, he found
there a wooden church already revered as ancient and he gave
extensive lands to its clergy. This church survived until it was
burned down in 1184.

In Britain under Roman occupation, some Christians were
executed during one or other of the persecutions of the third
century. One of them, probably put to death in 208-9, became
famous. The earliest reference to the 'blessed martyr Alban'
comes in a biography of St Germanus, Bishop of Auxerre,
written about 480 and describing a visit which the bishop had

paid to Britain about thirty years before. The author, Constantius, told of how the visitor had added other relics of saints to the martyr's shrine, but he did not say where the shrine was. The earliest surviving statement that it was on the outskirts of Verulamium was provided by Gildas, more than three hundred years after the event. Gildas adds some stories which seem too tall about the miracles surrounding the martyrdom, but there may well be more substance in his report that Alban was a Roman soldier who had sheltered a Christian priest escaping from Gaul and who had been baptized by him. Bede's *Ecclesiastical History* tells us that a 'church of wonderful workmanship' was flourishing in the 720s on the site of the martyrdom. Some seventy years later Offa, King of the Mercians, founded St Alban's Abbey as penance for the murder of another king (St Ethelbert) in which he had been involved.

Gildas and Bede tell us also of the martyrdom of Aaron and Julius at Caerleon and of 'many more of both sexes in several places'. Aaron's name suggests that he was a converted Jew.

Two third-century writers, Origen and Hippolytus, vaguely mention Christianity in Britain, but the earliest clear evidence comes in the Acts of the Council of Arles in 314. The council was attended by five persons from Britain: Eborius Bishop of York, Restitutus Bishop of London, Adelfius Bishop of Lincoln (but this is not certain since the scribe wrote *Colonia Londinensium* instead of *Colonia Lindensium*), a priest and a deacon. The fact that this party travelled to an official meeting is an indication that the bishops, priests and deacons of Britain already thought of themselves as officials in a fellowship spanning the Roman world. (And these Roman days were never to be completely forgotten: in the empire Britannia was a part known as a *diocesis*, and the Church was always to call the area of a bishop's jurisdiction a 'diocese'.) The council, which included thirty-three bishops, was held in August in a city not far from the French Mediterranean coast. All must have seemed warmth and peace, with the emperor himself summoning the Christian leaders and assuring them of his protection. Yet that council in August 314 met less than ten years after the abdication of the last of the emperors who persecuted the Church, Diocletian. Such had been the results of the conversion to Christianity (if that is not too strong a phrase) of the emperor Constantine. In a ceremony momentous for the Church and the world, in the Roman military headquarters on the site of the present York Minster, Constantine had been proclaimed Augustus or emperor by the troops on 25 July 306. He was then not much over twenty. His father, the emperor Constantius, had died in York earlier that day.

When the council summoned by Constantine to Nicaea in 325 had defined orthodox Christian belief, the British were among those listed by Athanasius as accepting its decrees. It is, however, probable that during the fourth century the Church in Britain remained a minority concentrated in the towns. In 359 three other British bishops who had travelled abroad to attend a church council accepted an offer by the imperial treasury to refund their expenses. Other British and Gaulish bishops present refused to do so – and a bishop from Gaul 'often' criticized the three. This we are told by Sulpicius Severus, a writer best known for his biography of St Martin of Tours. St Martin was a monk-bishop who insisted on living in poverty and it is possible that the three British bishops were monks like him, or missionaries in areas where the Church had few resources. At any rate, Sulpicius Severus tells us that he defended their attitude to the Welfare State.

Of the labours of these and other bishops in the conversion of Roman Britain, we know nothing. Only one bishop's name can be linked with any definite work. A manuscript survives in the library at Monte Cassino in Italy and is marked as being by a bishop called Fastidius. Apparently it is the book *On the Christian Life* which another fifth-century writer says Fastidius wrote to a certain Fatalis about 425, together with a book on how to be a widow. If so, it is the earliest recorded expression of simple themes which were to be repeated, generation after generation, in this island over fifteen centuries ahead. The reader is urged to practise modesty, contentment and good works; not to be sad, for Christ means 'anointed' and the Christian is anointed with the oil of gladness; not to turn the poor away, for the Christian must imitate Christ in all things. A prayer is added. It was attacked as being too con-

fident that the hands being lifted up to heaven were clean. A
more eminent scholar, Pelagius, had to issue a denial that he
had composed it.

The controversy over this prayer was part of a doctrinal
crisis. Pelagius, who had been born in Britain about 380, went
abroad and became a well-known theologian, emphasizing the
freedom and ability of man to co-operate with the grace of
God. This teaching conflicted with the emphasis then being
placed by St Augustine of Hippo on the complete sinfulness of
man, who must rely totally on God's forgiveness and redeem-
ing power. It is reported that Pelagius was horrified to hear in
Rome a quotation of the famous prayer by St Augustine:
'Grant what thou commandest, and command what thou
wilt'. The dispute intensified when, after the fall of Rome to
the barbarians in 410, Pelagius went to live indiscreetly near
Augustine in North Africa. It is believed that he died, having
been excommunicated by the pope, in Palestine (an early
example of theologians who have appealed over the heads of
the bishops to the teacher of Galilee). But the cheerful
liberalism of Pelagius soon reached his native Britain. The
contemporary chronicler Prosper says that it was spread by
Agricola, a bishop's son. It was well received, on a scale sufficient to alarm orthodox churchmen.

Bishop Germanus was summoned from Auxerre in Gaul,
and was accompanied by a neighbour and fellow-bishop,
Lupus of Troyes. It was during this visit in 429 that they
visited St Alban's shrine, but their main purpose was to preach
against the liberal heresy of Pelagius — which they did, 'not
only in churches but also at crossroads and in fields and lanes',
and not only in sermons but also in debates. The Pelagians are
said to have been 'distinguished by their riches, resplendent in
their dress, and surrounded by an adoring crowd'; but the
visitors soon won over the crowd. We seem to see a British
Church with a considerable following among both the sophisticated and the simple, and with enough peace of mind to be
tempted to take a benevolent view of human nature.

When he records these theological disputes, Constantius the
biographer of Germanus adds that the bishop was (with
Lupus) invited to join an expedition against the Picts and the

Saxons who had invaded the north. Before his ordination the
bishop had been a *dux* or military commander. Constantius
claims that Germanus now used the approach of Lent to instruct a great part of the British army, which was duly baptized. On Easter Day the soldiers paraded still wet with the
baptismal water. They then set up the Easter acclamation
Alleluia, and the enemy promptly fled. Whatever we make of
this story, it is by no means impossible that the visiting bishop
gave his hosts military as well as theological guidance. The
bishops of Gaul were expected to defend every aspect of a
Christian civilization. We begin to see the Church taking on
many strange tasks because it had received the legacy of the
Roman empire.

Constantius also claims that Germanus and another bishop
were asked back for a second visit fourteen years later, but this
time concentrated on the area later called Wessex. They were
so successful in their second mission that Constantius believed
that when he was writing about his hero in 480 the British
were entirely free of the Pelagian heresy.

Despite the '*Alleluia* victory' they were not at all secure from
a military or economic point of view. And from across the
North Sea poured in thousands of barbarians, finding the
coast which had come to be known as the 'Saxon shore' no
barrier. In 383 Magnus Maximus, a Christian general in the
Roman army who had been born in Spain and had married a
British girl (Helena), led his troops from Britain to the
mainland, declaring himself emperor. From that date the
Roman military presence in Britain was inadequate, although
some troops remained for some years and two of their com-
manders are known. The general Stilico was a giant of a man,
the son of a barbarian cavalry officer. Another general,
having taken the ambitious name Constantine, led his troops
out of Britain in 407 in order to take his chance in the politics
of the empire. A contemporary historian, Orosius, says that
this adventurer summoned his son Constans, who had been a
Christian monk, to join him.

No Roman coins later than 407 have been found in Britain.
In theory the island remained part of the empire; about 425
an official document, the *Notitia Dignitatum*, assigned to

Britain an army of six thousand under the command of a
'count'. But in 410 the emperor Honorius recognized that he
was cut off from this island on the edge of the world by the
great barbarian invasion of Gaul and Italy. When appealed
to, he therefore formally instructed the British *civitates* (cities
with their surrounding regions) that they must look to their
own defence. In the terms of Roman law it was the grant of
permission to civilians to use arms. In practice it meant that
the British *civitates* became petty kingdoms, each depending
on its chief's energy. The most powerful of these rulers
appears in the history of Nennius as Vortigern or 'overlord'.
He invited Saxon mercenaries to settle in the island, recogniz-
ing that despite the emperor's words the British were not able
to defend themselves against the barbarians from the north or
against their own tendency to civil war. The Britons, needing
a strength greater than their own, had summoned the English.

THE AGE OF ARTHUR

We now enter an age where historians can find few lights
to guide them. The history of Christianity is particularly
obscure. It is always possible that archaeology will be more
illuminating, but on the basis of discovery and reflection up to
1982 it would seem that Romano-British Christianity was a
minority religion, in striking contrast with the popularity of
the Church in Gaul, Italy or North Africa. Surveying the
evidence to the end of the fourth century, W. H. C. Frend
writes of 'two main zones of Christian activity. The first com-
prises the Romanized and urbanized south and south-east
from the Wash to Exeter, the second from York north-west to
include Carlisle and the Cumbrian coast, the military zone,
especially the western end of it'. Entering the fifth century, he
finds that the scanty evidence points to 'a Church which,
though rich in personalities and ideas, lacked the popular
support that ensured its survival elsewhere in the West . . .
Generally, as the Roman towns and villas were abandoned,

only sites of special holiness continued as centres of Christianity'.[2]

So the little candle of the Romano-British Church seems scarcely to flicker in the barbaric darkness. We do not know more than a handful of these Christians even by name. We do not know their thoughts, and we do not know much about the objects they used daily. Unlike the pagan invaders of their island, they did not bury goods which their dead could use in an after-life. What we do know is depressing. The trinkets which have survived from the Britain of this period are of poor quality; the homesteads which have been excavated were evidently built with defence rather than enjoyment in mind; and the only really impressive objects dug up by the archaeologists are bronze hanging bowls found in Anglo-Saxon graves, almost certainly looted from British churches or homes. The descent from the level of civilization reached in Roman towns and villas could scarcely be sadder.

There is, however, other evidence. A great scholar points out that it was 'in this period of freedom between the Roman and Saxon Occupations that the ideals and literature took shape which still characterize the Celtic peoples wherever the Celtic languages are spoken'.[3] And these ideals and literature were largely shaped by Christianity. The Celtic peoples adopted the faith, often with great zest. Although Roman influences weakened as the empire faded into history and the Continent seemed more remote, the Celts did not reject the Latin language or the pre-eminence of the Bishop of Rome or any other reminder of the fact that the Christian faith had been carried to them through the Roman empire. Because Britain had belonged to the Romans, some of them could read and write (as the early Anglo-Saxons could not, apart from 'runic' letters crudely carved on wood, bone or stone). It is therefore entirely right to speak about Celtic *civilization*, using a word which is itself derived from Latin. But it was a civilization almost completely different from life in Roman Britain;

---

[2] W. H. C. Frend, '*Ecclesia Britannica:* Prelude or Dead End?' in *Journal of Ecclesiastical History* (Cambridge, 1979), pp.129-144.

[3] N. K. Chadwick, *Celtic Britain* (London, 1964), p.34.

and the most striking difference was the centrality of a fervent Christian faith.

Theirs was a faith spread by monks. The Celtic literature was preserved in monasteries like any other literature in Western Europe at the time, but this guardianship of culture was only one part of the monk's significance in Celtic religion.

Again and again when we explore this new kind of Christianity we find communities of monks setting the pace spiritually. They were the custodians of the Bible, acknowledging its holiness by taking it literally and obeying it wholeheartedly; even the food regulations in the Old Testament were received as the law of God. The Bible was also venerated by being copied and decorated (or 'illuminated') with the best art of the time – all that now remains to prove the intensity of this Celtic monastic devotion. The monks maintained a strenuous round of corporate and private prayer, worshipping their holy and demanding God in the little huts as well as in the simple chapels that together made up their monasteries. From the Celtic word *ciric*, referring to the holy burial ground in such a monastery, descended the later word 'church'. From this base they went out to evangelize and to minister to converts, staying close to the people in their standard of living although their morality was, no doubt, high above the common level. We shall watch Irish monks playing a crucial role in the conversion of England. So far as we know, no monks in Roman Britain had been nearly so prominent in the maintenance and spread of Christianity. But their successors were a new breed. In this dark age of which we know so little the monks emerged as the Church's vastly influential elite.

It is also significant that the monks of Celtic Christianity ministered not to a town but to an area of the countryside. The Celtic peoples were organized in tribes. These tribes seem to have been of mixed racial origins. What united them was not an army and an administration with urban centres, as in the Roman civilization, but a strong common culture based on their shared faith. When their monks told them about the tribes of Ancient Israel making a covenant with their God and their neighbours, these tribesmen must have recognized their spiritual ancestors. Somehow the British Christians, after the withdrawal of the Roman legions, had changed Christianity into this powerful new shape, monastic and tribal – a mutation as difficult as that which had changed the Church from being one Jewish sect among many, daily expecting the end of the world, into being the guardian and rebuilder of a civilization which spoke Greek or Latin around the Mediterranean. Christianity would survive many empires and cultures because it had in it this extraordinary capacity to adapt; and while adapting, to inspire.

We can recover only hints of the creative process. There are small signs to be found in regions which neither Romans nor Saxons were able – or, perhaps, willing – to conquer. Latin names under Christian symbols appear on tombstones in Wales or Cornwall, or are Celticized to appear in the family trees of Welsh chieftans. The red dragon of Wales is a version of the *draco* or standard carried before Roman soldiers on the march, and some six hundred words in the Welsh language are derived from Latin. The ruins of a Celtic monastery amid the spectacular scenery of Tintagel on the north Cornish coast were associated by later legends with King Arthur, but are in fact the foundations of a monastery built before 500, the oldest known monastery in the British Isles. The Welsh were for long scorned by the civilized (a word based on the Latin *civis*, a citizen) as mere countrymen, *pagani*, the word from which 'Powys' descended. Their numbers seem to have been enlarged by emigration from Ireland when Roman rule was over. But it did not take long for them to become Christians. How this happened is the subject of legends interspersed with a few saints' names preserved in the dedication of ancient churches or villages. In the south there was, for example, St Illtyd, who is believed to have been an active Christian from about 475 to about 535, the founder of a famous monastery, probably in the modern Llantwit Major but possibly on Caldey Island.

Illtyd is said to have been born in Brittany (or Armorica, 'the land by the sea'). The evidence about British links with Brittany and Normandy in the fifth century is far from complete, but it is enough to suggest a substantial migration of the British beginning in the middle of the century. Many saints' names and place names preserved by the Bretons and Normans are close to Welsh names, and the Breton language is so close to Cornish that it is related that, when both languages were in everyday use, the fishermen could understand each other when they met in their little boats in the middle of the narrow sea. The biography of St Paul Aurelian gives a vivid picture of its hero arriving in a Roman town then inhabited only by animals. He was, however, accompanied by other refugees who shared his own noble birth and by 'sufficient slaves'; and before long the Roman town bore his own name.

We may suspect that story as a flourish in a ninth-century book about a fifth-century saint. More useful as evidence is the fact that Sidonius, a bishop in Gaul, corresponded with the leader of the first group of British settlers, Riothamus; these settlers seem to have been invited over as mercenaries to fight the invading Visigoths. In 461 the name of a British bishop, *Mansuetus episcopus Britannorum*, appears among the bishops attending a small council in Tours. Since it seems unlikely that Mansuetus would have crossed the Channel for a minor occasion in such troubled times, the probability is that he was ministering to the settlers in New Britain. It is also probable that in the end the colony became substantial. Whether invited to fight as mercenaries, or lured by the prospect of empty lands, or encouraged to leave the old country by Irish or English invasions, gradually the Britons over the Channel grew in numbers. It has been claimed that 'we can envisage a migration attaining five, if not six, figures — perhaps, over three centuries, up to a quarter- or half-million people (the population of England and Wales in late Roman times could have been of the order of two to three million)'.[4] Here, we may say, was Britain's first transatlantic colony, complete with colonial churches.

There was also a mission to the north – to the Picts. These lived in what is now Scotland and were allies, not subjects, of Rome. ('Picts' comes from the Roman soldier's sneer: 'painted

---

[4] Charles Thomas, *Britain and Ireland in Early Christian Times* (London, 1971), p.69.

men!') But they were only a short sea journey away up the west coast, and it seems that some of the Romanized British made that journey and took their Church with them. According to Bede, the first bishop to live among the Picts was 'Nynia, a most venerable and holy man, of the nation of the Britons, who had been instructed properly in the faith and the mysteries of the truth at Rome'.

This refers, it seems, to a time shortly before 450, but it represents a tradition handed on by Bishop Pecthelm to Bede for inclusion in his *Ecclesiastical History* almost three hundred years later. Pecthelm had become bishop of the area when the English had conquered it. Bede added that there still existed in his day a 'stately church in which rest the bodies of Nynia and many other saints'. Dedicated to St Martin of Tours, this church was usually called *Candida Casa* or White House, from the limewashed plaster covering its stones. Modern scholars are cautious about some of the details of this tradition. It is, for example, difficult to believe that St Ninian (as his name would be remembered) was trained in far-off Rome. He may well have been trained by St Martin, or at any rate influenced by his holiness, but if he dedicated his church to this recently dead saint it was an unusual gesture. In 1949 walls more than three foot thick and of a great age were excavated in a cemetery in the area of Whithorn Cathedral. They belonged to a small oratory of stones bedded in clay, still showing a few traces of whitened plaster. Nearby was found a tombstone erected probably in the fifth century commemorating one Latinus and his unnamed daughter aged four, under the words *Te Dominum Laudamus*, 'We praise thee, O Lord'. Not far away on the coast is St Ninian's Cave, with many Latin crosses carved on the rock face. And in Kirkmadrine on the next peninsula is an inscription on a tombstone: 'here lie the holy and eminent *sacerdotes* Ides, Viventius and Mavorius'. *Sacerdotes* probably meant 'bishops'. Evidently at the time of the plantation of the British Church in Brittany, some success had also come to this British mission to the north.

There are many traces in Welsh literature of the British kingdom of Rheged, based on Carlisle, celebrated for its king Urien, holding its own until the middle of the seventh century.

But no trace of its church life, said to have been strong, has been recovered in the ground. We are left with the thought that 'if, as we learn from Bede, the churches in this area were not built of stone, it is in no way surprising that neither the structures nor any documents which they have contained should have survived'.[5]

Fortunately, simple stone churches and lesser objects survive in Ireland and Wales, and our knowledge has been enriched by the art of photography from the air. When aerial surveys were first published in the 1960s they revealed the sites of many monasteries long buried in fields but just discernible in the late evening sunshine.[6] And we know that the most dramatic mission of the British Church in the fifth century reached Ireland.

The Irish were then generally called *Scotti* (what is now Scotland was partly colonized from Ireland). There is evidence of a concern for them as well as for the Britons in Auxerre, which under the saintly bishop Germanus was a centre of Christian life in Gaul. A deacon called Palladius seems to have belonged to the Church in Auxerre, although he may have been an official in Rome itself. He was the man who persuaded Pope Celestine to send Germanus on the anti-Pelagian mission to Britain. He was subsequently, in 431, himself sent by the pope as a bishop to 'the *Scotti* who believe in Christ' (in the words of the contemporary chronicler, Prosper). Nothing is known about the length or success of his mission, but it seems probable that it was cut short by death. It is the first recorded instance of missionary activity by the papacy.

The main apostle of the Irish, Patrick, was not only far more prominent in folk-memory and legend, but was also the author of two documents which have survived. One is a short autobiography or *Confessio* written 'before I die'. The other is a letter rebuking a British king, Coroticus, for a raid on the

---

[5] N. K. Chadwick, *The British Heroic Age* (Cardiff, 1976), p.123.

[6] See L. Laing, *The Archaeology of Late Celtic Britain and Ireland, c.400-1200* (London, 1975), and his more popular *Celtic Britain* (London, 1979).

Irish which had resulted in the death of some of Patrick's converts or their enslavement for sale to the Picts. Coroticus, a
nominal Christian, was firmly excommunicated until he had
made a full restitution.

From these sober documents in strong but rough Latin, the
outline of the true life of Patrick (in Latin, Patricius) emerges.
He was the son of a Roman British deacon, Calpurnius, and
the grandson of a priest, Potitus. He grew up in a village
called Bannavern; where this was we do not know. When
nearly sixteen he was captured by raiders and taken as a slave
to Ireland. After six years of misery minding his master's
cattle, he escaped and returned to his family, only to receive a
vision bidding him return to Ireland as an evangelist. In this
dream he received a letter asking him to 'come again and walk
among us'. He was made a bishop for the Irish about 425. He
seems to have walked over much of northern and central
Ireland; to have made his headquarters in Armagh where one
of the kings had his fort; and to have planted the Church
extensively before his death about 460. Tradition says he
founded dioceses with himself as archbishop, but no other
bishop in Ireland is mentioned in his *Confessio*.[7]

When the Irish Church emerges into the light of history, we
find that the bishops were not the rulers of the Church in a
definite area but were monks of exceptional holiness whose
functions were to ordain priests and to bless oils for the sick;
the leadership was exercised by the nobly born abbot of the
monastery belonging to the tribe. The period during which
this system emerged has been buried in obscurity, however.
Although the 'Breastplate of St Patrick' has been popular as a
hymn ever since its translation into English in the nineteenth
century, the earliest version known belongs to a time three
centuries after Patrick's death. What we can find in it – or in
the hymn 'Be thou my vision, O Lord of my heart' – is the
atmosphere of this obscure period. Here was a faith deeply
personal but also securely orthodox, accepting battle against
the magic of paganism, creating a Celtic Christianity full of

---

[7] See R. P. C. Hanson, *St Patrick: His Origins and Career* (Oxford, 1968).

confidence in its Lord and in itself.

This missionary expansion of British Christianity, taking the Church into the Celtic realms of Wales, Brittany, Scotland and Ireland cannot be pursued in a book about England.[8] But the story hints at the missionary energy of the British Church. Obviously the missionaries who planted the Church in the Celtic fringe of Britain were thoroughly enthusiastic, and therefore not entirely typical. But it is illuminating to notice what criticisms were made of the British bishops by some of these enthusiasts. Both the missionary Patrick and the monk Gildas suggest that the British bishops were admired for their learning and social graces although inadequate as spiritual leaders. This indicates a Church which had not only fathered some radically critical sons but had also become established, with deep roots in society.

Some evidence that this Church still had a few links with the rest of the international Christian community is provided by an incident which took place in or about 475. The Roman town of Avitacum was shortly to fall to the Visigoths in their march across Gaul. A letter from Sidonius Apollinaris, who had a villa there, congratulates Faustus, a Briton who had become Abbot of Lérins and Bishop of Riez, on the authorship of a theological book brought to Avitacum by a travelling British monk, Bishop Riochatus.

The surviving evidence also suggests that, with an improvement in their morale, the Britons were able to make a military rally against the invaders tormenting them – and against their own Saxon mercenaries, previously thought indispensable, who had revolted. Gildas, writing towards the middle of the next century, alludes to a series of fifth-century victories gained under the leadership of Ambrosius Aurelianus. This rally culminated about 500 in a victory at Badon Hill (often identified with the hill fort called Badbury Rings near Wimborne in Dorset, but possibly another of the five Badburys in England). And when he edited his history some three hundred

---

[8] See M. Dillon and N. K. Chadwick, *The Celtic Realms* (revised, Dublin, 1972).

years later, Nennius named the victor of Badon Hill: Artorius. This is 'King Arthur', whose chivalry was one of the most popular themes in the entertainment of medieval Europe.

Arthur's name is not given by Gildas who is thought to have been a contemporary. But Gildas certainly writes after a generation of peace (apart from civil wars); the whole point of his book is to warn the Britons that because they do not deserve it this peace is about to come to an end. It is therefore reasonably certain that about the year 500 there were leaders of Britain's defence who were more effective than the petty kings who had found themselves in charge after the with-drawal of the Roman army – and also more effective than the five Welsh and Cornish tyrants whom Gildas denounced. Did one of these leaders have the Roman name Artorius?

A Welsh poem, *Y Gododdin*, which was probably written about 600, praises one hero who glutted the black ravens with the bodies of his enemies 'although he was not Arthur'. This reference may have been added later, but it does not stand quite alone. At least four, perhaps five, people called Arthur are known to have been born in Celtic parts of Britain during the late sixth and early seventh centuries, although the name is previously unknown in Britain apart from the single case of a Roman officer of the second century.

There is a somewhat more substantial collection of Arthur-ian references in a manuscript now in the British Museum (Harley 3859). This seems to have been copied out early in the twelfth century from material originally put together in the monastery at St Davids in Wales during the second half of the tenth century. Part of this material is a record of events added to dates of Easter (the so-called *Annales Cambriae*). The last event probably occurred in 957. For the year 518 is recorded: 'The battle of Badon in which Arthur carried the cross of our Lord Jesus Christ on his shoulders for three days and three nights and the Britons were the victors'. For the year 539 is recorded: 'The *gueith* (Welsh for battle) of Camlann in which Arthur and Medraut perished and there was plague in Britain and Ireland'. Also in this manuscript there is material usually dated in the first half of the ninth century and referred to as a *History of the Britons* by Nennius. This informs us that

'Arthur fought against them in those days with the kings of the Britons, but he himself was leader of the battles (*dux bellorum*).' Twelve victories are named, ending with Badon, where '960 men fell in one day from one charge by Arthur, and no one overthrew them but Arthur alone'. The location of the sites named has been much disputed, but it seems that his campaigns took this *dux bellorum* from Scotland to Cornwall. Obviously he is envisaged as a cavalry commander. It is thought that this passage is based on an old Welsh battle-song.

Many have debated the problems involved in assessing the historical value of these references to Arthur and in the attempt to link them with archaeology. For example, in Somerset the hill-top fort at Cadbury was excavated in the 1960s and fortifications of the sixth (or late fifth) century enclosing about eighteen acres with a perimeter of about twelve hundred yards were revealed. Within these ramparts were found remains of a timber hall, sixty-three by thirty-four feet. Already in 1532 the antiquary John Leland was of the opinion that this was the site of Arthur's court, Camelot (although that name was invented by Crétien of Troyes in the twelfth century), but it may be more scientific to confine ourselves to the conclusion that here was a major fort used defensively, presumably by the British against the Saxons. While the debate continues all that can be said here is that it seems possible for reasonable people to believe that a British general called Arthur was successful during the conflicts of the sixth century.[9]

The international fame of Arthur is shown by a carving on the north doorway of Modena Cathedral in Italy, executed before 1120. It depicts an armed and mounted knight labelled 'Artus de Bretania' attacking one 'Burmaltus'. In the background is a castle containing a woman, Winlogee (the Breton name for Guinevere). In England, however, the legend was given its first big boost by the fervent Welsh bishop and story-teller, Geoffrey of Monmouth, who put it into Latin in the 1130s. In his *History of the Kings of Britain* he based Arthur

---

[9] A scholarly summary of the 'small kernel of Arthurian fact' is found in Leslie Alcock, *Arthur's Britain* (London, 1973), pp.1-88.

on the Roman and Welsh town of Caerleon-on-Usk and had
him conquer much of Western Europe before being betrayed
at home by Mordred and Guanhumara (Guinevere). This
great hero's chief counsellor was the magician Merlin and
when mortally wounded he was carried away to the Island of
Avalon.

The legend of the betrayed conqueror was picked up by the
wandering minstrels, the troubadours, who sang it into the
hearts of royal and noble households in France. Fresh scope
was provided by the growing interest in Arthur's knights, said
to feast with him at a round table to show their equality.
These poets with an aristocratic market developed, for instance, the tale of the tragic love of Sir Tristan (a Cornishman
who died in Brittany) for Iseult (an Irish princess). The story
of Arthur and his knights, ever more richly embroidered,
proved worthy of the genius of Goltfried of Strasbourg and
Chrétien of Troyes: and now the climax was the discovery of
the Holy Grail used at the Last Supper. A young knight called
either Perceval or Gawain was led to this treasure by the Fisher
King – for the story was lush with mythology and symbolism.
The Frenchman Wace's *Roman de Brut* was translated into
English and expanded by the Worcestershire priest Layamon
between 1189 and 1199 – it was Arthur's first appearance in
English literature. More prosaically, in 1191 the monks of
Glastonbury, then needing to attract the tourists because they
needed cash to rebuild their monastery, discovered the grave
and with it a financial resurrection. Beneath the coffin a
leaden cross was inscribed: 'Here lies entombed the renowned
King Arthur with Guinevere his second wife in the Island of
Avalon'.

In the fourteenth century a warrior-king, Edward III,
attempted to cast the glamour of chivalry and piety over his
favourite fellow-soldiers, then embarked on another European
adventure, by modelling the Order of the Garter on Arthur's
knights; and at Windsor they feasted at a round table. In the
fifteenth century in order to while away his imprisonment Sir
Thomas Malory had the idea of combining the romances
about Arthur, his court and his death, to form the first
English novel that can be called a major work of art. William

Caxton edited and printed his book in 1485, advertising: 'herein may be seen noble chivalry, courtesy, humanity, friendliness, hardihood, love, friendship, cowardice, murder, hate, virtue and sin'. Malory's book, although denounced by the Elizabethan schoolmaster Roger Ascham as 'open slaughter and bold bawdry', did much to form the layman's idea of the gentleman in the Tudor Age when medieval knights were no more. Shakespeare laughed at Arthurian legends but could think of no more fitting end for Falstaff than 'he's in Arthur's bosom, if ever man went to Arthur's bosom'. Drawing on Malory as well as on his own genius for the celebration of nostalgia, Alfred Tennyson moved the Victorians with his twelve poems about the stately court of the 'once and future king'. Hugely successful novels prove that the spell is still strong in the twentieth century. When John Kennedy's White House was nicknamed 'Camelot' almost everyone knew what was meant.[10]

Coleridge said that it was by the legends of Arthur that his imagination was 'habituated to the Vast'. In real history, however, Arthur's Britain was doomed. Gradually the British were cut off from a Christian Europe which itself was being swallowed into the darkness of an age ravaged by barbarians. The isolation of the British was not complete, it seems; archaeologists studying tombstones surviving in Wales from this period have found in them some evidence of continuing contact with changing fashions in Gaul. But evidence suggesting the confusion of the times is found in the date of Easter. This has always been a problem, as is shown to this day by the celebration of different Easters in the church of the Holy Sepulchre in Jerusalem. The council of Arles in 314 found it necessary to discuss it, and was able to agree that the pope should solve the problem. Owing to its origins in a Jewish community, Easter has been calculated by the date of a full moon, while the ordinary year for Romans Celts and Saxons alike had its calendar determined by the sun. To add to the compli-

---

[10] See *Arthurian Literature in the Middle Ages*, ed. R. S. Loomis (Oxford, 1959), and for a summary of the whole tradition Elizabeth Jenkins, *The Mystery of King Arthur* (London, 1975).

cation, the Church decided that Easter must fall on a Sunday;
it was to be the first Sunday after the full moon on or after the
spring equinox. But when, in the solar calendar, was that? In
444 Pope Leo the Great decided that the method of dating
Easter should be changed; one motive was to avoid the coincidence of Good Friday with a Roman sports day. The Church
in Britain accepted this change, and the Church remaining in
Britain's Celtic parts later defended it with great obstinacy.
But in 457 a new way of fixing the date of Easter, worked out
by Victorius of Acquitane, was adopted by the Roman
church. This calendar was gradually adopted in Gaul (the
bishops there agreed on it in 541) but not in Britain; the island
was spritually cut off from Europe.

Sixth-century Britain seemed so remote from the Byzantine
world of the civilized East that Procopius in far-off Caesarea
believed that after death the souls of men were ferried from
Gaul to this fog-bound island inhabited by the British with
Angiloi (Angles) and *Frissones* (Frisians). And archaeology has
made a comment on the primitive nature of any other trade
still being conducted. So far as we know, Arthur's Britain used
no coinage after 430.

Gildas (about 550) could denounce it as a society not fit to
survive, as the Ancient Israelites had been denounced by their
own prophets in the time of the Assyrian and Babylonian invasions. To this indignant critic the Old Testament was 'a
mirror reflecting our own life'. He gives an impression that in
Wales and what else was left of Post-Roman Britain Church
and State were equally corrupt. Vortipor, tyrant of the
Demetians in south-west Wales, was 'from top to bottom'
stained with murders and adulteries. This may seem to be
merely the rhetoric of a moralizing monk who too easily
assumed the mantle of a prophet. But in Carmarthen Museum
is preserved a tombstone reading MEMORIA VOTEPORIGIS PRO-
TICTORIS. It is a rough stone; the lettering is crude and the
spelling is worse. It is hard to believe that the ruler thus commemorated was fully worthy of the title *protector*, derived
from the bodyguard of a Roman emperor — or of the cross on
the stone. It would seem that Arthur, if he had ever existed,
had left degenerate heirs. Yet that is not all that can be said

about British or Celtic Christianity in the age of Gildas. For
Gildas himself clearly made a large impact on his time. A
modern scholar has gone so far as to claim that when Gildas
had written his great protest 'within ten years monasticism
had become a mass movement, in South Wales, Ireland and
northern Gaul. Its extensive literature reveres Gildas as
its founding father, named more often than any other individual'.[11]

THE ENGLISH CONQUEST

Until the middle of the sixth century the Germanic peoples
settling in England were, it seems, confined to Kent, Sussex
and southern Hampshire; to Essex, East Anglia, Lindsey and
the East Riding of Yorkshire; and inland to the upper Thames
region and to the area between what were long after to
become the university cities of Oxford and Cambridge. But
the fragmentary evidence suggests that the main British force
was weakened by a plague which swept through Europe in
549, and then overwhelmed by another revolt or invasion (or
both) about 570. Thus the disasters which the Jeremiah-like
Gildas had prophesied came to pass. However, the whole land
did not move immediately into the firm control of the English.
Much of it was moor, forest or fen with few or no inhabitants.
Felix's *Life* of the hermit Guthlac, written about 740, pictures
him alone at Crowland in the desolate fens near the Wash; he
lived in a long grave, presumably dating from Roman times,
which robbers had conveniently dug open. Even in the
cultivated parts of the island, not all the fields immediately
fell to the new rulers. As we have noted, the area around
Glastonbury was not colonized by the West Saxons until the
710s and 720s. Guthlac, before he became a hermit, had been
a soldier, and Felix tells us that even in his solitude the hermit
was troubled by dreams of attacks by the Britons – for in the

---

[11] John Morris, introducing *Gildas: The Ruin of Britain and Other Works*,
ed. M. Winterbottom (London, 1978).

700s it was still the case that 'the Britons, the implacable enemies of the Saxon race, were troubling the English with their attacks'.

Victories in these times must have been somewhat like the naval victories which the English were to win in the centuries ahead, defeating those enemies who had appeared but not necessarily leading to the immediate colonization of a whole territory. And we have now to notice some exceptions to the general rule that there was little real contact between the conquerors and the conquered. While it is probable that many of the British fled to the west and became the Welsh, those who stayed were not all slaughtered. A few personal names seem to be evidence of intermarriage between the triumphant Anglo-Saxons and the remaining Britons. These include the famous names of Cerdic who was regarded as the founder of the royal house of Wessex, Caedwalla, King of the West Saxons 685-8, and the poet Caedmon. It is known that the Northumbrian king Oswiu married a princess of the British kingdom of Rheged (and, when she died, an Irish princess). Cumberland retained its British name, as the land of the Cymry. The country north of the Humber seems to have had few English settlers in the early years, and the names of both the Anglo-Saxon kingdoms into which it was divided, Deira and Bernicia, were British. Even Kent, which the English colonized much more thickly, remained the land of the Cantii. Numerous slaves are found in Anglo-Saxon laws; for example, the *wealhs* of Wessex.

So it is likely that the Christian faith was still kept or remembered not only in Wales or Cornwall or Wessex which remained independent, but also inside England, in the huts of many slaves as well as in a few centres of special holiness such as St Alban's shrine at Verulamium. But it is also possible that many clung to gods and goddesses of pre-Roman paganism; perhaps the Christian landowners of the 'age of Arthur' had failed or neglected to convert their slaves or tenants. It is possible, too, that many who had been converted now tamely abandoned their Christian faith, or kept quiet about it until new Christian missionaries came. Sir Keith Feiling pictured the sad end in the emptying Roman city of Silchester: 'one day the Christian priest serving its small Christian church, finding no flock left to minister to, put out the light on the altar for the last time'.[12] All that we know is that Christianity was not handed on by the British to the English on any large scale – any more than their language was. Only six villages are known to have been called Eccles by the English, although fourteen other place-names include the word. It is a little indication that a British church (in Welsh, *egles*) was seldom a prominent feature in the landscape. And it is reckoned that not more than sixteen nouns in the language spoken by enslaved Britons entered the Anglo-Saxon language.

This failure to impress the conquering English is all the more striking in the light of subsequent history. When in their turn the English became the victims of invasion, the invading Danes were soon converted to their enemies' religion. Even the conquering Normans did not ultimately succeed in imposing the French language on the country. But it is clear that in the fifth and sixth centuries there was an extraordinary depth in the hatred between the Anglo-Saxon invaders and their victims, creating the gap over which no religion or language could travel. Still in the seventh century, according to St Aldhelm, the Welsh clergy refused to greet any Englishman unless he wished to take refuge among them – and had first done forty days' penance for being English.

We cannot tell fully what caused this total failure to forgive the atrocities which no doubt both sides perpetrated. But R. P. C. Hanson has commmented that the work of Gildas suggests that there was already a spiritual failure in the British Church before the invaders' triumph became complete – a failure in tragic contrast with earlier missionary achievements. He writes: 'Patrick does not hesitate to excommunicate a British tyrant who has conducted a cruel massacre, and it seems clear that he expects his instructions for both boycott and excommunication to be obeyed. One gathers from Gildas that, though the Church of his day has plenty of atrocities to witness, it cannot do more than deplore and denounce their perpetrators. The British Church of Patrick's day converts

---

[12] Keith Feiling, *A History of England* (London, 1950), p.18.

savage barbarians; the British Church of Gildas's day merely abuses them. Gildas shows quite a wide acquaintance with theology, rhetoric and learning, but in his day they appear to be in danger of degenerating into verbosity and pedantry. Patrick certainly has very little learning and no rhetoric whatever, but he is aware of his deficiency and honest about it, and succeeds in a surprising way in compensating for his lack of these things. Gildas writes much about God's wrath and punishment, Patrick constantly harps upon God's loving care'.[13]

So the heirs of Arthur may have been less than chivalrous. The English were, however, also less gentlemanly on arrival than they later liked to admit. And the poison stayed in the system. Bede may well be reckoned the most truly educated and attractive man to be found anywhere in his day. But when he was drawing his *Ecclesiastical History* to a close in 731, he still could not find it in him to forgive 'the Britons, who would not pass to the English a knowledge of the Christian faith'. Although he accepted a fellow-Englishman's story of the British Ninian's mission to the Picts, he ignored the British Patrick's more important mission to Ireland. And his narrative shows an Englishman's bitter hatred of the Welsh. He seems never to have pondered the reason why, clinging to a Christian tradition already ancient, the Welsh would not accept the authority of intruders.

Bede tells the story of how 'the warlike King of the English, Ethelfrid, made a very great slaughter of that perfidious nation'. This was in a battle near Chester about 615. The pagan king observed that the monks of Bangor Iscoed and other Welsh priests had come to watch the battle and to pray for victory to 'their God'. He therefore commanded that they were to be attacked first, and 'about twelve hundred' were cut down. 'Thus', Bede gloats, 'was fulfilled the prophecy of the holy Bishop Augustine that those perfidious men should be punished by temporal death because they had despised the offer of eternal salvation'. It is an astonishing verdict on a tradition which had built and maintained the Christian Church

---

[13] R. P. C. Hanson, *St Patrick*, p.199.

in Roman or Celtic Britain across almost four hundred difficult years.

All that the Romanized Britons handed over to the English was the land itself. But what a legacy it was! Gildas lets us glimpse the island for which men fought savagely. 'Virtually on the edge of the world . . . it is protected on all sides by a vast ring of sea, almost impossible to cross . . . but it has the benefit of . . . two splendid rivers, the Thames and the Severn, up which luxuries from overseas used to be brought by ship. It is ornamented with twenty-eight cities and many castles, and well equipped with fortifications. . . . Like a bride arrayed in her jewels, the island is decorated with wide plains and agreeably placed hills, excellent for vigorous farming, and with mountains specially suitable for the pasture of cattle. Flowers of many colours make them a delightful picture. To water it the island has sparkling fountains . . . and clear rivers that glide with a gentle murmur. . . .'

CHAPTER TWO

THE CONVERSION OF ENGLAND

· Saxon Church at Brixworth · Northamptonshire ·

WHY KINGS WERE BAPTIZED

A modern historian has made a fair comment. 'The question is sometimes put why the Anglo-Saxons were converted to Christianity so quickly. The truth is that they were not converted at all quickly. In spite of there being good political and cultural reasons for the conversion of kings to Christianity, in spite of an extraordinary galaxy of able and saintly missionaries, it took nearly ninety years to convert just the kings and the greater part of their aristocracy, not to speak of the countryside which was a question of centuries. In the course of that near-ninety years hardly a court was converted which did not suffer at least one subsequent relapse into paganism before being reconverted. The old religious instincts died hard.'[1]

The correctness of that judgement is confirmed by the evidence that church councils, bishops and preachers had to do battle against pagan magic long after the official conversion of the people. In 786 the first legates (ambassadors) to visit England from papal Rome commented on the survival of pagan practices. Some twenty years later Alcuin in a letter to Etherhard, Archbishop of York, pointed out that some of the people were carrying magic amulets and 'taking to the hills where they worship, not with prayer, but in drunkenness'. The hill of Harrow overlooking London was one such scene of pagan worship; *hearh* means 'holy place'. Inevitably the monks to whom we owe most of our knowledge of Anglo-Saxon history did not wish to record many details of a heathen religion, but the *Life* of St Wilfrid told how, when he and his companions were shipwrecked on the coast of Sussex, a pagan priest stood on top of the cliff shouting curses at them. Bede included in his *De Temporum Ratione* an account of the pagan English year (which began on 25 December) and in one of his stories about the miracles of St Cuthbert gives us a glimpse of a 'large multitude' of peasants standing on the shore at the mouth of the river Tyne. They were jeering at some monks whose little boats were being swept out to sea by the fierce wind. Cuthbert rebuked them, only to hear these further insults: 'Nobody shall pray for them! May God save none of them! For they have robbed us of the old religion and nobody knows how to cope with all these changes!'

The toughness of paganism at a higher social level is illustrated by Bede's mention of the fact that the East Anglian aristocrats killed their king, Sigbert, 'because he was too ready to forgive his enemies'. It is also significant that the Saxons who stayed behind on the mainland were the last of the west German tribes to be converted. They killed the two English

[1] Henry May-Harting, *The Coming of Christianity to Anglo-Saxon England* (London, 1972), p.29.

...ionaries, the brothers Black Hewald and White Hewald,
... to preach to them at the end of the seventh century, and
...r eighth-century conversion was completed only at the
point of the sword. We may well ask: what factors eventually
made for the success of the new message of Christian humility
among the proud, determined and conservative Anglo-
Saxons?,

Their society always depended on the unquestioning willingness of most people to work and fight for their lords,
specially for their kings. No new religion could make an impact on such a society except with the good will of the kings,
and it is not surprising that Christianity spread from the top
downwards.[2] The question, therefore, is what first attracted
the kings. And the answer seems to lie in the example of Gaul
across the Channel. Its now prosperous invaders had become
Christians.

An incident was related in the clumsy Latin *Life of St
Gregory* by an anonymous monk of Whitby between 704 and
714 (the first book known to have been written by an
Englishman). It was an incident which thoroughly deserved
the fame it has enjoyed since Bede included it in his
Ecclesiastical History fifteen or twenty years after that first
telling. One day in Rome the future pope, Gregory, noticed
some fair-skinned, blond and generally good-looking young
men. Asking to what people they belonged, he was told 'the
Angles'; and he commented that they looked more like angels.
He was further told that they came from the kingdom of Deira
(the modern Yorkshire) and made a further pun about *Dei
ira*, the wrath of God from which he wished to save them. The
incident is revealing because it shows that slaves were being
sold from England to traders in Gaul, presumably by the kings
who had captured them during fights between the rival Anglo-
Saxon war-bands. And whatever Gregory may or may not
have said on that day in Rome, there survives a letter of his
dated September 595. As pope he ordered his agent in Gaul to

---

[2] See W. A. Chaney, *The Cult of Kingship in Anglo-Saxon England*
(Manchester, 1970), and J. M. Wallace-Hadrill, *Early Germanic
Kingship in England and on the Continent* (Oxford, 1971).

buy Englishmen between seventeen and eighteen years of age for training in monasteries. We may conclude that the trade between England and Gaul, including the slave-trade, produced a more general interest in England on the Continent – and, to match this, an interest in Christianity among the English.

Ethelbert, King of Kent, ruled the part of England most involved in the European common market. A fifth-century glass factory has been excavated in Faversham; it had been equipped by some of the Franks who had conquered Gaul. Other archaeological sites confirm how extensive the international trade was. A part of this connection with the Continent was Ethelbert's marriage before he became King of Kent with Bertha, daughter of Charibert, the Christian king reigning in Paris. The queen was accompanied by her chaplain, Bishop Liudhard, and attended services conducted by him in the small Roman church a little to the east of Canterbury dedicated to St Martin. The failure of Bertha and Liudhard to convert Ethelbert may have been due to their own laziness; a letter from Pope Gregory rebuked the queen. But Liudhard may not have lived long in England; certainly he disappears from the story. And the king, for all his wish to link Canterbury with Paris, seems to have been intensely suspicious lest the acceptance of the Franks' religion as well as a Frankish princess should involve submission to them politically.

He was also suspicious of Christianity as a magic different from the magic of his own people. Bede tells us that when in 597 Augustine landed in Kent as the envoy of Pope Gregory, Ethelbert insisted on hearing him in the open air. But the missionary probably had a special reason to overcome his own great nervousness, for the pope's correspondence hints clearly that Augustine landed only when Gregory had been assured of Ethelbert's welcome.[3] And it is clear that when he had been baptized the king expressed his respect for the new priests handsomely. In his laws anyone stealing his bishop's property was compelled to make restitution elevenfold. For the king's

---

[3] Margaret Deansley has given us a portrait of this first English archbishop in *Augustine of Canterbury* (London, 1964).

own property, ninefold was enough. What is not so clear is how deep Ethelbert's conversion went. His second wife and his eldest son were both pagans.[4]

It was, it seems, easier for a king to accept a missionary from far-distant Rome because no risk seemed to be involved of political submission. As the monks in black chanted their Latin prayers on English soil around a silver cross and a painted image of Jesus (according to Bede), probably no one foresaw the full extent to which future popes would revive the worldly claims of the Caesars. But perhaps Augustine and his fellow-monks did even then have some beginnings of an insight into the future of the bishopric of Rome. They came from St Andrew's monastery which Gregory had founded in his own former mansion on the Coelian Hill, when he had turned to the monastic life from his work as the secular 'prefect' of Rome. Monks belonging to the Italian tradition regulated by the great St Benedict (who was born in or about 480) have seldom been missionaries. But these monks knew how imperious was the will of a pope who took an interest in an island on the edge of the world which Rome had ruled. When they had turned back from their perilous journey to England, they had been sent forward by Gregory the Great himself, exercising authority over them and their fears without hesitation.

More than eight hundred of this creative pope's letters are preserved in Rome. Some thirty concern the mission to England. They show that despite the suspicions of later historians Gregory had no long-term plans to establish papal supremacy by taking a personal initiative in missions beginning with Augustine's; on the contrary, as he struggled to pacify and convert the Lombard invaders in Italy, he expected the end of the world to come soon. (So, for that matter, did

---

[4] The evidence that Kent under Ethelbert remained largely pagan is assembled in Appendix I to H. G. Richardson and G. O. Sayles, *Law and Legislation from Aethelberht to Magna Carta* (Edinburgh, 1966). A summary of 'The archaeology of Anglo-Saxon England in the pagan period' has been provided by Catherine Hills in *Anglo-Saxon England*, ed. Peter Clemoes (Cambridge, 1979), pp.297-327.

every one of those Anglo-Saxon Christians who have left us their thoughts on the subject.) But standing as he believed he did in a brief period between the end of the empire and the end of the world, his mind was also full of memories of Roman rule. He knew that the chief Roman cities in Britain had been London the commercial centre and York the military headquarters. Accordingly he ordered that the chief bishops were to be established in London and York, each having under him twelve dioceses.

It was a new kind of Roman colonization, and in July 598 Gregory wrote from Rome to Eulogius, Patriarch of Alexandria, gleeful about the baptism on Christmas Day of some ten thousand of the English. They were a people 'placed in a corner of the world and until this time worshipping sticks and stones'. The number of such baptisms reported from Augustine's years based on Canterbury may well reflect the presence in the area of many who had links, at least in their family traditions, with the British Church. But the decisive factor was the willingness in Kent to draw closer to the Continent. This is made clear by Bede's narrative, which was based on the traditions of Canterbury communicated to him by Abbot Albinus and on letters of Pope Gregory brought to Jarrow from Rome by Nothelm, a London priest employed by Albinus to help Bede.[5] And the next steps in the spread of Christianity were connected just as clearly with Anglo-Saxon high politics.

Redwald, King of the East Angles, was persuaded by Ethelbert to accept baptism; but Bede tells us that on his return home Redwald was told by his wife to forget his conversion, except to the extent of placing a Christian altar alongside the pagan one in his private temple. Almost cer-

---

[5] These letters seem to be largely, but not completely, genuine. The most interesting among them, the so-called *Responsiones*, are not found in Gregory's own register of correspondence and contain at least one clear anachronism, but may well be substantially Gregorian. See P. Meyvaert's study in *England before the Norman Conquest*, ed. P. Clemoes and K. Hughes (Cambridge, 1971), pp.15-34. Jeffrey Richards, *Consul of God* (London, 1980), is the latest English tribute to Pope Gregory.

tainly this acceptance and rejection of Ethelbert's Christianity
corresponded with Redwald's acceptance and rejection of
Ethelbert's overlordship. And probably a memorial of his
semi-Christian attitude survives in the treasure buried with a
ship at Sutton Hoo, near Rendlesham in Suffolk where the
East Anglian kings had a residence. The treasure, discovered
in 1939, is now in the British Museum.

It is not certain that the burial did honour Redwald, who
died about 625, but the evidence all seems to be compatible
with this identification. Some of the highly skilled goldsmiths
and jewellers who made this treasure may have been English,
but others were Swedish. There is also evidence supplied by
coins and other objects of trade with Gaul and, through Gaul,
with Byzantium the capital of the eastern empire. A large dish
bears the mark of Anastasius, emperor 491-518. It was a
burial in the old pagan style, full of the equipment which the
warrior-king would need on his voyage into eternity (there was
even a lyre for his music); but perhaps most impressive of all is
the presence of a couple of silver spoons in the Byzantine style.
One is inscribed SAULOS, the other PAULOS. They link the
owner of this treasure with the baptism of Saul of Tarsus, who
became Paul the Apostle to the Gentiles. And it is possible
that the king did not entirely lapse from the faith into which
he had been baptized. No definite traces of a human body
have ever been found in this magnificent pagan tomb. It has
been asked: did the king receive a Christian burial quietly
elsewhere?[6]

Redwald took over from Ethelbert as overlord of the
Southern English, and was in his turn eclipsed by the victories
of Edwin, the king of the Angles to the north of the Humber.
The site of Edwin's simple palace at Yeavering, including a
grandstand for semi-democratic assemblies, was excavated in
the 1950s; but we should not think that Edwin lacked authority. His power over the Scots resulted in the naming of Edwin's Borough, still preserving his name as Edinburgh.

Edwin married Ethelberga, a daughter of King Ethelbert,

---

[6] See *The Sutton Hoo Ship Burial*, ed. R. L. S. Bruce-Mitford, vol. i
(London, 1975).

and accepted Bishop Paulinus (an Italian sent by Pope
Gregory to England in 601) in his court as her chaplain.
Various pressures were brought on him to embrace his queen's
faith, including a letter from Pope Boniface reproduced by
Bede, but what seems to have been decisive was the memory of
the time he had spent as an exile at Redwald's court. He had
then been in fear of his life, but had met a stranger who had
promised him safety and had laid his hand on his head in
blessing. (Bede tells this story – and has the generosity to add
that the refugee had been delivered from death by the insistence of Redwald's pagan queen that in honour a king must
protect his guests.) Now, years later at Edwin's own court,
Paulinus revealed that he had been the stranger. Together this
powerful ruler and his friend the bishop won thousands of
converts. It was to be remembered as a golden age. Bede
claims that a mother with a new-born babe could have walked
'throughout the island, from sea to sea, without receiving any
harm'; and that brass dishes were placed by fountains near the
highways for the convenience of travellers – were placed there,
and remained there. He had talked with a monk who recalled
a conversation with an old man who had been baptized in the
Trent at noon-day, with a crowd of other converts. This old
man even remembered what St Paulinus looked like: 'tall of
stature, a little stooping, with black hair, a thin face, a slender
and hooked nose, his whole appearance both venerable and
majestic'.

This fruitful alliance of Church and State lasted for no
more than six years (627-633). It collapsed when Edwin was
overthrown and killed by another alliance – between his
fellow-Christian, King Caedwallon the Briton, and his fellow-
Englishman, the pagan King Penda of the Mercians (meaning
Borderers) in the Midlands. Paulinus had to flee with Queen
Ethelberga to the south, where he was given a fresh sphere as
Bishop of Rochester. Only James the Deacon carried on as a
Christian missionary in the north, in his solitariness advertising what the withdrawal of royal patronage meant to the new
religion.

So politics and economics played their parts in the adoption
of Christianity by three successive Anglo-Saxon overlords; and

significant evidence about the alliance of Church and State
was included in Bede's *Ecclesiastical History*. Indeed, the
History seems to have been modelled on the work of Bishop
Eusebius — the historian who had celebrated the effects of the
conversion of the emperor Constantine in far-off Caesarea
(where Pilate had once had his headquarters) back in the
fourth century. Bede knew the work of Eusebius through
Rufinus, who had translated and completed the Greek book.

If we had fuller evidence about missions which Bede barely
mentions, we should probably find similar reasons for the
support given by other kings to other missionaries. Sigbert,
King of the East Angles, who had become a Christian while an
exile in Gaul, welcomed Felix, a bishop from Burgundy — and
in seventeen years Felix managed to plant the Church in the
area where Paulinus had failed. He died about 650. Cynegils,
King of the West Saxons, had the Northumbrian king,
Oswald, as his sponsor when baptized. This baptism was the
prelude to effective work by Birinus, a missionary bishop
consecrated in Milan, who established a primitive cathedral
in Dorchester-on-Thames and also founded a church in
Winchester before his death (also about 650). How much depended on a king's liking for a particular bishop is shown by
the fact that the next king of the West Saxons, Cenwalla, got
rid of two bishops whom he disliked — Agilbert (a Frank) and
Wine (who is reckoned as the first Bishop of Winchester).

Peada, the future king of the Mercians, was baptized when
he married the daughter of another Northumbrian king,
Oswiu; and he arranged for the conversion of the Midlands to
begin even during the lifetime of his pagan father, Penda.
Four priests were sent by King Oswiu to begin this mission in
653. Two were brothers. One of these, St Chad, later (in 669)
became the first Bishop of the Mercians, building his
cathedral in Lichfield and tirelessly preaching until his death
in 672. The other, St Cedd, did not stay long in the Midlands
but evidently this was not due to any lack of missionary zeal.
In 654 he was recalled to become Bishop of the East Saxons.
The churches he founded during his subsequent work included the monastery at Lastingham, quietly remote on the
Yorkshire moors.

The nave of the church which Cedd built in his own diocese at Bradwell-on-Sea, using Roman bricks from the nearby fort of Othona, is used for worship to this day. It is a simple building, but one which sums up this whole first age in Christian England's story: an age when kings and their peoples were baptized because the Christian Church was given prestige by the civilization of Gaul and Rome. To become a Christian meant to cease to be a barbarian.

LINDISFARNE OR ROME?

Chad and Cedd had, however, been trained not in any of the centres where men felt close to the prosperity of Gaul and to the religion of Rome, but on the holy island of Lindisfarne in the North Sea – a centre of the mission commonly called Celtic or Irish. We must now consider this very impressive mission as a possible rival to a distinctly Roman form of Catholicism as the religion of England.

Bede's *Ecclesiastical History* was the work of a man who was very much a Roman Catholic; indeed, it was to be translated in 1565 by Thomas Stapleton, an exiled Roman Catholic priest, to prove the claim that the Roman Catholic mission to Elizabethan England was identical with the mission on which St Gregory had sent St Augustine. But one of Bede's charms is that his imagination has been caught by the holiness of men who did not look, as he looked, towards Rome. He quotes someone who listened to Fursey, an Irish saint who lived in voluntary self-exile among the East Angles in the 630s. This informant remembered the saint describing a vision of fire – and sweating although it was winter.

Bede also tells how Augustine did not rise from his chair when the British bishops came to meet him. In contrast, when he became a bishop Chad had to be pushed on to a horse. Missionaries trained at Lindisfarne had previously refused to use horses despite the length of their preaching tours; they knew that horses separated them from the people they might meet on the way. Bede shows us how Augustine was so ignor-

ant of lay life that he had to seek instructions from Pope
Gregory on an amazing variety of sexual and other problems.
In contrast, the missionary saints who looked to Lindisfarne,
despite their preference for the continuous prayer-life of a
hermit, identified themselves with the world of the poor.
Bede, it seems, could not help loving them more than
Augustine, who had to be rebuked by Pope Gregory for the sin
of pride. He knew that these men whose hearts had been fired
by an Irish sanctity had spread fire among simple people, who
judged missionaries by how they lived.

The early history of the Celtic Church from which their inspiration came is not well mapped. (How much of the early
history of the English Church would we have known if Bede's
History, the fruit of his old age, had perished?) What is known
shows that, in its isolation from the rest of the Christian world,
the strongly tribal society of the Irish had retained or
developed a number of customs which now made them look
peculiar in the eyes of Rome; yet they retained the energy of
the unsophisticated, the uncorrupt. Two passions had grown
strong in them. One was for the learning to be found in
Christian books. They could see and touch and even in some
cases read those books, to them the thrilling embodiment of
the world beyond their shores. The other Celtic passion was
for 'pilgrimage for the love of God'. By this they meant the
heroic self-discipline of one who exiled himself from the land
of his birth and his heart. Perhaps there was in this potent
emotion a more worldly love of adventure, even a touch of
tourism. With whatever motives, Irish monks were to be found
as far east as Kiev in Russia, as far west as Iceland; and the
story was to grow that St Brendan's leather boat reached an
earthly paradise, North America.

All these characteristics of the Irish missionary movement
come out in the story of St Columba. He was a prince who had
become a monk but had still got involved in a battle with a
rival tribe, it is said over the possession of a manuscript.
Ashamed (or perhaps exiled) after this bloodletting, Columba
led his monks to settle on the very beautiful island of Iona,
and made at least one expedition to the nearby, and almost
equally beautiful, country of the Picts. He died on Iona in

597, eight days after the baptism of Ethelbert in Canterbury.

Iona became linked with the story of England because a young Northumbrian prince, Oswald, became a Christian while in exile among the Irish monks on Iona. Returning home, Oswald drove back the British and was acknowledged king in 633. Once in power, he asked the monks of Iona for a missionary. The first man to be sent soon retreated to his base, complaining that the English were too uncouth. Oswald and the Northumbrians were then sent a saint: Aidan. And Aidan was humble enough to win love. Bede tells the story of how the king gave an exceptionally fine horse to Aidan – who passed the gift on to a beggar. A spiritual force stronger than Gregorian Rome's imperialism as represented by Augustine had come to woo and to captivate the English.

The heart of the Christian mission lies for Bede, it seems, not in Augustine's Canterbury but on Aidan's island of Lindisfarne. He dedicated his great *History* to King Coelwulf, who was soon to begin twenty-seven years as a monk on Lindisfarne. There, within sight of Bamburgh, the Bernician royal castle on the rocky coast, St Aidan established a monastery in 635. The huts of this monastery, made of wood and thatch, were so lowly that no archaeologist has found traces of them beneath the tough grass and the salt winds. It was England's Iona.

Aidan, for whom King Oswald was content to act as interpreter, was a great saint – but not the greatest to be associated with this holy island. St Cuthbert, an English monk who moved with his abbot from Melrose to Lindisfarne in 664, found the island too crowded for his liking, and in 676 withdrew to pray alone on one of the nearby Farne Islands. He would, Bede tells us, pray all night in the cold sea, but once had his feet warmed by two seals on the sand, to the amazement of a monk who was spying on him. (To this day Britain's largest colony of grey seals is found here.) Reluctantly he agreed to be consecrated bishop in 685 but loved to return to this place of prayer. And he loved to fast, so that in his weakness the vision of God might grow strong. Shortly before his death in 687 he was cut off on his island by a great storm, when too ill to move. He had as his food five onions. When the alarmed monks eventually reached him, it was his gentle boast that four of the onions were untouched.

When his skeleton was disinterred in 1827 it was found that this austerely uncomplaining man had been riddled with tuberculosis and tormented by ulcers. But he had been buried with some eloquent, although small, treasures: a cross for his breast made with all the skill of the pagan jeweller, a large ivory comb, a portable altar. Incorporated into the cross was a shell which had come from the Indian Ocean. In death the English shepherd-boy had become a prince of the Church, a king in the marvellous new realm of Christian holiness.[7]

The courage of saints such as Aidan and Cuthbert, moving out so simply to God and to the people, may be contrasted with an incident which took place in Canterbury in or about 616. Mellitus, Bishop of London, had been forced out of his diocese by the pagan reaction under Ethelbert's son Eadbald. During his retreat to Canterbury he had been joined by Justus, Bishop of Rochester, who was similarly discouraged. They had urged Laurentius, Augustine's successor at Canterbury, to join them in flight. They had already crossed the Channel to the safety of Gaul, leaving Laurentius to say his prayers in church during what he believed would be his last night in England. During the night, however, the despondent archbishop had a dream about St Peter, who rebuked his cowardice. So he stayed put; King Eadbald was amazed and converted by his new courage; and Mellitus and Justus were recalled. We cannot imagine those true saints, Aidan and Cuthbert, needing any such reminder about their duty.

But for all the attractiveness of the humble and holy men associated with Lindisfarne, they lacked something: authority to teach a creed, to organize an institution, to command. When the English Church was united, the union came around the authority of St Peter and his successors in the Bishopric of Rome. That union lasted for almost exactly nine hundred years and when it had perished in the sudden storm of the Reformation its restoration seemed a cause still worthy of the dedication of many English martyrdoms.

---

[7] See *The Relics of St Cuthbert*, ed. C. F. Battiscombe (Oxford, 1958).

The unification was made possible by the decision at the small English synod meeting at Whitby in 664 to accept the latest papal way of dating Easter as a symbol of Christian Rome's general authority. It may seem that the decision might easily have gone in favour of the Celtic or Irish Church with its own Easter; but the defenders of the outmoded Celtic date in the synod at Whitby had little real hope of success. The king (Oswiu) who presided over the synod was married to a queen (King Edwin's daughter, Eanfled) who, having been brought up in Kent, already observed the Catholic Easter. Over most of Ireland at this time the latest Catholic date had already been accepted; the northern Irishmen who clung obstinately to a separate date (on Iona itself, until 716) were not typical of the Irish as a whole. The authority of Rome in this matter was almost bound to prevail, in England as in Ireland. A reference was made by King Oswiu ('smiling a little,' says Bede) to the danger of offending St Peter when one knew that one would have to appear oneself at the gates of heaven, but the practical point was the need to accept the verdict of the living pope for the sake of unity. The best of the English missionaries trained by the Irish seem to have been ready enough to bow to this verdict. Chad and Cedd conformed. So did Tuda the new Northumbrian bishop (a Southern Irishman) and Eata the new abbot of Lindisfarne (an Englishman trained by St Aidan), although Bishop Colman, who had spoken against the Roman date at Whitby, felt obliged to resign and to return to Iona after his defeat. For all the attractiveness of the Lindisfarne tradition, the prestige of Rome proved unanswerable.

In England the unification of the Church around the authority of the papacy was dominated by the contrasting personalities of two great churchmen, both of them highly authoritarian: St Wilfrid and St Theodore.

Wilfrid was an Englishman who travelled to Rome when not yet twenty, and was always fascinated by it. With youthful eloquence in the debates at Whitby he urged the claims of Rome as the claims of Peter the prince of the apostles. He was appointed to be bishop of the Northumbrians with his cathedral in York, but felt it necessary to go to Gaul in order to secure an appropriately valid and splendid consecration.

Twelve bishops conveyed the grace of the apostles to him, and
he was carried into the sanctuary on a golden chair — perhaps
more like an emperor than an apostle. In his absence King
Oswiu grew impatient and appointed the more modest and
agreeable Chad as his successor, but on his return Wilfrid
raged, and Chad was packed off to become the first Bishop of
Lichfield.

During disputes about the extent of his jurisdiction and income as bishop of Northumbrians, the far from humble
Wilfrid twice returned to Rome in order to argue his case. In
the course of those disputes, when exiled from his own
northern territory, he found himself among the Middle
Saxons, the still wholly pagan South Saxons and even the
pagan and terrifying Frisians on the German coast; and in
every case he immediately began work as a missionary, for he
was a bishop of the Universal Church. But his chief delight
was to build, decorate, equip and secure estates for his
magnificent churches at Hexham and Ripon, with everything
in the Roman style, for monks living according to the rule of
St Benedict. The crypts of his churches remain. In York he
restored the little cathedral built by Paulinus. As he lay dying,
aged seventy-five, he had his treasures brought to his bed and
divided them up so that these monasteries and his other
followers could 'buy friends' for themselves when he was gone.
He was a proud, although devout, prelate (a bishop for forty-
five years) who although he died in 710 belonged in spirit to
the high Middle Ages. We know of him through a biography
written by his admiring disciple, Eddius Stephanus.[8] Plainly
he embarrassed Bede.

Theodore had a less dramatic but more steadily creative
personality. Born in St Paul's own city of Tarsus, he had spent
most of his life as a scholarly monk in the East but had moved
to teach in Rome. When the Englishman Wighard, seeking
consecration as Archbishop of Canterbury, had died of the
plague in Rome, and when two other Roman monks had declined invitations to replace him, Pope Vitalian turned to
Theodore, then aged sixty-six. Next year (668) the old man set

---

[8] It was edited and translated by Bertram Colgrave (Cambridge, 1927).

out for England – and during twelve years achieved a work of organization more remarkable than the achievement of any Archbishop of Canterbury before or since. With his fellow-monk Hadrian who accompanied him from Rome he presided over a school at Canterbury. A teacher with English pupils was like a boar surrounded by hounds, it was said, but so effective was the teaching that Bede assures us that some of the men emerging from this Canterbury school were fluent equally in their native language, in Latin and in Greek. The tireless old archbishop summoned the first general council of the whole English Church to meet at Hertford in 672 and planned annual councils although the difficulties of travel were so great that this optimistic plan had to be abandoned. He founded dioceses, issued laws ('canons') to regulate church life, deposed unsatisfactory bishops, and handed down the appropriate judgements on the moral problems of the lesser members of his flock in his *Poenitentiale*. For example, he decreed that if a man could not buy back a wife who had been violently taken into slavery he was free to marry again after five years.

Although little visible evidence of Theodore's achievement has survived the centuries, we can still enter its atmosphere by visiting the parish church at Brixworth in Northamptonshire. Built about 680, it looks like a fortress outside. Inside it resembles a *basilica*, a Roman hall for the administration of justice; and the bricks of which it is made are Roman. The whole building speaks of the restoration of Roman rule to this island, although the new empire needed no legions. It is not surprising that although Wilfrid was one of the thorns in St Theodore's elderly flesh the two men were reconciled before death, for ultimately they both claimed authority not as English potentates but as ambassadors of Rome.

What drew the Anglo-Saxons to Rome was, no doubt, in part a worldly lure. In 747 an English missionary who was always suspicious of the worldliness of the eternal city (St Boniface) complained that there was scarcely a city on the road to Rome without its Englishwoman who had come as a pilgrim and remained as an adulteress or prostitute. But there was also a strong religious motive to inspire the long and

dangerous journey. Two kings of the West Saxons in succession – the young Caedwalla, exhausted after fighting his
way to the throne, and Ine the mature law-giver – died as
pilgrims in Rome. King Alfred's father, Ethelwulf, left estates
in Wessex in order that there would always be plenty of oil in
the lamps of the churches of Peter and Paul in Rome on Easter
Eve. Gradually the pilgrims became so numerous that a *schola
Saxonum* was established in the English quarter of the city,
with an English church (now Santo Spirito in Sassia). Towards
the end this tradition was clouded by the intrusion of an
Englishman, Stigand, into the archbishopric of Canterbury in
place of the Norman, Robert of Jumièges, whom the pope
continued to regard as the legitimate archbishop; and this was
one of the reasons why Duke William's Normans conquered
under the blessing of a papal banner. But it is revealing that
the English showed themselves to be nervous about Stigand's
right to function as archbishop. To the end they were loyal to
the distant pope, proud of being a small part of the greater
Christian world under Rome, conscious in particular of what
they owed to Pope Gregory. England was more regular than
any other country in sending a tax to Rome (Peter's Pence); so
regular that popes began to claim that it proved England's
acknowledgement of a duty to pay tribute.

A wide world began to be opened to the English by their
conversion to the religion taught in Rome.

In the 660s an Englishwoman – beautiful, devout and determined – was regent in the kingdom of the Franks. Balthild
had been a slave girl bought for household duties in the
palace, but had attracted the notice of King Clovis II, who
had married her. When Clovis died and their son was not old
enough to rule, she assumed control of the government until
the turbulent barons persuaded her to retire to the monastery
of Chelles near Paris, one of a number which she had founded
while queen.

In the 670s a young westcountryman, Aldhelm, was studying the culture of the day in Canterbury under Archbishop
Theodore and Abbot Hadrian. He wrote an excited letter to
the Bishop of Winchester, proudly apologizing for not being
able to spend Christmas with the old man; he was too pre-

occupied with his books, which included a Roman law book as well as arithmetic, music, versification, astronomy and every aspect of ecclesiastical learning. Aldhelm went on to become a great scholar, Abbot of Malmesbury, Bishop of Sherborne and, after his death in 709, a saint. We have a hundred or so riddles by him in Latin. He wrote a Latin which was too elaborate to be elegant, but it was modelled on the work of Irish scholars (his first teacher had been an Irishman, Maelduib) – and was far more fluent than the barbaric Latin being written in Italy at this time. He gloated over these rich, strange words, watching them glow and flash like one of the Anglo-Saxon warriors turning over captured treasure. King Alfred reckoned St Aldhelm the best of all the Old English poets, although no poem of his in his native language has survived.

In the 680s a Frankish (or, as we can begin to say, French) bishop named Arculf was caught in a storm at sea and wrecked on Britain's western coast. He found his way to the monastery on the island of Iona and told his story to its abbot, Adamnan. He had been to see the holy places in Palestine. Adamnan wrote it down and took his book with him on a visit to the Northumbrian court. Eventually the book reached Bede and the gist of it was incorporated into his *History*. There the material seems irrelevant – but Bede evidently thought it exciting that such a book had been written in his own lifetime, when the Muslims, as he knew, were sweeping through Spain into Gaul. He delighted to think of any English connection with Jerusalem and Galilee.

In the 720s a young Englishman from Wessex, Willibald, was a pilgrim in Rome. Leaving his brother Wynbald there, he decided to visit even holier places, although these were now under a firm Muslim occupation. Working his way through Sicily, Asia Minor and Cyprus, he saw the scenes of the earthly life of the Saviour and then returned to Rome after two years in Constantinople. He spent ten years in the monastery which St Benedict had founded at Monte Cassino, but in 740 was ordered by the pope to join his brother and sister in the English mission to what is now Germany. There St Willibald laboured until his death in 786; he was the first Bishop of

Eichstatt. He told his story to an English nun who wrote a
book about it — the first English travel book.

SONGS OF ENGLAND'S CONVERSION

So English Christians could now explore a European and
Mediterranean world. But the spiritual world of the Bible
excited their imaginations still more, with results which
survive in fragments of craftsmanship and of poetry.

The oldest surviving book written in England (but covered
with red leather made from the skin of an African goat) is a
copy of St John's gospel, now a treasure of Stonyhurst College.
The writing suggests that it was created by Bede's fellow-
monks in Northumbria; just possibly, it was Bede's own copy
of his favourite gospel. St Augustine had received in Canterbury an Italian copy of the four gospels still preserved at
Corpus Christi College, Cambridge, and now the English were
competing. St Wilfrid gave to his church at Ripon a book of
the gospels (now lost) which, we are told, was written in golden
letters on purple-tinted parchment and guarded in a jewelled,
golden case.

The finest of the religious poems of the Anglo-Saxons is *The
Dream of the Rood*. It seems to have been written well before
750. Passages from it were carved on the high red sandstone
cross still standing at Ruthwell near Dumfries, and a single
copy of the full poem has been preserved in the cathedral
library at Vercelli in Italy. The poet presents a dream about
the cross (which, as we have seen, even the Christians among
the Romans had for long avoided in art). He has seen the cross
golden, jewelled, suffused with light and adored by angels.
But he has also dreamed about its history. He has heard it
speak to him. The cross remembers the time when it was cut
down and set on a hill. It remembers, too, the time when the
Lord of mankind, 'the young hero, God Almighty', mounted
it with eager zeal. That warrior was pierced with nails, reviled

by his enemies, killed and covered with darkness, leaving the tree blood-drenched, heart-broken.

> All creation wept,
> Bewailed the King's death. Christ was on the cross.

The cross remembers, too, watching Christ being taken down, 'tired after the great agony', and buried in a sepulchre of bright stone while a dirge was sung. Then the cross itself was cut down and buried. But now the young warrior who died as a true hero is risen, the cross is greatly honoured as the tree of triumph, and the poet, remembering his dead friends who now 'live with the High Father', prays that the cross may soon carry him to heaven 'where the Lord's host is seated at the feast'.

Here an anonymous Old English poet's imaginative genius has interpreted the biblical stories in terms already familiar to the Anglo-Saxons – cutting down the trees of the forest; listening to nature (was it only the wind that spoke among the trees?); gold, jewels and the feast as the rewards of the battle; the victory gained by the warrior's courage and endurance; the permanent honour won by accepting a lonely defeat without flinching. Such were some of the themes of a much longer poem, *Beowulf*, an epic which seems to have been composed at about the same time as *The Dream of the Rood*.

Beowulf is a pagan poem in many senses: Christ is never mentioned, there is no statement of any explicitly Christian theme, the hero is a noble pagan and he is never criticized. In a leisurely way the poem includes, or alludes to, many subsidiary stories which presumably were part of the pagan folklore which the Anglo-Saxons brought with them. But the poet who has shaped this material is a Christian, as is shown by allusions to the Creation, Cain and Abel, the Flood and the Judgement, and by a few denunciations of reliance on heathen gods; not all these passages are likely to be later Christian interpolations in the poem, although some may be. Presumably he was a minstrel at an eighth-century court, perhaps the Mercian court of the great King Offa whose ancestors get a brief mention.

He wrote to entertain warriors after dinner in some royal

hall very like the one where some of the action of his poem
takes place. That means that efforts which have been made to
interpret his work as an elaborate allegory designed to put
across Christian teachings are probably far-fetched. Although
this was not an art intended primarily to appeal to monks,
some of the more worldly-minded monks, and the young
noblemen they were educating, would have enjoyed it. In the
790s Alcuin found it necessary to rebuke the monks of Lindisfarne for their love of the heroes of Germanic pagan
mythology: 'what has Ingeld to do with Christ?' Only one
ancient copy of *Beowulf* has survived (with scorch marks from
a fire in 1731); and in the same manuscript is found a Bible-
based poem celebrating the courage of Judith who killed an
Assyrian general after a drunken feast — which suggests that
this copy may have been treasured in some monastery, anyway
the most likely place for the survival of any literature.

Beowulf tells of Grendel, a demon who inhabited wild
moors and fens but also attacked the banqueting hall of
Hrothgar, King of the Danes. Beowulf, a young prince of the
Geats (in the country now Sweden), seizes at the opportunity
for adventure and glory. After a voyage — described with
gusto — Beowulf arrives at Hrothgar's hall, Heorot, and after a
great fight mortally wounds the demon. A feast with lavish
gifts follows, but then Grendel's mother returns to avenge her
son. Undeterred, Beowulf pursues the older demon. 'It is
better for a man to avenge his friend than to mourn him long',
he reminds King Hrothgar. 'We must all expect an end to life
in this world; let him who can win fame before death, for that
is a dead man's best memorial'. And Beowulf does win fresh
fame, tracking Grendel's mother to the lake where she lives
and eventually killing her after an underwater contest.
Rewarded with another feast and further gifts, and with a
long moral exhortation by old Hrothgar, he returns to his own
people and becomes their king for half a century of prosperity.

In his old age Beowulf undertakes his last battle, with a
dragon who guards a buried hoard of treasure. Determined to
win more fame and gold, or else to accept the common lot of
death, he fights and kills the dragon; but he is deserted by all
his followers (apart from one Swede, Prince Wiglaf) and

mortally wounded. He lives long enough to rejoice over the treasure, and after his death and cremation all of it is buried with his ashes amid many laments.

So 'they buried the gold and left that princely treasure to the keeping of earth, where it yet remains, as useless to men as it was before'. Beowulf is remembered as 'the gentlest and most gracious of men, the kindest to his people, the most eager for fame' – but the final impression left by the epic is of a funeral. The fame is tragic. At the end Beowulf's people, the Geats, know that they are now doomed to be conquered by the Swedes. There are many other mentions of feuds and deaths, and we are reminded that even the great hall of Heorot is soon to be burned down by enemies. The demons and the dragons symbolizing evil are conquered, but the heroes are also mortals, under the impartially ruthless sovereignty of fate. *Beowulf* is an entertainment for a feast, and it is the celebration of heroes. But it is also, in the words of J. R. R. Tolkien, an elegy about 'man at war with the hostile world and his inevitable overthrow in time'. It is a poem about a doomed pagan world, and therefore to its own Christian author it is the revival in a new and happier world of the tragedy of the heathen, the sadness of 'an ancient dirge'.[9]

Such was the world rescued from the devils of the darkness by the 'young hero, God Almighty' who fights in *The Dream of the Rood*.

Celebration of the biblical light in the darkness became (and remained for many centuries) the chief theme of the English poets. An early passage in *Beowulf* tells of a harp player in Heorot singing of the creation. God made the world a shining plain; he established the sun and the moon to light its inhabitants; he decked the earth with leaves and branches; he gave life to all that moves. And Bede attributes the same theme to Caedmon, the first Englishman to compose religious poems.

---

[9] J. R. R. Tolkien, 'Beowulf: the Monsters and the Critics', in *Proceedings of the British Academy* (London, 1936), pp.245-295. M. E. Goldsmith, *The Mode and Meaning of Beowulf* (London, 1970), also emphasizes the Christian content.

In the 670s Caedmon was a lay brother attached to St Hilda's monastery on the hill by the sea at Whitby. The story goes that one night he was asleep in the stable where he looked after the horses. He had escaped a feast because he had been once more embarrassed when the harp was passed round with the invitation to sing. But in his dream he heard a voice: 'Caedmon, sing some song to me'. 'I cannot sing'. 'But you *shall* sing!' 'What shall I sing?' 'Sing the beginning of the creation!' Caedmon's hymn has been preserved. Its nine-line tribute to the 'Father of glory' who 'made the beginning of every wonder' is not remarkable except for one thing. This illiterate herdsman had memorized not only the beginning of the Bible but also the secular songs he had heard in the hall; and he had fused the two. 'What Caedmon did was – so far as we know, for the first time – to apply the whole technical apparatus of that Germanic heroic poetry which the Anglo-Saxons had brought with them from their continental home-lands to a specifically Christian version of the story of Creation'.[10]

Later poems in this tradition are more sophisticated. There are only four whose authorship is known. These are by Cyne-wulf, a scholarly churchman who probably worked in Mercia and who added his name asking for his readers' prayers about 750. One of these poems, *Elene*, tells the story of the discovery of the cross by St Helen, the mother of the emperor Constantine; this alleged event, together with the subsequent distribution of innumerable pieces of the 'true' cross, encouraged devotion of the kind that gave birth to *The Dream of the Rood*. But Cynewulf knew his public; probably he belonged to it himself. Writing within a tradition of fighting and seafaring, he gave the English glowing accounts of Constantine's legendary battle against the Huns and of his mother's long voyage to the Holy Land. When he adapted a Latin legend to form his *Juliana*, what interested him most was the opportunity to celebrate the saint's heroism in her conflicts with the devil. Another of his poems, on *The Fates of the Apostles*,

---

[10] C. L. Wrenn, *A Study of Old English Literature* (London, 1967), p.102.

presents the Twelve as the Lord's companions who were glad
to fight his battles and to lay down their lives for him.
Cynewulf's *The Ascension of Christ*, based on a sermon by
Pope Gregory the Great, is also full of images that would
delight an Anglo-Saxon audience, presenting Christ's ascension into the sky as a sea-voyage into heaven.

Another long poem that has survived, *Andreas*, tells of the
loyalty of two of the apostles to each other. Braving a storm at
sea, cold and hunger, imprisonment and torture, Andrew
rescues Matthew from death among the cannibals. Other
Anglo-Saxon Christian poetry puts Lucifer (Satan) at the head
of his war-band in rebellion against his true overlord, God,
and pictures the Exodus as a voyage through a storm at sea.

All this presentation of the Christian message draws on the
tradition of Germanic heroic paganism, to which Tacitus
refers when he mentions that some of the barbarians would
sing poems about the descent of their kings from their
gods. Anglo-Saxon Christian poetry, celebrating holiness as
heroism, demonstrates how wise Pope Gregory was in 601 to
cancel his initial instruction to Augustine that all pagan
temples were to be destroyed. His second order, that the
temples were to be converted to Christian use and pagan
festivals turned into Christian feasts, was more typical of the
whole successful strategy to reclothe the Christian message in
Anglo-Saxon dress. The Gospel was accepted because it was
thoroughly interpreted in terms with which the English could
feel at home.

Inevitably the Gospel became dangerously English, for the
pagan culture influenced Christians even while they used it for
their own purposes; they knew that it was a great deal more
than the worship of 'sticks and stones', despite the distant Pope
Gregory's ignorant boast in 598. Missionaries spreading
Christianity through Asia and Africa in the nineteenth and
twentieth centuries became very nervous about any mixture
of the Christian and the heathen; it seemed to them 'syncretism' – a betrayal of the Gospel. In Anglo-Saxon England
there certainly was syncretism. A compromise between the
Gospel and paganism is shown in, for example, the Franks
casket in the British Museum. This is a box made of whale

bone, carved with Christian images such as the Adoration of
the Magi but also with scenes of Roman history and pagan
mythology. Many of the Christian leaders of Anglo-Saxon
England would have condemned such a compromise. But
because it treated many pagan traditions tenderly, the Christian mission seemed less of a threat to the Anglo-Saxons than
its greatest enthusiasts would have made it. If a Christian poet
wrote *Beowulf*, that helps to explain why no missionary in
Anglo-Saxon England had to be remembered as a martyr.

BEDE AMONG THE SAINTS

When Bede completed his *Ecclesiastical History of the English
People* in 731, he could tell of many saints. Despite all the
political and economic influences in the Christianization of
this society, the heart of the conversion of the English people
was personal religion; for despite all the attractions of contacts
with Gaul and Rome, of the sea-links with Iona and
Jerusalem, the most fascinating allurement offered by the new
religion was the hope of heaven. We gather from Bede's
stories, and from other sources, that between 610 and 830
about thirty English kings or queens became monks or nuns.
They were seeking a kingdom beyond the empire of death.

Bede's best known story is a little drama of this psychological reality behind the conversion of the English. In the
debate about the preaching of Paulinus before King Edwin in
his hall, the chief of the pagan priests, Coifi, said that the old
religion had not brought him adequate rewards; 'there are
many who receive greater favours from you'. Coifi proved that
he was a man of exceptional energy when he rode from the
royal hall on the king's stallion (a thing no priest had ever
done) and set fire to the temple which he had served. But
'another of the king's chief men' spoke about the old religion
at a deeper level. Man's life on earth was, he said, like the swift
flight of a sparrow through the hall, from door to door,
leaving and returning to the dark winter outside. 'So this life
of man appears for a short space, but of what went before, or

what is to follow, we are utterly ignorant'. The Christian message appealed because it seemed to provide information about this matter.

The women's response is specially striking. In pagan Anglo-Saxon society women were not always treated as insignificant; the stories about Redwald's formidable queen show that. But there is no suggestion that any escape was possible for women whose ambition was other than handing round the goblets and the gifts to the heroes (as Queen Wealhtheow did in *Beowulf*). The way in which the new religion, with its offer of heaven, captured the devotion of outstanding women, and made them intrepid heroines, is shown in the record of the Anglo-Saxon abbesses. Many of these were of noble, if not royal, birth. Some of them ruled monasteries including monks. This tradition of the 'double monastery', which deeply shocked later reformers, was taken over from the flourishing monastic life of Gaul, and since it provided 'orphanage, boarding-school, old people's home, hotel and, not least, avenue of occupation for meddlesome women', it has been reckoned 'the greatest single blessing bestowed by Christianity' on seventh-century England.[11]

St Etheldreda, for example, was the natural daughter of a Christian king of the East Angles. While a girl she must have set her heart on the life of a nun, for although she married twice (the second time to King Egfrid of the Northumbrians), she steadfastly refused to consummate either union. In the end she was allowed to found a double monastery at Ely amid the desolate fens. She was encouraged by Wilfrid in this spiritual ambition; that did not endear him to her husband. She ruled Ely as abbess, noted for her austerities, until her death in 679. And the next year saw the death of another famous saint and abbess of royal birth, Hilda. She had ruled Hartlepool and Streaoneshalh (as Whitby was called before the Danes came). The latter monastery, where Caedmon worked, has been excavated. It consisted of many small houses and cells within enclosing walls. Little signs of gracious living in this

---

[11] Joan Nicholson, concluding '*Feminae glorosiae:* Women in the Age of Bede', in *Medieval Women*, ed. D. Baker (Oxford, 1978), pp.15-29.

seaside monastery came to light during the excavation:
spindles and pens, many coins and fine specimens of imported
pottery, even nail-cleaners and ear-picks.

But the most impressive saint coming to meet us from
Bede's *History* is, readers tend to feel, Bede himself.

He was a genuine scholar, endlessly collecting the best
knowledge of his day. This is shown not only by the *History*
where at the beginning Bede listed his sources, but also by his
earlier books in which he expounded grammar, rhetoric,
science, chronology, martyrology and above all the Holy
Scriptures. Day after day and far into the night, he pondered
the meaning of books. He once wrote that the words of the
Bible had three meanings. There was the *literal* meaning,
which was like cooking on the griddle. The more advanced
allegorical meaning was like using the frying pan; and finally
there was the *mystical* meaning, like cooking in the oven. His
raw material consisted of the books which Benedict Biscop
had brought back from six journeys to Rome, together with
many more recent additions to a library which modern
scholars have catalogued on the basis of references in his own
works. The only surviving book known for certain to have
belonged to this collection is a copy of the Acts of the Apostles
in Oxford. In Florence is a copy of the complete Bible which
Bede's beloved abbot, Coelfrid, took with him as a present for
the pope when in his old age he determined to go on pilgrimage to Rome. It is said that manufacture of this one Bible
must have consumed the skins of more than 1,500 calves. But
the best monument to Bede's scholarship lies in the custom of
dating events from the year believed to have seen the birth of
Christ. This *Anno Domini* method was invented by a sixth-
century Roman monk, Dionysius Exiguus. Bede adopted it
and popularized it; his *History* is the first major work to use it.
A memorial of the older method of dating is preserved in the
dedication stone of St Paul's church in Jarrow, where he worshipped. Inscribed partly in Latin and partly in Old English
letters, the stone records that the building was dedicated on
'the ninth of the Kalends of May in the fifteenth year of King
Ecgfrith and the fourth year of Colfrith, abbot'. This refers to
23 April 685.

Bede's literary work was, of course, not purely academic. It was part and parcel of his work as a monk, celebrating the grace of the God whose praises he sang several times a day, looking back to a golden age of holiness and evangelism. How his mind was working not long after the completion of his *History* comes out in his long letter of 734 to his former pupil, Egbert, now Bishop of York.

This was a letter full of pride in the 'innumerable blameless people of chaste conduct, boys and girls, young men and maidens, old men and women' to be found in the Northumbrian Church. But Bede was not complacent. Egbert must study scripture devoutly and make sure that the people could repeat at least the Lord's Prayer and the Apostles' Creed, in English if not in Latin. He must ordain more priests, for some of the outlying villages and hamlets have not seen a bishop for years although they all have to pay their dues. He must try to get more bishops consecrated – for did not St Gregory himself plan for an Archbishop of York with twelve bishops under him? (Egbert was in fact made archbishop shortly after Bede wrote.) And he must stop laymen from founding spurious monasteries in order to get their lands exempt from taxation; the defences of the kingdom are in danger. Right into his sixties, when he wrote his *History* and this letter, Bede was a concerned and active churchman, with a policy for the future.

The modern reader has to summon patience when Bede seems to be wasting words on miracle-stories while denying us information which we should greatly have preferred. But he was a man of his time, fundamentalist in his approach to the Bible, credulous in his zest for the collection of tales of the supernatural. And his time was a period of universal belief in the supernatural. Pagans expected gifts from the gods in exchange for the gifts which men offered to them – as did the priest Coifi in Bede's own story. The ambassadors of Christianity could offer no less. They, too, had to produce victory in battle, good crops, many children, deliverance from disease and death; or at least to produce the necessary impression. Exactly what happened (if anything did) to give rise to the miracle stories, is a question which perhaps no man is now wise enough to answer – but some of the holy men of the day may well have exercised the psychic powers as all around them would have expected. Far more remarkable is the fact that Bede supplies us with so much down-to-earth evidence about the foundation of the English Church. Incidentally it was the birth of England as a unit; although he was a monk not a traveller and there were large areas from which he had received little information (Wessex, for example), Bede was interested in the whole country. He passionately believed in its religious unity. Peculiar Irish customs about dating Easter, or about the fashion in shaving a monk's head, must, he insisted, not be allowed to disrupt the unity. Long before they had any political unity other than the temporary dominance of an overlord (*Bretwalda*), the English people as seen by Bede had this unity in their faith and their Church: and in this perspective, his zeal for Catholic uniformity is understood to be more than trivial.

Bede wrote in order to build up Christian England. Probably the chief audience which he had in mind was monks in other monasteries, when his *History* would be read out at refectory meals, but his theme was the English people. And he lets us see that under God English men and women had created their unity by the holiness they had in common. For that, it seems, was the miracle that interested Bede most. In his history of the abbots of the monastery where he had lived since the age of seven, there was no story of the supernatural. No conversation with angels marked his last hours on the eve of Ascension Day 735, as related by the monk Cuthbert. Instead we are told of his talk with his pupils. 'Learn quickly,' he begged them, 'for I do not know how long I shall live'. We are told of his dictation to one boy in particular, Wilbert, who took down a translation of St John's gospel into English. He completed that work; then in his little cell he sang his last *Gloria* ('Glory be to the Father and to the Son and to the Holy Spirit'). 'All who saw the death of our father Bede used to say that they had never seen any other man end his days with such great devotion and peace of mind.' The sparrow had escaped from the hall, to find light.

His translation of St John is now lost. Most of the church which he loved at Jarrow was finally demolished in 1783.

What were believed to be his bones were, however, taken to Durham Cathedral and have been honoured there since the eleventh century, not far from St Cuthbert's own last resting place. And another treasure rescued when the Vikings devastated Northumbria is the visual equivalent of Bede's *History*.

In the British Museum one of the most spectacular 'illuminated' manuscripts is painted delicately in blue, red, green, yellow and purple. Some of the decoration is abstract, particularly when the initials are adorned or whole pages (the 'carpet' pages) are filled with labyrinthine patterns. But we find also stylized representations of birds such as cormorants and of animals including dogs. Echoes of Irish art are to be found here, but clearly much of this is native Anglo-Saxon art, not unlike the Sutton Hoo treasure. And we find four lifelike portraits of men — the four evangelists of the New Testament. This is the book of the Lindisfarne gospels, written in a lovely Latin script and using a text derived from a church in Naples, with an accompanying lectionary suggesting readings for use in worship. A note records that the writing (presumably also the decoration) was done by Eadfrith who became Bishop of Lindisfarne in 698, and that the book was bound by his successor, Ethelwald.

Copied in a windowless hut close to the cold, often tempestuous, wind and the incessant surge of the North Sea, these gospels are high art, fully the equal of any achievement elsewhere in seventh-century Europe. Working only a hundred years after Augustine's fearful journey to Kent, little more than sixty years after Aidan had crossed the sea from Iona to test whether high courage might not do something among the uncouth, heathen tribesmen, Bishop Eadfrith has creamed the culture of the Christian world. Models originating in Iona or Naples or the courts of the Anglo-Saxon warrior-kings have been brought together to make the beauty of holiness and to adorn the Church's worship in Bede's England.

CHAPTER THREE

THE ANGLO-SAXON ACHIEVEMENT

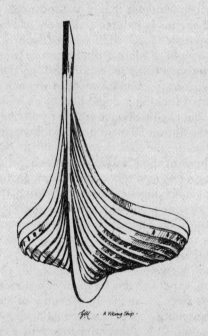

A Viking Ship

A TERROR-STRICKEN WORLD

The Anglo-Saxons seem to have found life hard and sad on the whole. Their numbers were probably never more than a million and a half. The analysis of their graves has suggested that eighty per cent were dead by the age of forty. Many of their bones give evidence of torturing arthritis, and the excavation of their homes has indicated that most of the peasants and slaves lived in perpetually damp huts, with the floor dug out of the earth. Their quickest way to riches lay in looting, after massacring, other Anglo-Saxons. Their poets celebrated their successful kings as men who had brought treasure back for distribution among their own followers. But the reality must have been sordid.

Aelfric's Colloquy is a conversation-piece written to show the correct use of Latin by a Dorset schoolmaster at the end of the tenth century; an English translation accompanies it. It affords a few glimpses of the life of the people. A ploughman is made to speak about his work, beginning at daybreak when he drives the oxen to the field: 'For fear of my lord, there is no winter so severe that I dare hide at home.' He has to plough a full acre or more every day, accompanied only by a lad who goads the oxen and is 'hoarse because of the cold and the shouting'. The shepherd then explains that from the early morning he has to stand over the sheep 'with dogs, lest wolves devour them' – but he adds: 'I am loyal to my lord'. The fisherman confesses that he prefers catching eels, pike, minnows, turbot and trout to any whale-hunt 'because of my timid spirit'. The other trades represented are those of the huntsman, the fowler, the shoemaker, the salter (salt was the indispensable preservative), the baker, the cook, the black-smith and the merchant. Here is a fairly complex society, but for those who are neither lords nor monks most of life is drudgery, close to the earth. Even the merchant, doomed to buy and sell, does not consider his travels fun.

Anglo-Saxon poetry (of which some 30,000 lines survive) not only celebrates heroes who merrily distribute the loot in the banqueting halls. It often conveys the sense that daily life is a test of endurance, as uncomfortable as the sharp battle. In one poem a wife complains about her joyless lodging and finds no cheer in thinking about her even more desolate husband, who has been exiled for a crime. In another, a wife is miserable because she is separated from her lover, and her husband's embraces give her 'some joy' but are essentially hateful. In a more encouraging poem, the minstrel Deor who has lost his position at court is consoled – by recalling stories he has himself sung of heroes who endured. One lament preserved in Exeter Cathedral's library (*The Wanderer*) is by an exile, weary and friendless. He dreams of the feasts he enjoyed when at home with his lord – and wakes up to see only the yellow waves, the sea birds, snow, hail and frost. Another lament also found at Exeter (*The Seafarer*) is by a professional sailor. He has been condemned to earn his living on the cold and stormy sea; but he knows that what condemned him was his own impatience with the land. The spring, with the wild flowers returning to woods and fields, makes a man restless; then his heart becomes 'eager to depart on his journey, far upon the waves of the sea'. And even while he writes, 'the mind's desire is urging my spirit to the voyage, that I should seek the far-distant land of strange peoples'.

It is significant that the later Anglo-Saxons, whose ancestors had once taken to the sea with such gusto, appreciated and therefore preserved this poem which seems to expect all its hearers to regard seafaring as one more disaster. They no longer loved the sea; it has, indeed, been suggested that the author of *The Seafarer* may have regarded life on the cruel sea as a pilgrim's exile, undertaken with religious motives in order to purge the self. The Anglo-Saxons certainly never expected fresh pirates to follow their own ancestors' example in seeking a 'land of strange peoples' across the North Sea. On the contrary, they placed some of their most venerable monasteries — Lindisfarne, Wearmouth, Jarrow, Whitby and others — on the coast. There they left them unguarded. Yet it was their fate to incur the full fury of the onslaught of the Vikings — first Norwegians, then Danes, then invaders from the Viking kingdom of Dublin. A disaster greater than any anticipated in their poetry overwhelmed them.

An explosion of energy threw Scandinavians all over the west during the three and a half centuries, 750-1100. Norwegians went to the Orkneys, the Shetlands, the Hebrides, the other Western Isles, the east coast of Ireland, Iceland, Greenland and Vinland (Newfoundland). Swedes crossed the Baltic Sea. Danes poured into England, Normandy and the region of the Loire. The Vikings even penetrated the Mediterranean and ravaged the Riviera.

The explosion was all the more frightening because it was not entirely due to simple land-hunger. This was certainly a major factor in the case of the Norwegians, but had the Danes been interested only in land they would presumably have cleared some of the forests in nearby Sweden. The Vikings were thugs whose chance had come now that the empire of Charlemagne had destroyed the once mighty Frisian fleet and had then promptly decayed as Charlemagne's successors proved that they were not his true heirs. The North Sea and the world now lay open, and men who had been exiled for crimes, younger sons, the disappointed or the inordinately ambitious, seized their opportunity. Vikings were trained to massacre and to plunder, and that they did like machines. And their ships – long enough to hold rowers who supplemented the sail, strong enough to cross the oceans, light enough to carry, shallow enough to use beaches as landing places and islets in estuaries as winter strongholds – still arouse the respect of later generations. The example preserved in the museum at Oslo is frightening in comparison with the far simpler rowing boat excavated from the peat bog at Nydam in Schleswig, the area from which the Angles had crossed the sea to England.

The impact of this Viking terror did as much as the Moslem armies from the south to frustrate the hope that dawned for Europe, including England, when Charlemagne was crowned Emperor in Rome on Christmas Day 800. The wonder is that in England so much of the Christian civilization survived – and expanded.

It survived because it was now the higher civilization, embodying the more powerful religion. But it might never have expanded. It might have survived in aloof, self-conscious isolation from the barbarians, as Welsh Christianity had survived when the English had first come to England. The earliest stone towers in English churches are found near the east coasts; evidently they were built as lookouts and refuges during the Viking raids. People took their families and their few treasures there – and their faith. In Anglo-Saxon literature we come across more than a few hints that withdrawal was a spiritual temptation for these battered believers. The poem about *The Wanderer* ended: 'All security remains for us in the Father of heaven.' Its companion-piece, *The Seafarer*, ended: 'Let us think where we have a home and how we may get there.' Such an emphasis on taking refuge in eternity could easily have become merely defensive and escapist, the high watchtower. But the temptation was resisted. The English Christians – or enough of them to count – were outgoing evangelists. They took the Gospel back to Germany. Their educated understanding of the implications of that Gospel lay at the heart of the civilizing mission of the empire of Charlemagne. And finally, the Anglo-Saxons led by King Alfred took the Gospel to the Vikings who had inflicted terrible loss and suffering on them. They quietly converted the Danes who had seized half England, and then they sent some of their best sons over the North Sea to build the Church in Scandinavia. The heroic endurance which was the chief quality they admired in men or women found its noblest expression in this expansion of the Church among cruel barbarians; in these beginnings of the English Christian mission which was one day to reach America, Africa, Asia and the islands of the Pacific.

No Bede arose to celebrate the achievement. Had Alfred lived longer, perhaps he would have been the man to write a comprehensive sequel to Bede's *History*; or at least he might have got it written at his court. He almost certainly commissioned the translation of Bede's work into English, but many of the best known stories about the late Anglo-Saxon period were written down long after the coming of the Normans: Alfred himself and the cakes, King 'Canute' and the waves, Lady Godiva's naked ride through Coventry. Much that would now make these Anglo-Saxons vividly alive for us was lost for ever under the Normans, when English books got thrown out of the libraries and English memories got forgotten in the harshness of life after the island's conquest. And the surviving anecdotes or chronicles were never pulled together, as Bede would have done. In the absence of an Anglo-Saxon history of it all, the modern student has to make his own attempt to tell an astonishing story.

THE CONVERSION OF GERMANY

The English missionary movement on the continent could look back on Wilfrid's winter among the Frisians (678-9) as the beginning of it all – but that was not a true beginning, for Wilfrid was essentially a Northumbrian prince bishop delayed on his journey to Rome, without the slightest intention of ending his days among heathen foreigners on the German coast. The real founder of the movement, St Willibrord, was a monk at Ripon under Wilfrid; he had been placed there while very young by his father, who spent his later years in a hermitage near the mouth of the Humber. When Wilfrid fell from ecclesiastical power in 678, the young monk retreated to Ireland. There he absorbed not only more learning but also a stronger desire for 'pilgrimage for the love of God'. This desire, perhaps combining the austere self-discipline of a voluntary exile with a touch of the more human curiosity about travel, had already changed Europe. Led by St Columbanus (about 590) many Irish monks had crossed over to the Continent to wander or to found new houses of prayer and study. Their influence had reached out through the kingdom of the Franks to penetrate many Germanic tribes, although the obstinately heathen Frisians and Saxons remained impervious to the Irish charm.

The idea of 'pilgrimage for the love of God' was in the air. In Ireland Willibrord met another Englishman, Bishop Egbert, who, when his life was preserved during a plague, had in gratitude made a vow of perpetual 'pilgrimage' or exile. Egbert had converted the monks of Iona to the Roman customs including the dating of Easter and had wanted to continue Wilfrid's work among the Frisians. Deterred from going himself (Bede says, by a storm accompanied by a dream), he had sent one Wicbert who had returned after two fruitless years. Now Egbert enthusiastically entrusted the Frisian mission to Willibrord and eleven companions.

The twelve were further encouraged by the protection of the Frankish ruler, Pippin, and by the blessing of the pope. Willibrord succeeded in his missionary work wherever (and for so long as) Frankish supremacy in the area could support it, and in 695 he was made the first Archbishop of Utrecht, taking the Roman name of Clemens. He was over eighty when he died in 739. Unfortunately he remains a shadowy figure to us. His correspondence perished, as did much of his achievement; the separate Frisian archbishopric did not survive. His first biographer was his kinsman Alcuin, writing half a century after his death when many legends were already surrounding the memory of him. A splendid copy of the gospels, presumably brought over from England by him, is preserved in the monastery which he founded at Echternach.

Far more is known about Wynfrid who was renamed Boniface when he, too, was made an archbishop in Rome. His biography was written by Willibald whom we have already met as an English traveller and bishop. Wynfrid was from Devon; he was educated in the monastery at Exeter, having been born (according to tradition) in Crediton. Made Abbot of Nursling near Southampton, he felt impelled to exile himself from his country, which he never saw again when he had sailed from London in 718, not yet forty years old. Willibrord tried to persuade him to become his assistant and successor in Utrecht, but the ex-abbot's probing travels and ambitions were now larger. He was determined to conquer wide German territories for Christ and, when Irish or other missionaries had got there first, to order all things in obedience to the papacy. He, too, was glad to accept the protection of the rulers of the Franks; but Christian Rome, which those rulers ignored for most of the time, was his real authority. He paid more than one visit to Rome to seek a clear commission and later wrote to it frequently for detailed instructions. When he was made a bishop and an archbishop in Rome, he did not hesitate to take oaths of obedience virtually the same as those taken by Italian bishops. It is not too much to say that these two Englishmen renamed Clemens and Boniface repaid the papacy for its past gift of the Gospel to England by this eighth-century gift of a spiritual empire over the Netherlands, the Franks and the Germans. 'The whole character of western Christendom had been transformed,' writes a modern historian of the papacy. 'It was an extraordinary accession to the papacy's sphere of authority, an immense increase in the number of those who looked to Rome as the source of true religion. . . .'[1]

---

[1] Geoffrey Barraclough, *The Medieval Papacy* (London, 1968), p.50.

Boniface was promoted to his archbishopric a few months from the day when the Arabs were defeated at Poitiers. As he fought with other weapons against the heathen beyond the Rhine, he knew that he was the representative of Roman civilization as well as of Roman Catholicism. Bishop Daniel of Winchester once wrote to encourage him. 'If the heathen gods are all-powerful . . . how is it that they spare us Christians who are turning almost the whole earth away from their worship? . . . We Christians possess lands rich in oil and wine and abounding in other resources, but the gods have left to the pagans lands stiff with cold. . . .' It was in keeping with this mission in the defence and enlargement of Christendom that Boniface once asked some English nuns to make a copy of the letters of St Peter in gold, to impress the simple folk to whom he had to preach. And it was in keeping with the Roman genius for organization that he regarded his key work as the establishment in the years 739-741 of eight German dioceses and a German synod (church council), followed by five years and five reforming synods to bring the discipline of the Frankish church up to Roman standards.

The decrees of the German synod were dated from the Incarnation. It was the first such public use of the method of dating popularized among the English by Bede. It was no coincidence that in surviving letters Boniface asked for copies of books by Bede – or that he asked Nothelm, the priest who had gone to the archives in Rome on Bede's behalf and was now Archbishop of Canterbury, for 'a copy of the letter containing, it is said, the questions of Augustine, first prelate and preacher of the English, and the replies of the sainted pope Gregory . . . for the registrars say that it is not to be found in the archives of the Roman church'. 'I beg also', he added, 'that you will let me know in what year of the Incarnation the first missionaries sent by St Gregory to the English people arrived'.

Boniface was joined by many recruits from England who became bishops, abbots, monks and nuns in Germany, and his correspondence shows that he set himself to maintain close links between the mother country and the German mission by frequent prayers, letters and small gifts (manuscripts, a cloak, incense, pepper, hunting falcons for a King of Kent, two small casks of wine for an Archbishop of York 'in token of our mutual affection, to use it for a merry day with the brethren'). The practical interest taken in this mission all over England both demonstrated and advanced the unity of the English. A Bishop of Leicester among the Middle Angles wrote to Boniface assuring him of prayers for the conversion of the Saxons, 'for they are our people'. When the great man had died, the Archbishop of Canterbury wrote to Boniface's successor, a West Saxon named Lull, rendering thanks to God 'that the English people were found worthy to send out this gifted student of heavenly learning, this noble soldier of Christ, with many pupils well taught and trained, to far-off spiritual conflicts'. Lull's own letters include a request for the complete works of Bede, sending in return a silk robe to cover Bede's relics.

Another incident shows the courage of such missionaries. There survives a letter written to King Ethelbald of Mercia by Boniface and six other bishops of English birth now on the Continent. The letter compliments the king on his good works: almsgiving, the repression of robbery, the defence of the poor, the maintenance of peace. But it boldly continues: 'we have learned from many sources that you have never taken to yourself a lawful wife.' So far from being chaste as befits a bachelor, the king has been promiscuous – and 'these atrocious crimes are committed in convents with holy nuns, with virgins consecrated to God'. He is told that even the heathen in Saxony punish women severely for adultery. How much more should an English Christian king be rebuked for these sins! The letter burns with patriotism as well as with moral indignation. Boniface wrote a covering letter to Herefrid, the unfortunate priest who was to read out the rebuke, addressing an illiterate king who was then the most powerful man in England. 'The well-doing and fair fame of our race are our joy and delight', he wrote, 'but their sins and their evil repute fill us with grief and sorrow'.

We are not told what were the king's immediate reactions to this letter. But it is probable that only the intervention of Boniface secured the holding of the very important Synod of

Clofeshoh in 746, at which King Ethelbald was present.
(Clofeshoh was probably a royal manor, but where is not
known.) This council of the English Church agreed on new
regulations similar to the reforms which Boniface was securing
in this period for the Church in the territories controlled by
the Franks. Bishops were to see that the houses of monks and
nuns remained devout, studious and quiet (did the king
blush?). They were also to visit all parish churches once a
year, insisting that priests should be able to understand the
Latin of the services and to explain them to the laity. Most of
these churches would be fairly large monasteries or 'minsters',
but some of the minsters no longer held monks and with some
reluctance the bishops agreed to visit them too, acknowledging their secularized status. And the council recognized the
growing number of small churches to which a priest would be
appointed by the lord of the manor and 'instituted' by the
bishop. Three years later King Ethelbald issued a charter in
which he freed all the churches from taxation apart from the
duty to repair bridges and fortresses. The English parish
system was coming to birth.

Above all, England was moved by the story of the martyrdom of St Boniface. It seems likely that his biographer
(Willibald) was right to say that he was killed because the
books he was carrying about were thought to be treasure. On
the whole the Germanic pagans treated Christian missionaries
with nothing worse than suspicion and insults. But it was
spiritually impressive that the Archbishop of Mainz, so far
from being content with the work which had come to him as
an ecclesiastical organizer and reformer throughout Germany
and France, chose when more than seventy years old to take
up again missionary work among the Frisians to the north-east
of the Zuider Zee. They were, he knew, dangerous; a letter has
been preserved in which he begged the Frankish ruler to take
care of his English and other fellow-missionaries when he was
gone. Thousands of the Frisians were baptized, but on 5 June
755, when he was about administer confirmation, Boniface
was killed together with his companions whom he had told to
be 'heroic in the Lord' (according to his biographer). His body
was taken by boat first to Utrecht and then, rowed for a month

up the Rhine, to his cathedral at Mainz; it was a ship-burial to eclipse Sutton Hoo and *Beowulf*. Finally he was buried in the great monastery he had founded at Fulda; the book he was reading, damaged by a sword-blow, is still shown.[2]

THE EDUCATION OF EUROPE

During Boniface's lifetime, and for quarter of a century after it, Alcuin lived quietly in York. He was first a brilliant pupil, then a teacher, in the school attached to York Minster (which was splendidly rebuilt in this period); a deacon, never a priest. His greatest enthusiasm was the minster's library, which he proudly catalogued in one of his many poems, *On the Saints of York*. In 782 he was on his way back to York from Rome, where he had been to ask the pope for the *pallium* (the sign of an archbishop's dignity) for his close friend, Albert. In Parma he met Charlemagne, the ruler of the Franks. That great man asked him to become his adviser on religious and educational matters, teaching in the palace school at Aachen. Fourteen years later he invited him to take over St Martin's old monastery at Tours. There he could use the profits of vast estates as abbot and as the creator of a school and library.

It was the largest educational opportunity ever offered to an Englishman, for it gave him the leading position in the whole revival of religion and learning as Charlemagne struggled to recreate the empire and civilization of Rome. Alcuin was always the schoolmaster, and very much the agent of Charlemagne; his own nickname was 'Flaccus' after the Roman poet Horace, but Charlemagne was 'David', the hero-king. In his own sphere, however, he possessed something of Boniface's organizing genius. He organized the copying out of manuscripts, a rescue-operation for literature; and the Carolingian miniscule handwriting used in them was the an-

---

[2] *The Letters of St Boniface* were edited and translated by E. Emerton (New York, 1940), and J. C. Sladden wrote a biography of *Boniface of Devon* (Exeter, 1980).

cestor of the type adopted many centuries later by the printers of Europe. He revised the Latin text of the Bible, often corrupted by the carelessness of copyists. And he secured uniformity in the services of the Church; the prayer for purity which still begins the Holy Communion service is there because of his influence, as is the recitation of the Nicene Creed during that service. Alcuin was the first to keep All Saints' Day in France.

Many of his letters survive.[3] Like Boniface's they are tenderly affectionate towards his companions in the Continental work and towards those he had left behind in England. One modern scholar's assessment of him is that he was 'in every respect a collector. He amassed huge quantities of information on all manner of subjects. He collected riches; he collected friends; and, especially during the last years of his life, he collected intercessors in all countries to pray for the salvation of his soul'.[4] But that verdict is needlessly cold. It is better to leave him with the epitaph he wrote for his grave: 'My name was Alchuine, and wisdom was always dear to me'.

ALFRED THE CHRISTIAN KING

On 8 June 793 Vikings from Norway sacked the island of Lindisfarne. 'It is nearly 350 years since we and our fathers inhabited this most lovely land', wrote Alcuin. 'It was not thought that such an invasion from the sea was possible. The church of St Cuthbert is spattered with the blood of the priests of God, stripped of all its furnishings, exposed to the plundering of pagans – a place more sacred than any other in Britain.' And the only solution of the Viking problem that seemed possible to Alcuin was moral rearmament. 'Consider the luxurious dress, hairstyles and general behaviour of leaders

---

[3] See *Alcuin of York*, ed. Stephen Allott (York, 1974).

[4] Heinrich Fichtenau, *The Carolingian Empire* (Oxford, 1957), p.95. A far more friendly portrait is to be found in E. S. Duckett, *Alcuin, Friend of Charlemagne* (New York, 1951).

and people', he urged King Ethelred. 'See how you have desired to imitate the pagan way of cutting hair and beards'. In other letters he quoted the warnings of Gildas to the British two centuries before.

In the following year Norwegian Vikings plundered Bede's old monastery and school at Jarrow, whether or not it had paid sufficient attention to Alcuin's advice: 'Look at the treasures of your library, the beauty of your churches, the excellence of your buildings, the order of the religious life. . . . The boys should learn to assist the worship of the heavenly king, not to dig out the earths of foxes or to course hares. . . . Liven sleepy minds by the example of Bede. Sit with your teachers, open your books, study the text, grasp its sense. . . .'

The English had to learn harder lessons about warfare than Alcuin could ever teach. Fortunately for them, they were taught by a man who combined something of Alcuin's love of learning with a mastery of his own military trade: Alfred the Great, King of the West Saxons 871-890.

Alfred is remembered as the father of the English navy, for he commanded the building of a fleet and trained the Saxons to resume their old courage and skill as sailors. He could equally be remembered as the father of the English army, for instead of resting content with the old militia (*fyrd*) which had tended to melt away at harvest time, he imposed a more systematic conscription (and taxation) and arranged for half this larger army to be on duty at one time. Or he could be remembered as the father of the English town, for he instructed as many of the English as possible to gather in a *burh* – Hastings, for example, or Chichester or Southampton or Oxford or Exeter – and fortify it.

Or Alfred could be remembered as the father of the English nation; it is certainly significant that the adjective *Englisc* came into regular use in his time. In the evolution of the national monarchy the fact that he was the only English king remaining in arms was decisive. In the days of Boniface and Alcuin the greatest English power had been in the Midlands. Offa, King of the Mercians 757-796, had dared to quarrel with Charlemagne and had persuaded the pope to make his own Bishop of Lichfield an archbishop. He had styled himself

'King of the English' and even 'emperor', ruling between the Thames and the Humber, constructing a great dyke against the Welsh (which largely survives), and minting a gold coinage which Arab traders would recognize as being like theirs. But in the ninth century the leadership had passed to Egbert, King of the West Saxons, a strong man who had the wisdom to be guided in policy by St Swithin (Bishop of Winchester 852-862). Finally the Mercian kingdom, like the Northumbrian, had fallen victim to the Danish and other raiders and settlers. At Easter 878 even Wessex seemed to depend on the Danes' mercy, which was non-existent. Alfred controlled only the Isle of Athelney. But he fought on; and eight years later, he rode into London. In the words of the *Anglo-Saxon Chronicle* (the history, in various local editions, which was itself a new expression of nationhood): 'all the English people submitted to Alfred except those who were under the power of the Danes'. And when Alfred issued laws to this people – on the whole conservative laws, although there were new provisions for the protection of the weak and for limiting the bloodfeud – he prefaced them by reciting the Ten Commandments.

Here, however, we can remember Alfred chiefly as the father of English prose and as the godfather of a religious revival. Fortunately we possess a *Life* by Asser, a Welsh priest persuaded by him to spend half the year at the court of Wessex. It is the first biography of an English layman, naive and unfinished, artistically inferior to Einhard's biography of Charlemagne which was presumably one of its models. But the book also imitated the biographies of saints; and whereas Einhard had been a layman writing about an emperor, now 'the churchman's patronizing when writing of a layman . . . comes through the story'.[5] Alfred, we are informed, when he learned to read late in life resembled the penitent thief. The

---

[5] Beryl Smalley, *Historians in the Middle Ages* (London, 1974), p.71. *Asser's Life of King Alfred*, edited by W. H. Stevenson, has been republished with an essay by Dorothy Whitelock (Oxford, 1959). N. P. Brooks stressed the greatness of Alfred's achievement in *Transactions of the Royal Historical Society* (London, 1979), pp.1-20.

priest's strange failure to understand Alfred's truly heroic and Christian achievement may help to account for the fact that the king was never canonized as a saint. Alfred's was the manly religion encapsulated in the proverb attributed to him:

If thou hast a woe, tell it not to the weakling.
Tell it to the bow in thy saddle, and ride singing forth.

Asser tells us that Alfred had a notebook by him day and night. He would copy into it extracts from other books which specially helped or comforted him, 'flowers gathered from all sorts of masters'. And he also kept by him a book of psalms; William of Malmesbury records a tradition that he was working to produce a complete Psalter in English when he died.

Charlemagne could not write; he kept tablets with letters on them beneath his pillow, hoping that something would seep through. Alfred, in contrast, astonished his contemporaries by being a studious prince and king. There is a story that as a young boy he admired the pictures in a book of English poetry. His mother promised that he would have the book once he could recite it by heart, and it was not long before he claimed his prize. He learned Latin while a king, although he claimed that when he came to the throne there were very few priests able to translate it into English ('and I cannot remember a single one south of the Thames'). He had to fight against decay within the English Church, therefore, as well as against the Danes; possibly one reason for this decay was that so many of the English Church's most active sons had become missionaries abroad. And despite the pressures of war and administration, literary work was for him an essential part of a Christian king's duties, as was the encouragement of craftsmen. He wrote, as he fought, for Christendom.

He translated into English Pope Gregory's book of advice on *Pastoral Care* and had copies sent to his bishops. The lovely Alfred Jewel found at Athelney in 1693 and now in Oxford may have been part of the encouraging bookmarker which we know accompanied this gift. The king also translated the *Consolation of Philosophy* written by a sixth-century Christian statesman, Boethius, in prison before his execution with the *Soliloquies* of St Augustine of Hippo. Alfred declared that this work was like cutting enough timber to make a mere cottage; it was for others to cut more according to their own needs. Boethius and Augustine had already been favourites with Alcuin, and were to have an immense influence on the Middle Ages throughout western Europe, but being a king introducing the English to unknown treasures, Alfred was not too nervous to edit and adapt them boldly. And to remind his fellow-countrymen of the world to which they belonged, he sponsored an English version of the *Universal History* of Orosius, adding an account of voyages related to him by two travellers who happened to be at his court, Ohthere and Wulfstan.

No doubt this busy king who had only just learned Latin had expert assistance in such books, but they all bore the stamp of his personality. And although the *Anglo-Saxon Chronicle* was not his work directly, it must have been due to an impetus coming from him that during his reign it expanded from brief notes to a narrative which is the earliest example of continuous, original prose in English.

After a decisive battle at Edington and more than a week of private talk, Alfred persuaded Guthrum, the general of the Danish army which had almost crushed the life out of Wessex, to accept baptism and to settle with his followers in England in peace. At this momentous baptism, at Aller near Athelney in 878, Alfred stood godfather to Guthrum, who took the English name of Athelstan. The Danish army moved into East Anglia, the East Midlands and Essex; and by a treaty with Alfred in 886 this 'Danelaw' was accepted as a peaceful kingdom with a firm frontier. This legitimized a very considerable area of conquest for the Danes. But the treaty provided for the equality of English and Danes, class by class, in the *wergild* (the payment due after a killing). It was a charter for the pirates' orderly settlement. This process is still commemorated in the English language, where not only the word 'sail' but also the word 'law' has Scandinavian origins.

The English word 'cross' is also Scandinavian in origin. It memorializes the fact that the Danes in England gradually followed Guthrum's path into Christianity; one, Oda, became Archbishop of Canterbury in 941. The story of the conversion is now lost, but a modern scholar refers to this as 'the fundamental fact concerning the religious life of the ninth century . . . : that Christianity was so deeply rooted in the countryside that within a few years the pagan conquerors had been converted to Christianity through the force of their English neighbours' practice and precept, without benefit of missionary activities from those parts of England which remained unconquered, and despite the fact that the bastions of organized religion in their own areas had been destroyed'.[6]

We have evidence of the new settlers' original paganism in some sculptures and some place names. If we need any reminder that the English must have been terrified of these heathen murderers, we have a letter written by Pope Formosus in the 890s telling the English bishops that he has considered excommunicating them because he has received no reports of attempts to convert the Danes. We also have some evidence in art to mark the impact of Irish evangelism among the Vikings. At Kirk Andrea on the Isle of Man a cross has the Vikings' high god (Odin, the equivalent of the Saxons' Woden) on one side with Christ on the other. But there are very few traces left in art of the reception of the message of Christ the new 'white' god; one such is a cross at Gosforth depicting the Christian Saviour in the style of the Vikings' Baldur.

We have, it seems, no evidence at all of the conversations between the English and the settlers in which the Christian religion was expounded and accepted. The main evidence provided by archaeology is negative: few Danish pagan burial grounds have been found. Such scraps of evidence as survive

---

[6] D. J. V. Fisher, *The Anglo-Saxon Age* (London, 1973), p.155.

suggest that the early Danish settlers 'adopted Christianity eagerly and early and that heathenism had ceased to be a powerful force among them by about 900 or at least by the end of the reign of Edward the Elder (899-924)'.[7] But we are left to wonder how Danes felt when they joined in the veneration of the tomb of St Edmund the Martyr, the last native King of the East Angles, killed while resisting the Danes in 872. The greatest of the Danish kings, Cnut, made the monastery built where St Edmund was buried richer than any other landowner in Suffolk.

In the end, not only the Danish settlers but also the Scandinavians remaining in their homelands were baptized. In Denmark itself the first missionary was the monk Anskar from Picardy, brought there by Harold Gormsson, the king who had been baptized while on a visit to a Frankish ruler, Louis the Pious. Anskar subsequently visited Sweden and became the first Archbishop of Bremen, but when this 'Apostle of the North' died in 865 the Scandinavians had returned to their old religion. The real progress of Christianity in Denmark seems to have begun more than a century later, and to have been greatly influenced by the conversion of the Danelaw in England. In 965 the Danish king, Harold Bluetooth, became a Christian. He was the father of Sweyn and the grandfather of Cnut, and an inscription still survives in Jelling in Denmark: 'King Harold had this monument made in memory of his father, Gorm, and his mother Thyri. Harold won all Denmark and Norway and made the Danes Christian'.

Paganism was still more obstinate in Norway than in Denmark, although the two kings Haakon and Olav Trygavason, who were both made Christians in England, endeavoured to persuade their fellow-countrymen to follow them — and Olav, who was killed in 1030, was remembered as a saint because he had thousands baptized more or less forcibly. The Christianization of Sweden was a slow process in the eleventh and twelfth centuries, and much of it was the work of English

---

[7] F. T. Wainwright, *Scandinavian England* (London, 1975), p.282. See also G. F. Jensen, 'The Vikings in England: A Review' in *Anglo-Saxon England*, ed. Peter Clemoes (Cambridge, 1975), pp.181-206.

missionaries. Sigfrid, a monk of Glastonbury, converted the Swedish king, Olav Ericson, and many other English names are found in the lists of the early Swedish bishops. The last of these Englishmen died in 1213.

What, we may ask, would a Christian priest teach an ex-Viking who asked for baptism? The official answer was given in 796 by Alcuin to Charlemagne, citing the authority of St Augustine of Hippo. 'A man must be taught first about the immortality of the soul, the future life, rewards for good and evil and both kinds of eternity. Then he must be told the particular sins for which he must suffer eternal punishment with Satan and the good deeds for which he may enjoy ever-lasting glory with Christ. The belief in the Holy Trinity must be carefully taught. The advent of the Son of God, our Lord Jesus Christ, into the world to save mankind must be ex-pounded, with the mystery of his passion, the truth of his resurrection and ascension to heaven, and his coming to judge all nations'.

But such an outline of the official catechism scarcely ex-plains what would have drawn the heathen Saxon or Dane in the first place. Part of the paganism of the Vikings was the myth, preserved in the great Norse Sagas of Iceland, that one day the heroic dead would be summoned by the gods from their feasting in Valhalla. The help of these warriors would be needed against the evil snake that was encircling all the earth. And that last fight would fail. Then would come the 'twilight of the gods' as chaos reigned. But in fact the Christian saviour conquered the Vikings' gods; and two scholars who have studied the story of the Vikings have asked themselves why the Christian Gospel was eventually believed as news of victory. These historians answer that the Scandinavians accepted Christianity for much the same reasons as the Anglo-Saxons. It promised prosperity in this life, and claimed to lighten the darkness surrounding it. Here was the unexpected treasure that the Viking voyages had brought home. But they add: 'perhaps in time Christianity's most conspicuous gift to the north was to add a dimension of pity to the lives of a hard people, brought up to admire and condemn but not to sympathize'.[8]

REBUILDING THE ENGLISH CHURCH

The hidden process of this conversion of ex-Vikings in England must have been helped greatly by the power, prestige and piety of Alfred's successors in the Christian monarchy of Wessex. The bones of these great kings are still treasured with his own in the mortuary chests of Winchester Cathedral: his son Edward the Elder and his grandson Athelstan.

Edward's generalship was matched by that of his sister Ethelfled, Lady of Mercia. Their joint campaign of 917-918 reconquered the Midlands and East Anglia, and before the end of Edward's reign every Danish colony south of the Humber had been annexed to Wessex. Under Athelstan English power reached out to subdue Northumbria, where Viking raiders from Ireland had established a kingdom based on York. Athelstan also conquered the British in Cornwall and made the Welsh princes his vassals. Since he was also acknowledged as King of Mercia, his boast that he was 'King of All Britain' was largely justified. It is possible to find a reason for these English kings' triumph in the fact that the Danes in England, or the Vikings from Ireland, did not develop a strong political unity of their own once the first fury of their conquest had abated. But the praise which the kings received personally was, it seems, well earned. That praise found its most lasting expression in the poem (incorporated in the Anglo-Saxon Chronicle) on the battle of Brunanburh, fought and won in 937 against a combined army of Vikings, Celtic British and Scots:

> Athelstan the King, lord of men,
> Giver of gold to warriors, and his brother too,
> Edmund the prince, won lasting glory. . . .

---

[8] Peter Foote and David Wilson, *The Viking Achievement* (London, 1970), p.416. For Scandinavian paganism, see E. O. G. Turville-Petre, *Myth and Religion of the North* (London, 1964), and two books by James Graham-Campbell, *The Vikings* with Dafydd Kidd and *The Viking World* with magnificent illustrations (both London, 1980).

In this celebration of heroic warriors the language is deliberately archaic; one in every seven of the phrases has been found in earlier poems which have also survived. But the effect is still strong:

> The king and the prince went back to their country,
> The land of Wessex, triumphing in war.
> They left behind them corpses to be food
> For the black-coated raven, with its horny beak,
> And for the eagle, white-backed and dark-breasted,
> The greedy war-hawk and that grey wild beast,
> The wolf. . . .

The Christian character of Alfred's kingdom came out more attractively in the work made possible by peace. Plegmund, an able Mercian priest who was appointed Archbishop of Canterbury in 890, led a reorganization of the now flourishing Church, creating five new dioceses (Ramsbury, Wells, Crediton, Selsey and Dorchester-on-Thames). Later, bishops were appointed to minister to the Cornish (based on St Germans) and in East Anglia (based on North Elmham). This last development was one of the fruits of the peace in the years between 955 and 980. The laws then issued in the name of King Edgar summed up the whole Anglo-Saxon conception of Christian justice; as did the supreme symbolic ceremony, the coronation of Edgar at Bath on Whit Sunday 973. The sacred character of English kingship was made clear in the oath which developed for use at coronations, whether or not these precise words were used in 973 – an oath to assure true peace to the Church of God; to 'forbid robbery and all unrighteous deeds'; and to exercise 'justice and mercy in the decision of all cases', so as to win God's mercy.

During King Edgar's peace the central figure in English religious life was St Dunstan, who presided at the coronation. He was trained for high politics as a young nobleman at Athelstan's court, and never hesitated to advise or to contradict kings. While still only a young man he had to drag one of them, Eadwig 'the Fair', back to a banquet with his lords when he had just gone to amuse himself with the ladies. Dunstan was exiled when one of the ladies involved in this incident became queen. But when his ally Edgar (Eadwig's brother) came to power and he became Archbishop of Canterbury, he showed where his heart lay – not in politics but in the Church. At a time when the papacy itself was in eclipse (it did not really revive until 1046), Dunstan was the ablest and most purposeful archbishop England had known since the death of Theodore in 690.

His purpose was the reconstruction of the Church, and his main strategy was the revival of the monasteries. Most of the earlier English monasteries had been destroyed by the Danes, and those that were left were not fully under the rule of St Benedict, which on the Continent had now become the criterion of a strictly religious life. King Alfred's patronage of monks and nuns had been premature. Dunstan himself was not impetuous; to the end of his life, the monks of Canterbury Cathedral were not strictly Benedictine, leaving that to their neighbour and rival, St Augustine's Abbey. Nor was he a puritan bigot; he was skilled in metalwork, painting (a drawing of himself kneeling before Christ survives), music and organ-building. But he owed his first education to Irish monks who were maintaining some Christian life at Glastonbury near the village of his birth and boyhood, and while a young nobleman he took a monk's vows. He then made his mark over fifteen years as the pioneering abbot of Glastonbury, more than bringing back past glories. His chief interest while archbishop was, it seems, the establishment of other Benedictine monasteries surrounded by other great estates. Monks had converted England to Christianity. Monks would now rescue it from the morally ruinous effects of the Danish invasions. It has been estimated that as a result of the enthusiasm of Dunstan and his associates, between 960 and 1060 there grew to be about sixty religious houses for men and women, owning about a sixth of the land south of the Humber and the Mersey. 'The servant of God, Dunstan', as his first biographer put it, 'shone as the first abbot of the English nation'.

Dunstan's closest collaborator was Oswald, a man of Danish descent who was both Archbishop of York and Bishop of Worcester (the Vikings had done so much damage in the north that the two dioceses could support only one bishop). A third name is linked with theirs: Ethelwold, Abbot of Abingdon (where he educated King Edgar) and Bishop of Winchester. He was much more of a fanatic.

A book of bishop's blessings (a 'Benedictional') was copied and adorned for Ethelwold in Winchester between 971 and 984. Richly decorative frames surrounded the text and some exquisite miniatures. The English art of painting was in full vigour. But Ethelwold was not content to bestow blessings. Reaching into the Danelaw, his was the iron will that restored the monasteries at Ely, Peterborough and Thorney as strict and prosperous houses. On the first Saturday in Lent 964 he stormed into Winchester Cathedral and told the clergy to become Benedictine monks or to leave at once. The king's lay representative stood at the door with a drawn sword. When the clergy had gone, monks were introduced from Abingdon. That decisive day in Winchester established a peculiarly English institution, the cathedral which was also a Benedictine monastery. It also indicated where the leaders of the nation's religious life were to come from; in the last century of Anglo-Saxon England, three quarters of the bishops were monks. A clear rule of life for the monks and nuns was drawn up by Ethelwold in the *Regularis Concordia* (Monastic Agreement), published at Winchester in an Easter council under the king.[9]

Two authors among the other leaders in this revival of the Church are also remembered, partly because their writing brought Anglo-Saxon or 'Old English' prose to its classic best. One was Aelfric, a product of Ethelwold's reformed school at Winchester, who while a monk at Cerne Abbas in Dorset and at Eynsham in Oxfordshire devoted himself to the production of English Christian literature. He wrote lives of the saints; he translated the first seven books of the Old Testament and expounded other scriptures; he supplied parish priests with sermons and bishops with letters which would invigorate their clergy; he even compiled the first Latin grammar in English.

Another author rich in rhetoric but much more urgently masterful was Wulfstan, Bishop of London, promoted to hold the sees of York and Worcester together in 1002. In the first

[9] Translated and edited by Thomas Symons (London, 1953).

book of English political theory (*The Institutes of Polity*),
Wulfstan held up the ideal of the Anglo-Saxon state in which
the king ('Christ's substitute') exercised the eight essential
virtues – truthfulness, patience, generosity, wisdom after
taking counsel, favour to the righteous, moderation in taxes,
equity in judgements. Supporting the king were the three
classes: those who prayed, those who worked and those who
fought. And Wulfstan had the courage to say when the ideal
was not reached. In a famous sermon of 1014 he denounced
the collapse of morality in the state he knew, deliberately
repeating the warnings which Gildas had delivered when the
Anglo-Saxons came and which Alcuin had revived in the days
of the first Viking raids. It was probably the most outspoken
sermon ever preached by an English archbishop; in its own
way as ruthless as the army of Sweyn Forkbeard, then terror-
izing England.[10]

FROM EDGAR TO HAROLD

The quality of the English kings declined disastrously after the
murder of St Dunstan's ally Edgar at the age of thirty-two in
975. (And Edgar was no saint: he married a nun.) King
Edgar's eldest son, Edward, was murdered at Corfe Castle in
Dorset and the guilt lay with his younger son, Ethelred – who,
although ruthless enough in gaining the crown, turned out to
be 'the Unready': the nickname means 'No Counsel'. Ethelred
has been very notorious to historians, as he was to his subjects.
Endlessly the English leaders, with no policy of concerted and
sustained resistance, paid out Danegeld to buy off trouble
from the Danes. Endlessly trouble came – for example, the
murder in 1012 of an Archbishop of Canterbury, St Alphege
(more properly Aelfeah), by the Danes during a drunken feast
at Greenwich when he had refused to allow a ransom to be
raised for his release. Sir Frank Stenton has summed up the

---

[10] See M. McC. Gatch, *Preaching and Theology in England: Aelfric and
Wulfstan* (Toronto, 1957).

impression left by a chronicle of the early eleventh century (written by a monk at Abingdon, this was the first detailed, contemporary history of England to take up the tradition of Bede). It is the impression of 'an ancient and rich society, helpless before a derisive enemy because its leaders were incapable of government'.[11]

The ineptitude of Ethelred and his chief ministers coincided with a new development in the art of war. Instead of picking up horses in England as had been the habit of earlier Vikings, the Danish army now landed cavalry, which was already trained and equipped; and probably not even Alfred, Edward or Athelstan would have been able to resist that fury. Ethelred's son, Edmund Ironside, was a far better general than his father and although he failed to secure the rest of the country he forced Sweyn Forkbeard's son Cnut to acknowledge him as King of Wessex. Then, worn out by the war, he died in 1016; and all the English acknowledged the immensely able Cnut as their king. Their acceptance was eased by the fact that he had become a Christian.

Sweyn had come to accept Christianity in Denmark, but never more than half-heartedly; Cnut, although ruthlessly brutal towards rebels actual or potential, was in his own estimation a model of piety. He took pride in being a friend of bishops. He used the Danish fleet to destroy pirates and then sent it back to Denmark. He then used England as a base from which to secure the throne of Denmark and to conquer Norway for a time. He issued to the English a law code which began with a long reminder of their religious duties; and almost all the laws appear to have been based on those of Edgar and other Anglo-Saxon lawmakers. Here as in other matters he seems to have been advised by Archbishop Wulfstan – who thus by his own statesmanship averted some of the doom he had predicted to his stunned congregation in York Minster in 1014. Cnut gave lands to reward the Danes,

---

[11] F. M. Stenton, *Anglo-Saxon England* (Oxford, 1947), p.388. The third edition of this masterly survey (1971) includes some revisions. See also his essays *Preparatory to Anglo-Saxon England*, ed. D. M. Stenton (Oxford, 1970).

particularly their chief men the 'earls', for keeping the peace in England, but the two most prominent earls to be found in the country after his reorganization were both Englishmen: Godwine of Wessex and Leofric of Mercia. Eleven years after being accepted as king of the English, Cnut travelled to Rome in order to attend the coronation of Conrad, the Holy Roman Emperor. He sent back to England a proud report of his favourable reception by 'the princes of all the peoples'. He boasted, too, of his success in obtaining concessions to ease the journeys of future English pilgrims to Rome. To that extent, therefore, the Alfred tradition prevailed even in the day of the Danish supremacy.

This could have been the beginning of a Scandinavian empire centred on an England which was increasingly prosperous; an empire proud of its laws and its churches. But when Cnut was assassinated at the age of forty in 1035 (he was buried where his treasure was, at Winchester), he left no strong successor. None of his children reached middle age. The fascinating possibility which had been opening up was over. Eventually Edward, son of Ethelred, was elected king in 1042 and reigned until the end of 1065. He shared Cnut's piety — to the extent that in his last years he concentrated on the building of Westminster Abbey next to his main residence, and is known to history as 'the Confessor'. He was by no means as monkish as he was later made out to have been by monks; his was the piety of a king capable of worldly action. His 'greatest and only significant failure', writes one modern historian, 'was his failure to generate an heir'.[12] But he did not possess Cnut's outstanding ability. During his reign Earl Godwine of Wessex and his son Harold were not really subject to his rule, and his attempted coup against them in 1051-52 only consolidated their power. Any heir of King Edward would have to fight Earl Harold.

Part of the strength of these Earls of Wessex lay in their ability to speak for their fellow-Englishmen against the Normans who surrounded the king. Edward's mother was

---

[12] D. J. V. Fisher, *The Anglo-Saxon Age*, p.348. See Frank Barlow, *Edward the Confessor* (London, 1970).

Emma, the sister of Richard, Duke of Normandy; she had been married into the English royal family as a token of the Normans' response to a plea for help against the Danes. When Elthred her first husband had died, this adjustable lady had been married again to a Dane, Cnut. Edward, however, had been brought up in Normandy until invited back to England by Cnut's son Hartha Cnut at the age of twenty-five. Inevitably his ideas and his favourites were now Norman. Reflecting this, Westminster Abbey was built in the style of the churches attached to royal or ducal palaces in France. Inevitably, too, he was no friend to the overmighty Earl Godwine. His own elder brother Alfred had been captured by Earl Godwine's men and handed over by them to the Danes, who had blinded him and allowed him to die in misery. Although Edward was married to Earl Godwine's daughter, not surprisingly the marriage was cold and childless.

When King Edward died a week after the consecration of his fashionable and therefore French abbey, the Normans felt that their hour had come. Duke William immediately began preparations to conquer a country which he claimed — almost certainly with truth — Edward had definitely promised him. Himself descended from Norsemen, William was to take up the task snatched by a murderer from the great King Cnut thirty years before.

THE NORMAN CONQUEST

While in France Earl Harold had already sworn loyalty to William (in 1064). He was, however, elected and consecrated king in Westminster on the very day of King Edward's burial. He reigned for nine months. An able man, he might have founded a strong new Anglo-Saxon dynasty had the fortunes of war been different; but the dice were loaded against him. His own brother Tostig, who had been the rapacious Earl of Northumbria until the Northumbrians had rebelled against his rule, now became his enemy, allying with the Scots and the Norwegians in a brutal attempt to seize the throne. At first their campaign was successful. Near York the troops of the northern English earls, Edwin and Morcar, were cut down. But on Monday, 25 September 1066 King Harold himself met the invaders in battle at Stamford Bridge. It was the last battle between the English and the Vikings from east or north. These invaders had darkened two and a half centuries; but Stamford Bridge saw a complete victory for Harold and for England. Tostig and the Norwegian king were killed. Only a remnant of their routed army survived to sail home. Unfortunately, however, these were not the only adventurers willing to try their luck against the questionable new English king. To the south lived hard men sprung from the Vikings of a previous generation: the Normans.

The expeditionary force assembled by Duke William's promises of wealth seems to have numbered some six thousand. It embarked two days after the battle in the north and found an undefended landing place at Pevensey on the south coast. During the next few weeks Harold gave another impressive display of kingship and generalship, settling the affairs of the north and marching some 250 miles into Sussex. There he waited for his own troops to recover and to be joined by the main English militia from the southern shires (the *fyrd*), which would have greatly outnumbered the Normans. But he was not joined by the northern earls and the southern *fyrd* was slow to assemble. Perhaps there was treachery; perhaps not. He trusted too much in his defensive position, a hill which seemed to block the road to London. On Saturday 14 October he was attacked by the Normans, who were forced to gamble.

At an early stage in the battle Duke William had to exercise all his personal courage to rally his left flank. But as the day wore on his mounted knights were able to dislodge the English infantry by pretending to flee and, when the English pursued them on foot, turning for a massacre. It was a manoeuvre so risky that only trained and disciplined soldiers could have brought it off. To the end the English fought courageously, but by nightfall their king, his brothers and the flower of their army lay dead. Even then there might have been another more successful battle against the Normans when the main English army at last assembled – if only the English had possessed another leader.

As it was, William conquered because he now had no real rival. In order to show his determination and particularly in order to alarm London, he devastated the countryside. It was not long before the city opened its gates. Terrified bishops were assembled to officiate at his coronation in Westminster Abbey on Christmas Day, although the traditional acclamation was misunderstood by nervous soldiers as the start of a riot.

The country's great churches were almost all either burned down (in accidents which were not inconvenient) or else brazenly pulled down to make way for Norman work. In Canterbury a fire happened; in Winchester the old cathedral was demolished when the largest church in Europe, a cathedral with a nave four hundred feet long, had been built in 1079-93 on the orders of the Conqueror's two cousins, Walkelin bishop of the diocese and his brother Simon, prior of the monastery. One of the Conqueror's own chaplains, William of Poitiers, left on record an indiscreet boast about the quantity and quality of the treasures sent from England to adorn churches in Normandy and Rome. This loot must have included a large amount of the *opus Anglicanum*, the needlework for which English women were famous throughout Europe. A few fine specimens remained in Durham, hidden in St Cuthbert's coffin where they had been placed by the great King Athelstan in 934; and when the Norman conquest was commemorated in a tapestry exhibited in his cathedral by Odo Bishop of Bayeux, he ordered English needlewomen to do the work. Such work still suggests something about the quality of the civilization which perished with King Harold on the hill near Hastings that October evening in 1066. Fortunately, too, some books remained in English monasteries. Some of them have preserved to our own day the excellence of the art honouring the Bible in the period of the 'Winchester School' – the period which in secular life had been the sordid time of Ethelred and Danegeld. There is nothing degenerate about these books, with their calmly beautiful colours and the excitement of their free-flowing line drawings. Nor is there anything second-rate about the small quantity of sculptures, ivory carvings and metalwork which has also survived the Normans' pillaging, some of it in museums far from England.

The people of the Anglo-Saxon Church did not escape the consequences of 1066. Some of the elite could escape abroad. English exiles took up service in Constantinople, to defend the still-surviving eastern empire of Rome. Agatha, daughter of King Harold, married the King of the Russians. But at home revolts against the Normans, such as that led by Hereward the Wake in the Fens with the monastery of Ely as its base, proved futile. English bishops and abbots found themselves gradually replaced by Normans. English parish priests found that they had to accept the authority of new, and probably much harsher, lords. And the English Christian laity disappeared into an underworld.

It is rather surprising how much pride was still taken in the English heritage under the Norman regime. The Anglo-Saxon Chronicles were still compiled in at least three monasteries (the chronicler at Peterborough wrote in Old English until 1154), and books such as those of Bede in Latin, or Alfred or Aelfric in English, continued to be copied. A little group of monks mainly English (but including a few Frenchmen such as the ex-knight, Reinfrid) reoccupied Bede's old monastery at Jarrow in the 1070s. A Norman monk-bishop then summoned them to found a monastery around the shrine of St Cuthbert in Durham Cathedral; and they took what they believed were Bede's bones with them. The latest datable Old English poem to have survived, written about 1105, praised Durham, where 'God's servant lies and waits for Judgement'. And two historians, monks with English mothers, contemporaries who died during the 1140s, both set themselves the task of doing for their own time what Bede had done for his. Orderic of St Evroul wrote an *Ecclesiastical History* of the Normans in the setting of Christendom, and William of Malmesbury wrote on *Deeds of the Kings* and *Deeds of the Bishops* in England. But they were not true successors of Bede. Their histories were far more untidy, because they lacked his simplifying vision of the emergence of a Christian people. Orderic knew that the Normans had done much for monks, and as half a Norman himself he was proud enough of their victories, but he had no illusions about their turbulence and harshness. William, who had met many of the leading men of the day, exercised tact in describing them. But he had a sharp eye for their selfishness. In their own ways, Orderic and William paid their tributes to the side defeated in 1066, to their mothers' memories.

However, only the Church preserved the public use of English. Parish priests – or at least the good shepherds among them – would expound the gospels in the language which the natives spoke at home. But the language of public worship and of formal business in the Church was Latin and the lay elite spoke French. It has been reckoned that by the middle of the twelfth century 'it appeared very possible that French and not English would be the language of England'.[13] Even when English revived and flourished as the 'Middle English' of the fourteenth and fifteenth centuries, it preserved for ever traces of the colonial period – the time when the enslaved natives had looked after the *sheep* and their French-speaking masters sitting around the fire in the hall had eaten the *mutton*; when the English had been responsible for the *cows* or the *pigs* and the Normans had enjoyed the *beef* and the *pork*.

In what remained of the eleventh century, it cannot have been easy for anyone to echo in English the creed to be found in King Alfred's translation of Boethius: 'I hold, as do all Christian men, that it is God's providence that rules, and not fate.'

---

[13] R. W. Chambers, *On the Continuity of English Prose from Alfred to More and His School* (Oxford, 1932), p.lxxxix.

PART ONE: FURTHER READING
(in addition to the books in the footnotes)

1 Prelude: Romans and Celts

BARLEY, M. W., and HANSON, R. P. C. (ed.), *Christianity in Britain, 300-700*, Leicester, 1968.

CHADWICK, N. K., *The Age of the Saints in the Early Celtic Church*, Oxford, 1963.

COLLINGWOOD, R. G., and RICHMOND, I. A., *The Archaeology of Roman Britain*, revised, London, 1969.

FRERE, S., *Britannia*, London, 1969.

HARDINGE, L., *The Celtic Church in Britain*, London, 1972.

LIVERSIDGE, J., *Britain in the Roman Empire*, London, 1968.

MORRIS, J., *The Age of Arthur: A History of the British Isles from 350 to 650*, London, 1973.

2 The Conversion of the English

BLAIR, P. H., *The World of Bede* (virtually a commentary on the *History*), London, 1970.
Northumbria in the Days of Bede, London, 1977.

BONNER, G. (ed.), *Famulus Christi: Essays in Commemoration of the Thirteenth Centenary of the Birth of the Venerable Bede*, London, 1976.

COLGRAVE, B., and MYNORS, R. A. B. (ed.), *Bede's Ecclesiastical History of the English People*, Oxford, 1969.

DUCKETT, E. S., *Anglo-Saxon Saints and Scholars*, New York, 1947.

GIRVAN, R., and BRUCE-MITFORD, R., *Beowulf and the Seventh Century*, London 1971.

WEBB, J. F., *Lives of the Saints* (translated in Penguin Classics), London, 1965.

3 The Anglo-Saxon Achievement

BARLOW, F., *The English Church 1000-1066*, revised, London 1978.

DUCKETT, E. S., *St Dunstan of Canterbury*, London, 1955.

FISHER, E. R., *The Greater Anglo-Saxon Churches*, London, 1962.

LEVISON, W., *England and the Continent in the Eighth Century*, Oxford, 1946.

LOYN, H. R., *The Vikings in Britain*, London, 1977.

PARSONS, D. (ed.), *Tenth Century Studies*, London, 1975.
RICE, D. T., *English Art 871-1100*, Oxford, 1952.
ROBINSON, J. A., *The Times of St Dunstan*, Oxford, 1923.
SAWYER, P. H., *The Age of the Vikings*, revised, London, 1971.
WALLACH, L., *Alcuin and Charlemagne*, Ithaca, N.Y., 1959.

General

BLAIR, P. H., *An Introduction to Anglo-Saxon England*, revised, Cambridge, 1977.
DEANSLEY, M., *The Pre-Conquest Church in England*, revised, London, 1963.
   Sidelights on the Anglo-Saxon Church, London, 1962.
GATCH, M. McC., *Loyalties and Traditions: Man and His World in Old English Literature*, New York, 1971.
GODFREY, J., *The Church in Anglo-Saxon England*, Cambridge, 1962.
KENDRICK, F. D., *Anglo-Saxon Art to AD 900*, London, 1938.
   Late Saxon and Viking Art, London, 1949.
KENNEDY, C. W., *Early English Christian Poetry*, London, 1952.
SWANTON, M. (ed.), *Anglo-Saxon Prose*, London, 1975.
TAYLOR, H. M. and J., *Anglo-Saxon Architecture*, 2 vols, Cambridge, 1965.
WHITELOCK, D. (ed.), *English Historical Documents, c.500-1042*, London, 1955.
WILSON, D., *The Anglo-Saxons* (mainly archaeological), revised, London, 1971.

1981 Publications

HILL, D., *An Atlas of Anglo-Saxon England*, Oxford.
SALWAY, P., *Roman Britain*, Oxford.
THOMAS, C., *Christianity in Roman Britain to AD 500*, London.

Part Two

THE MIDDLE AGES

CHAPTER FOUR

FREEDOM UNDER THE KING

Canterbury Cathedral . Choir and High Altar .

THE CONQUEROR'S CHURCH

The main interest in the next period, 1066-1215, is political. Anglo-Saxon England had been ruined by its political failures, more fundamentally than by its military defeats. It was the work of William the Conqueror to impose order on the country, although it was the no less essential work of other men coming after him to impose law on the king. And the Church knew that both in the establishment of law and in the winning of freedom its own welfare was at stake.

A chant called *Royal Praises* has survived. Its use under

William I probably began at his coronation, and there is evidence about its frequent use under Henry III two centuries later. The clerks who sang it first solemnly saluted their monarch, enthroned in state: 'To the most serene William, the great and peacegiving king, crowned by God, life and victory!' They continued to sing of Christ's victory, in such a way as to suggest that the king's was not very different. And the fervent royalism expressed in this chant was defended by an anonymous priest in Rouen, making a contribution to political theory about 1100. This priest believed, of course, that the king's beliefs and morals ought to be blameless; but the king was sacred, his right to rule was given directly by God, all his priests were his subjects, and the pope had no power to intervene.[1]

For most of the time, the bishops of medieval England were enthusiastic advocates and agents of the king who had been 'crowned by God'. The explanation is not merely that almost all of them owed their appointments to him. The service of England's Christian monarchy was held to be a sacred duty not only by time-servers but also by some bishops whose spiritual integrity matched their intellectual power. This tradition reached back deep into Anglo-Saxon England, but at the head of the line after the Norman Conquest stood the Conqueror's archbishop, Lanfranc.

Although William did not want an immediate change at Canterbury, eventually Stigand had to go. A worldly man, he had been given the archbishopric by Earl Godwine while retaining his income as Bishop of Winchester, and his appointment had never been recognized in Rome. He made room for Lanfranc, who was archbishop for almost twenty years from 1070. During the king's many absences from England this austere and able monk shared political responsibility with two Norman bishops who had come over in 1066: Odo of Bayeux the king's half-brother and Geoffrey de Mowbray, Bishop of Coutances. He was, however, more in the king's confidence than they could ever be – a status recognized

---

[1] See G. H. Williams, *The Norman Anonymous of 1100* (Cambridge, Mass., 1951).

by his position as the richest landowner in England after the king. They were essentially Norman aristocrats, rewarded for their support of William first by rich bishoprics in Normandy and then by large estates in England. But they were always liable to turn traitor; on suspicion of this, Bishop Odo was imprisoned in 1082. Lanfranc, on the other hand, was a monk through and through, a man whose loyalty to William had become a matter of firm religious principle. When Norman earls rebelled against William in 1075, it was he who called out the English militia and assured his absent king that there was no cause for alarm.

An Italian, he practised as a lawyer in Pavia and then crossed the Alps to earn his living as a schoolmaster in Avranches in Normandy. He was drawn to the life of a monk at Bec, only eight years after the foundation of that monastery by Herluin. The community he joined was still so poor that he was persuaded to make some money for it by taking in pupils — and was still so disorganized that he was persuaded to administer it as prior. Duke William joined the circle of his admirers. The story told of their first real encounter throws light on the characters of the two men. William's marriage with Matilda was condemned by the strictest churchmen because they were too closely related. Lanfranc accordingly opposed it and was banished from Normandy for the offence. Meeting his duke, he asked for a better horse so that he might ride more quickly into exile. William's interest was stirred by the brave joke, it is said; the two men became friends and after many talks Lanfranc was sent to persuade the pope to issue a dispensation for the marriage. The pope consented if William would found two monasteries, and of one of these — St Stephen's, Caen — Lanfranc became the first abbot.

Much of what he wrote has been lost, but from his years at Bec and Caen there survive a number of books. These show his great talents as a master of grammar and argument; as a commentator on the psalms, St Paul's letters and the Latin Fathers of the Church; and as one who defended the transformation of the bread and wine into the Body and Blood of Christ (the doctrine later defined as 'transubstantiation') against another Norman teacher, Berengar. Berengar had used the newly developed skill in reasoned debate ('dialectic') in order to insist that Christ's own phrase 'this is my body' demonstrated that 'this' remained bread. In the eyes of those of his contemporaries who interested themselves in such matters Lanfranc had been even more rational, as well as much more orthodox, in his counter-argument, insisting that the 'bread' was now bread only in appearance; its essence was the body of Christ. Such was the renowned teacher who in his late fifties, when he had already refused the archbishopric of Rouen in Normandy, was persuaded by the Conqueror to set the English Church in order.

Some of his reorganization while Archbishop of Canterbury proved abortive. He attempted to make himself ecclesiastically supreme throughout England, Wales, Scotland, Ireland and the northern isles. He quoted Bede's history and impressive charters forged by the Canterbury monks (we need not suppose that he knew they were forgeries). His successor persisted in the attempt, but it had to be abandoned – with the result that throughout the Middle Ages (indeed, until the twentieth century) only a papal 'legate', who need not be the Archbishop of Canterbury, could unite the clergy of the provinces of Canterbury and York into a single council to consider the welfare of the English Church. Lanfranc also failed in an effort to insist that in future all the parish priests of England should have the sex-lives of monks. Even he did not insist that the clergy should put away the wives or the other women to be found established in most of the parsonages, and the evidence suggests that the practice of clerical marriage or concubinage remained common long after his day. Illustrations in medieval manuscripts show many priests in gaily coloured gowns – in green, yellow or scarlet; the sombre black does not seem to have become standard until the fifteenth century, by when clerical marriage was unknown. But in many other spheres where he sought order, order was established by the Conqueror's archbishop.

Lanfranc introduced from the Continent the new ecclesiastical or 'canon' law; in his day it was not as elaborate as it later became, but at least he consigned Anglo-Saxon church law into oblivion. In the library of Trinity College, Cambridge, is preserved a law book of Decretals brought over by Lanfranc from the library at Bec: it is a missionary lawyer's Bible, the key to the whole difference between this systematic, long-lasting, reform and the revival over which King Edgar and Archbishop Dunstan had presided. In Anglo-Saxon England there had been no neat separation of church courts from the ordinary courts of the state. From the national *witenagemot* downwards, one court would handle all matters — secular, ecclesiastical or moral. Now (in 1072) ecclesiastical and moral questions were withdrawn from the ordinary courts and a separate system of church courts was set up, presided over by bishops and archdeacons or their deputies. Thus were sown the seeds of future conflict between Church and State.

Lanfranc took a special interest in reshaping the English monasteries on the best Continental models, and compiled his *Monastic Constitutions* in order to arrange the monk's life in minute detail. The monasteries thus reformed included Canterbury Cathedral, which was rebuilt after a fire.[2] Church councils were held to regulate church life outside the monasteries. When he was free to do so the king presided, but Lanfranc's was the master mind in details. Each diocese was now to have clear boundaries, with a centre of population as its own centre. The vast, disordered Anglo-Saxon dioceses of Selsey, Sherborne, Wells, Lichfield, Dorchester and Elmham were given new centres in Chichester, Salisbury, Bath, Chester, Lincoln and Thetford (later Norwich) with new bishops to rule them. It was the logical completion of the policy begun under Edward the Confessor, when the diocese of Crediton had been given a new centre in Exeter.

While the English Church was being reformed in these and other ways, claims that only the papacy could order the life of the Church in accordance with the mind of Christ were resisted. In Rome it was hoped that William would be in a weak position because of what he owed to papal support of his claim in 1066 — and because of the personal power of the new pope, formerly Archdeacon Hildebrand, before whom the

---

[2] *The Monastic Constitutions of Lanfranc* have been translated and edited by David Knowles (London, 1951).

emperor Henry IV humbled himself in the snow at Canossa. But William had no intention of yielding to the demand for allegiance which reached distant England from the pope. 'I never promised it', the king replied in 1080, 'nor do I find that my predecessors ever paid it to yours'. The king exercised a veto over the recognition of any pope, over the reception of papal letters or envoys in England, and over punishment by the Church of the leading aristocrats, the king's tenants-in-chief; and he advised Lanfranc to ignore repeated requests to come to Rome for instructions. And Gregory VII, normally both inflexible and passionate, accepted the rebuff. One reason was his fear that William might recognize a rival claimant to the papacy. But he also had to acknowledge the effectiveness of the reforms being carried out by Lanfranc in alliance with his invincible king.[3]

Four other bishops and twenty-two abbots came over from Norman monasteries to work in England under the Conqueror. Given the conditions of the time, the Normanization of church leadership was inevitable. Bishops and abbots could not be financed except by the grant of estates which in almost all cases now carried with them the obligation to provide a stated number of knights for the king's army – the essence of 'feudalism'. They had to be men on whose loyalty the king could rely. Accordingly William took care not to reproduce in England the pattern which existed in Normandy, where many of the bishops were recruited from a small circle of aristocratic families. As bishops, he preferred monks or his own chaplains. However, among the imported Norman bishops only one, Herfast, who was sent to East Anglia, was discreditable: Lanfranc had to tell him to switch his attention from dice to the study of the Bible. And among the Englishmen left undisturbed until their deaths were two saints: Ethelwig, Abbot of Evesham, and Wulfstan, Bishop of Worcester. St Wulfstan was a monk, elected bishop by his brethren in 1062. His continuance as bishop, surrounded by Englishmen, until 1095 is explained partly by the strong support he gave to William I against rebellious barons and to William II against the Welsh.

---

[3] See Margaret Gibson, *Lanfranc of Bec* (Oxford, 1978).

But his *Life*, written by the monk Coleman as the last echo of Anglo-Saxon ecclesiastical history, makes it clear that a man so holy (yet not stupid) would never have collaborated with his country's new colonial rulers had he not believed that this acceptance of fact was in the interests of the English Church. Wulfstan was not ashamed to be the colleague of Lanfranc.

A twentieth-century authority judged that this Italian lawyer played a greater part in organizing the Church in England than any other Archbishop of Canterbury between Theodore of Tarsus in the seventh century and Thomas Cranmer in the sixteenth. But, he added, when praising Lanfranc it would be unjust to ignore the Conqueror himself — 'a ruler resolved of set purpose to raise the whole level of ecclesiastical discipline in his dominions'.[4]

A bastard (his mother was said to be a tanner's daughter in Falaise), William became Duke of Normandy while a little boy. He developed into a great man in the hardest of schools: fourteen years of almost continuous war against the other descendants of pirates who now constituted the aristocracy of Normandy. Almost all the guardians of his boyhood were murdered during those terrible years. The man who survived was fiercely determined, but cunning enough not to be impatient; outstanding in his age as a general but also as a diplomat; ruthless and illiterate, but sharing to the full the Norman aristocracy's admiration for monks, the cavalry of God. Such qualities won some tributes from the English. When he died in 1087, 'things both good and bad' were written in one of the Anglo-Saxon Chronicles. Although a brutal and grasping oppressor, the Conqueror was also 'very wise . . . and stronger than any predecessor of his had been'.

SEEKING A CHRISTIAN KING

The Conqueror's tragedy was that he had no power to make his sons men like him. The eldest, Robert, whom he intended

---

[4] David Knowles, *The Monastic Order in England* (Cambridge, 1940), pp.93, 143.

to be Duke of Normandy, when aroused could be as ferocious as his father — but was so lacking in military skill and in general intelligence that he could not hold the duchy down. He spent the last twenty-seven years of his life in prison. For some of this time he was in Cardiff castle, and a Welsh poem containing the line 'Woe to him that is not old enough to die' is attributed to him. He lived until the age of eighty, and his wooden effigy is still to be seen in Gloucester Cathedral.

William the Ruddy or Rufus did fulfil his father's intention that he should be King of the English and was a strong soldier, but it was typical of him that he sold vacant bishoprics for cash, incurring all the Church's condemnation of 'simony' and not gaining bishops with moral authority over the clergy. When Lanfranc died he kept the archbishopric of Canterbury vacant, preferring to transfer its revenues to his exchequer rather than to secure its support for his throne. It seems that he resented the years when, at his father's command, he had been Lanfranc's pupil in Canterbury. It was also typical of his lack of discretion that when in 1093 he did allow an appointment (he was terror-stricken because he thought he was dying), the appointment was an error, politically speaking. He nominated for Canterbury a theologian without a trace of Lanfranc's interest in politics and without any of his willingness to co-operate with worldly men.

The archbishop was Anselm, who had spent thirty-three years as a monk at Bec. He had been generally expected to follow Lanfranc ever since the latter's death in 1089, but that did not make the appointment sensible — or, it seems, genuinely attractive to him. Gradually Anselm, without being willing to renounce any of the bishops' wealth, adopted an extreme position. He held that no bishop should express obedience by doing homage to a mere king — whereas Lanfranc had never hesitated to support a king's right to sentence a bishop such as Odo of Bayeux (or the far more religiously minded William of St Calais, Bishop of Durham) for disloyalty. An archbishop so lacking in a taste for practical affairs would probably not have acquired a reputation so immense as Anselm's, had there not been the dramatic contrast between him and his king. William Rufus scandalized a brutal age by flaunting his contempt for religion, his greed for money and his homosexual practices. 'By the holy face of Lucca!' he once swore to the meek and saintly Gandulf, Bishop of Rochester. 'I shall not repay God with good for the evil he has done me!' Against him was pitted St Anselm, to whose character we shall return.

The Conqueror's third son, Henry, outwitted his brothers, defeating and imprisoning Robert and almost certainly inspiring the murder of William Rufus while they were both hunting in the New Forest one August afternoon in 1100. He did much to secure order and justice in his dominions, and after his death people looked back on his reign as a golden age. His merits or promises as a king were such that the saintly Anselm helped to establish him by turning a blind eye to the probability of conspiracy to murder, by accepting his hasty coronation by the Bishop of London, and by marrying him to a descendant of the old English dynasty, Princess Matilda of Scotland. But Henry lacked his father's strength of character, and modern historians incline to the view that his chief interest in the extension of royal justice in England lay in its profitability to finance the wars in France. The prosperity of the English Church in his reign (one sign of which was the creation of the diocese of Ely in 1109) does not seem to have been due to his initiative. The author of a modern study concludes that 'it is peculiarly difficult to construct an account around the personality of Henry. The king is an elusive character with a marked capacity for concealing his motives and emotions'.[5]

The Conqueror's sons, although so unattractive, were served by able churchmen. Ranulf Flambard, Bishop of Durham, was the chief minister of William Rufus. Clearly he was not fit to be a Christian bishop, but he deserves some credit for his agile industry in running the country – and for the architecture he commissioned at all three of the churches with which he was connected: St Martin's church in Dover, Christchurch in Hampshire and the nave of Durham Cathedral. Although Flambard fell from power on Henry I's

---

[5] Martin Brett, *The English Church under Henry I* (Oxford, 1975), p.3.

accession and had to escape to his native Normandy, it says something for his cheerfully secular energy that he was able to make first himself, then his brother and then his son Bishop of Lisieux, before dying (after a peaceful and apparently penitent old age) in the recovered possession of his Durham bishopric. A characteristic glimpse of him at the height of his power comes in the story of how once he attempted to seduce his mistress's niece, Theodora. Saying she would first close the door, she escaped through it instead – and, having beaten off another man's arduous attempt to marry her legally, lived to become a famous recluse and prioress, Christina of Markyate.[6]

Far more respectable – although he, too, openly acknowledged that the law of priestly celibacy was not for him – was Henry I's chief minister, Roger, Bishop of Salisbury. One chronicler says that the king first came across him in Normandy and was delighted by the rapidity with which he could say Mass; but this bishop's serious merit was that he wasted no time as an administrator. As 'justiciar' he was, it seems, the true architect of almost everything that men later praised about the reign of Henry I. The Anglo-Norman state disintegrated into civil war on the king's death; his only legitimate son had been drowned when the *White Ship* met a storm in the Channel and its crew, like their passengers, were drunk. But Bishop Roger remained steadily at the helm of such law and order as survived. He was also a faithful family man. His wife's name was Matilda; his son Roger was chancellor of the kingdom, another son (or nephew) worked in the exchequer, his nephew Nigel (Bishop of Ely) was treasurer, and another nephew, Alexander Bishop of Lincoln, was prominent at court. Although for some unknown reason they were known by the surname Poore, this family had great wealth and influence and deserved them, for they were 'the real moulders of the highly organized royal household administration and the financial machine, which even all the disturbances of Stephen's unquiet reign could not destroy'.[7]

---

[6] For Flambard see R. W. Southern in *Medieval Humanism and Other Studies* (Oxford, 1970), pp.182-205. C. H. Talbot edited the *Life of Christina of Markyate* (Oxford, 1959).

The Poore family supported the claim of Stephen of Blois to the throne on the death of Henry I, presumably because they distrusted the capacity of Henry's daughter Matilda. She was an ill-tempered and foolish woman who remembered too often that she was an emperor's widow. But Stephen did not have an unarguable claim: his mother Adela was the Conqueror's daughter. Nor, as it turned out, did he have much of a character to argue for him. When he moved against the Poores, with his eyes on the castles and treasures which they had taken care to amass, he lost the Church's support.

One of those alienated from King Stephen (partly by his treatment of the Poores) was his brother, Henry of Blois, the immensely rich Abbot of Glastonbury and Bishop of Winchester. More gifted than Stephen, this royal monk was elected Archbishop of Canterbury, only to find that at Stephen's request the pope refused to allow the move or 'translation' from Winchester. As a consolation he was appointed papal legate, thus taking precedence over Canterbury; and he tried to get Winchester made into an archbishopric. For eight years no subject in the kingdom was more powerful. His enthusiasm for art is shown by his commissioning of the Winchester Bible, the giant among twelfth-century English manuscripts, enriched by the art of at least six masters. His affection for the English past is shown by his ordering the removal of the mortuary chests containing the bones of the West Saxon kings from Hyde Abbey to his own cathedral (where they have remained). He was an enlightened patron of architecture and a connoisseur of antiques. While on a visit to Rome, he once amazed the crowd by going to the market place to buy ancient statues. When his brother gradually lost control of the country and finally died, Henry of Blois found it wisest to spend a period reorganizing the finances of the famous monastery of Cluny in France, where he had been trained as a young man. Under Henry II he returned to Winchester to perform the role of an elder

---

[7] H. A. Cronne, *The Reign of Stephen* (London, 1970), p.219. E. J. Kealey has provided a biography of *Roger of Salisbury, Viceroy of England* (Berkeley, Cal., 1972).

statesman together with the less expected duties of a conscientious diocesan bishop. 'For all the adventures and intrigues and extravagances and ambitions of his middle life', writes a modern scholar with a personal tendency to austerity, 'Henry had always remained not only blameless in his private life but also unsoured, uncoarsened, unhardened and undefiled'.[8] He is best remembered as the founder of the Hospital of St Cross in Winchester, the greatest of all medieval almshouses for the poor.

The archbishop elected when Henry of Blois was disappointed was Theobald, who like Anselm had been Abbot of Bec.[9] He regarded a stable monarchy as essential to the good order of the Church. Becoming convinced (as was the pope) that such a monarchy would never be established under Stephen or his son Eustace, he arranged the treaty by which Stephen accepted the succession of the Empress Matilda's son, Henry II. He collaborated with the new king until his own death in 1161. His household at Canterbury became a centre of ecclesiastical law and administration. It trained four future archbishops and six future bishops, and as was natural some of these took part in the government of the country. It was Theobald who recommended the most brilliant member of his staff, Thomas Becket, Archdeacon of Canterbury, formerly clerk to the sheriffs of London, to serve King Henry as his chancellor in 1155. He once summed up his approach in a letter to Henry: 'When the members of the Church are united in loyalty and love, when princes show due reverence to priests and priests render faithful service to princes, then do kingdoms enjoy that true peace and tranquility which must always be the goal of our desire'.[10]

The theory of the Christian monarchy encapsulated in that sentence was worked out at length in a treatise on politics and morality.

At the turn of the 1150s and 1160s, a period while Thomas

---

[8] David Knowles, *The Episcopal Colleagues of Thomas Becket* (Cambridge, 1951), p.36.

[9] See A. Saltman, *Theobald, Archbishop of Canterbury* (London, 1956).

[10] W. L. Warren, *Henry II* (London, 1973), p.422.

Becket was superintending the siege of Toulouse in France, Archbishop Theobald's learned secretary, John of Salisbury, dedicated and sent to him a new book. It was his *Policraticus*, or 'Statesman's Manual'. Like many another medieval treatise, it compared the State with a man's body. Of course the priests constituted the soul of this body. But the peasants were its feet, the soldiers its hands, the judges its eyes — and the king was its head. Although the king received his authority from God through the clergy (whose own authority was higher), it was he who supplied the brain-power which kept the whole body functioning harmoniously. Under such leadership, the peaceful progress of a society inspired by the Christian culture of Paris and Chartres (which was what John of Salisbury really cared about) would be secure.[11]

THE CHURCH UNDER HENRY II

After Theobald's death in 1161, Henry II chose Thomas Becket as Archbishop of Canterbury. We shall later make an attempt to understand the sense in which this extraordinary man was a saint. Here we ask only why he was the central figure in a heated controversy about Church and State.

The king was astonished when his friend became critical of him only a few months after his promotion, and had the two men remained close it is hard to see that England would have been less Christian. If Becket had stayed on as Chancellor of England as was the king's intention, the new archbishop would not have been called upon to administer any policy hostile to the vital interests of the Church. Or if Gilbert Foliot, Bishop of Hereford, had become Archbishop of Canterbury instead of Bishop of London on Theobald's death (as, it seems, both he and the monks at Canterbury hoped), the Church would not have suffered. Foliot was no courtier. His life as an austere abbot at Gloucester, and as a bishop active in his diocese,

---

[11] See H. Liebeschütz, *Medieval Humanism in the Life and Writings of John of Salisbury* (London, 1950).

proved that he belonged fully to the movement for greater discipline and holiness in the Church under the pope's inspiration. His dislike of Becket cannot be put down to mere jealousy. He sincerely despised his archbishop. To him Becket was a fool, whose quarrel with the king involved no question of faith or morals.[12]

Naturally the matter would not have been expressed like that in Rome. To papal Rome in the Middle Ages, the increase of its power at the expense of kings was always a question of faith and morals. But it is significant that the pope did not make the exiled Becket a cardinal or a member of his own court. It was not until Becket had been out of England for six years that Pope Alexander III threatened Henry II with the penalties of excommunication and interdict. These penalties were to bring King John to his knees; and the threat of them now made Henry II swallow his pride, so that he allowed Becket to go home. The pope's patience during the previous six years is remarkable. More curiously still, neither interdict nor excommunication followed the archbishop's murder. It seems that the pope was not entirely convinced about the martyr. His letters show irritation at Becket's independence, indiscretion and obstinacy.

The famous quarrel between the king and the archbishop became so bitter because of personal factors. These included Henry's deep resentment that his former friend, on whom he had loaded honours and whom he had taken into his close confidence, had picked one quarrel after another with him. Another factor, as the drama moved towards its finale, was the archbishop's determination to get killed. John of Salisbury was a loyal secretary to Thomas Becket as he had been loyal to old Theobald, but it is clear that he was puzzled. Here he was dealing with a man fundamentally different from the ecclesiastical politicians whom he so shrewdly portrayed in his *History of the Pontiffs*. Becket, as John learned, was a man driven by no common, earthly ambition; yet he had none of Theobald's quiet acceptance of monastic discipline in con-

---

[12] See *Gilbert Foliot and His Letters*, ed. A. Morey and C. N. L. Brooke (Cambridge, 1965).

fidence of the heavenly reward. In the end John had to abandon his strange master to his chosen destiny, saying: 'no one here wants to die for the sake of dying except you'.

Admittedly Henry was being provocative when, having twice extracted from Becket promises to obey the ancient customs of the realm, he had these customs drawn up in a formal code (the Constitutions of Clarendon, 1164) – and demanded that the archbishop should publicly accept them. Becket refused to endorse the Constitutions by formally sealing them and soon made it very clear that he repented on his former assent. Although at the beginning of the controversy his fellow-bishops were more consistent than he was in refusing to accept the 'customs', they later became very alarmed at the dangers in the crisis and ineffectively tried to heal the breach. The bishops' confusion is, however, not entirely surprising. Their stand against the Constitutions of Clarendon corresponded with the generally accepted teaching in the Church of the day, now that the Church's canon law had been codified much more clearly than in Lanfranc's or Anselm's time (thanks largely to the work of the monk Gratian).[13] On the other hand, almost all the customs included in these Constitutions of 1164 had been the practice in England before the Church had taken advantage of the anarchy of Stephen's reign. And they continued to be the general practice in France, for example. On the question of appeals to the papal court, what Henry II wanted was to be asked for his consent first; and that had certainly been the demand of William the Conqueror. On the question of clerics who were criminals (a question created by the Conqueror's insistence that 'spiritual persons' should be dealt with by the bishops), what he wanted was that they should be tried by an ecclesiastical court, degraded from holy orders if found guilty, and handed over to a royal official for punishment.

---

[13] The theological background has been studied by Beryl Smalley in *The Becket Controversy and the Schools* (Oxford, 1973), and the legal background by L. C. Gabel in *Benefit of Clergy in the Later Middle Ages* (Northampton, Mass., 1929) and Henry Mayr-Harting in *Journal of Ecclesiastical History* (London, 1965), pp.39-53.

When the drama was over — when Henry had been scourged
in public at the martyr's tomb in Canterbury and poor Bishop
Foliot had had to undergo his worst ordeal by reading out the
royal declaration of penitence — it was found that the working
of English law had changed less than men expected.

The only major concessions on the king's side were two.
First, appeals to Rome were to be allowed as a last resort in
ecclesiastical controversies. Second, a cleric convicted of a
crime in a church court would not be punished by the secular
authority. But neither of these concessions, not even the
second which was humiliating, necessarily spelt disaster to the
State. The king had to come to terms with the pope's growing
authority; even the Constitutions of Clarendon had envisaged
some appeals to Rome. Henry could now gain from a deal
with the papacy, as was to be demonstrated in the bargain
struck by his son, John. And clerical criminals could still be
condemned in the king's court, and suffer the confiscation of
their goods there and then, before being allowed to escape to
the bishop's court by pleading 'benefit of clergy'. In the
bishop's court the old-fashioned method of 'compurgation'
was used; twelve neighbours of substance had to be gathered
to swear to the innocence of the accused cleric. Most of the
accused were then released, but if they were so guilty as to be
notorious they could be imprisoned for life in the bishop's
prison. Should they be released by the bishop, or escape, they
could be outlawed and forced to flee the country. The over-
riding practical need, we may conclude, was to have justice
which actually worked. The papacy's legal processes, which
had hitherto been subject to many delays and confusions, were
now becoming far more efficient and it was inevitable that
they should appeal to some of the English in some situations.
But the English Church on its own was not in much of a position to act as policeman or judge. This was tacitly acknowledged when the Church abandoned the claim that it alone was
competent to try and punish murderers of priests or other
offenders against their dignity. The claim was made ridiculous
by a fine piece of irony: Becket's own murderers were never
properly punished.

In one of his fits of rage Henry cried out that he wanted to

be rid of this priest. Four knights immediately hurried to
Canterbury from the king's Christmas court near Bayeux. But
all this was not because of a dispute over the competence of
rival courts. What finally stung the king to fury, and what the
knights shouted about in Canterbury Cathedral, was Becket's
refusal to accept the ceremony of crowning the king's eldest
son. This coronation was important to Henry II; it was intended both to bind the 'young king' to him and to strengthen
his chance of succeeding to the throne in peace – two hopes
which history was to mock. It had occurred in Becket's
absence. A long record of defending the rights and privileges
of his office with a complete obstinacy now came to a climax.
Having just staged what had seemed to be his final reconciliation with Henry, the archbishop, back in Canterbury, excommunicated the bishops who had taken part in the honour
paid to the 'young king'. They were not to enter any church or
to be befriended by any Christian. It was this act directed
against bishops that led to the end. The king exploded in
anger and the four knights rode into Canterbury on the afternoon of 29 December 1170. They subsequently claimed that it
had been their intention to carry out an arrest which the king
had ordered, until the emotion of the moment got the better
of them. This may well have been the truth; in the twelfth
century one did not lightly murder an archbishop in his
cathedral, or expect a king to approve. It seems that to the
end Becket could not be grasped or placed by his contemporaries. They were dealing with problems of law and politics.
As he went to his martyr's death, he was dealing with – what?

After that drama quieter actors were needed. The next
Archbishop of Canterbury was a placid monk, Roger of
Dover, who specialized in ecclesiastical law but was determined to stay at peace with his king. The next Bishop of Winchester after Henry of Blois was Richard of Ilchester, a civil
servant specializing in financial problems. The king had com-
mended him to the monks of Winchester with the well-
remembered words: 'I order you to hold a free election, but
forbid you to elect anyone but Richard my clerk'.[14] Arch-

---

[14] C. Duggan has studied his career in *Transactions of the Royal Historical
Society* (London, 1966), pp.1-21.

bishop Roger gave no trouble and Richard of Ilchester gladly remained in the king's service while a bishop.

Henry's closest friend among the bishops was, however, St Hugh of Avalon. At his special request this true saint became in 1180 prior of the exceptionally austere new monastery (a Charterhouse) founded by the king at Witham and then, in 1186, Bishop of Lincoln. The king loved Hugh so obviously that the baseless rumour spread that he was his father, but the *Life* written by Adam, the bishop's chaplain during the last three years of his life, reveals the truth. There was a rare combination of strengths in him; and it aroused respect in king and monk, priest and people, alike. Self-discipline was united with self-confidence (he was a Burgundian nobleman's son); and the intellectual equipment of a scholar (although he was no author) was assisted by a ready sense of humour. He once had a previously sulky king in fits of laughter by a brief, sharp joke based on William the Conqueror's descent from the tanner in Falaise. And all the time the desire for a silent union with God was compatible with efficiency in the pastoral care of a diocese and in the business of the royal court.[15]

Such bishops supported their king in principle, although in St Hugh's case at any rate they did not lack the courage to disagree when they thought it necessary. In a more tactful way they were what Becket's murderers claimed to be, roaring out as they left Canterbury Cathedral that December evening: *réaux, réaux* ('king's men, king's men'). And it is possible to see why the king commanded such allegiance; why good men were his men.

He was the founder of the Plantagenet or Angevin dynasty in England, so named because his mother had married Geoffrey Plantagenet, court of Anjou. When he inherited the English throne at the age of twenty-one in 1154, he was already Duke of Normandy and lord of rich lands to the south in France; and he had married Eleanor of Acquitaine, who had brought with her still richer lands further to the south. At the court of this famous and extremely independent-minded

---

[15] *The Life of St Hugh of Lincoln* was edited by D. L. Douie and H. Farmer in 2 vols. (London, 1961-62).

lady the civilization of love, as sung by the troubadours, reached its height of glamour, chivalry and courtesy; of unreality. A man of astounding energy and capacity for business, Henry did not go in for glamour. He was determined to defend his own rights, and to see justice done to others, in any place brought to his attention between Scotland and Spain. And even that did not satisfy him. He was encouraged to conquer Ireland by Pope Hadrian IV – Nicholas Breakspear, the son of a minor official of St Albans Abbey and the only Englishman ever to sit on the papal throne. The king landed there in 1171, the beginning of England's tragic involvement in the neighbouring island. Such a ruler made and enforced law by his own exertions, although in England he relied a great deal on his great justiciar, Ranulf de Glanvill. Himself too restless to concentrate on church services or to remain in any one spot for long, Henry seems to have had a real admiration for genuinely devout monks or hermits and made many gifts to them. When Gilbert of Sempringham, the Lincoln-shire country priest who had started the only religious 'order' ever to have a medieval Englishman as its founder, arrived at Henry's court on business, the king forestalled him. He hurried to his lodgings, to receive the saint's blessing.[16]

With his grey eyes, freckled face and uncertain temper, with his indifference to comfort or pomp despite his wealth and power, with the positive delight he took in an unkempt appearance, Henry fascinated his generation by his person-ality as much as by the extent of the lands he ruled. And the clergy had special reasons to be interested in him. His con-ception of justice guaranteed massive privileges for the Church and the Becket controversy never touched them. The clergy administered their vast and steadily growing possessions with almost no interference from the king's officers. If bishops and abbots were usually appointed after consulting the king, no one thought the royal interest in these great landowners un-reasonable. From laymen the clergy collected tithes (tenths of crops), mortuaries (normally a dead man's best beast or

---

[16] Rose Graham, *St Gilbert of Sempringham and the Gilbertines* (London, 1901), p.19.

gown), oblations (financial contributions four times a year), and fees. They punished, often by fines, laymen accused of fornication, adultery, incest, usury, defamation, perjury, blasphemy or heresy. Ecclesiastical courts decided all the many legal problems connected with contracts, marriages or wills. It is reasonable to suppose that this position of rich privilege mattered to the clergy far more than did the question of how to punish clerics convicted of serious crimes; and that the legal question did not involve many priests who were murderers. From the days of Edward I to the days of Henry VIII the bishops' records show that the clerics or 'clerks' whom Becket saved from the gallows were almost all men in minor orders: parish clerks, readers, acolytes and the like, many of them earning their livings like laymen. Even schoolboys were given the tonsure that brought them within the privileged clerical caste. It was widely believed that laymen ought to escape secular justice even if they were not in such minor orders, provided only that they could read a little Latin; Psalm 51:1 was regarded as the 'neck verse'.

So we can see the reason why modern students of the controversy of the 1160s find it difficult to believe that the Christian Church's vital interests were at stake when Henry II was resisted to the death by his former friend and agent, Thomas Becket.

THE GREAT CHARTER

Henry II's sons, however, proved as unworthy of the throne as did the Conqueror's. Geoffrey, his son by his mistress Rosamund Clifford, was made Bishop of Lincoln at the age of fourteen, Chancellor of England and finally Archbishop of York, despite his protest that he preferred dogs to priests. The legitimate son called by King Henry's own name and crowned at his wish (despite Becket) lived long enough to break his father's heart before dying prematurely. The next son and fellow-rebel, Richard, was while King of the English interested only in his crusade, courageous but futile. To him the country was a source of income and chroniclers reported his remark that he would sell London if he could find a buyer.

During King Richard's absence the administration of England was entrusted to Hugh de Puiset, Bishop of Durham, and William Longchamp, Bishop of Ely — the former a handsome and acceptable aristocrat, the latter a civil servant of humble birth who was said to look like an ape and to be so overbearing that he was forced to leave the country.[17]

On his return in 1193 Richard found time to secure the appointment of his principal assistant during the crusade, Herbert Walter, as Archbishop of Canterbury. A nephew of Henry II's justiciar Ranulf de Glanvill, and himself highly trained as a lawyer and administrator, the new archbishop served Richard with great efficiency as justiciar for five years. He made enemies by his financial demands on behalf of the absent king, and his own monks at Canterbury protested to Rome against his absorption in secular affairs, with the result that he fell from political power. But early in the next reign he was back in power as chancellor for six years, conducting the administration of King John. Hubert Walter was to Richard and John all that Henry II had hoped for from Thomas Becket.[18]

King John was never popular in his lifetime, and has joined the rogues' gallery in many assessments of his reign from his own century to this. He is reputed to have been utterly incompetent because during his reign (in 1204) the duchy of Normandy was conquered by the French king; yet the link across the Channel made in 1066 had always been fragile and the so-called 'Angevin empire' of Henry II had been nothing more than a federation, united by a dominating personality. John is known to have been cruel and rapacious and his murder of Prince Arthur outraged his informed contemporaries; yet the records of his reign show him dispensing much justice and some charity. He did not look like a Christian king (he was physically undersized) or behave like one (he

---

[17] See G. V. Scammell, *Hugh de Puiset, Bishop of Durham* (Cambridge, 1956).

[18] There are two recent studies of *Hubert Walter*, by C. R. Cheney (London, 1967) and C. R. Young (Durham, N.C., 1968).

talked with his cronies during services); yet he founded a
monastery at Beaulieu in Hampshire. He offended the barons
as much because he was no soldier as because he was no
gentleman, and fell foul of the Church not because of some
unspeakable sin but because of a dispute over the archbishopric of Canterbury.

On Hubert Walter's death in 1205 the king's candidate for
Canterbury was his secretary, the Bishop of Norwich, but the
monks of the cathedral monastery (with whom lay the formal
right to elect) hurriedly chose one of their own number. The
situation was sufficiently unclear to allow a formidable pope,
Innocent III, to appoint Cardinal Stephen Langton, with
whom he had formed a close friendship while they were both
teaching at the University of Paris. Langton was not accepted
by the king and had to spend six years waiting for his revenues
or for admission to England. The enraged pope now placed
the kingdom under an 'interdict' and excommunicated the
king. The excommunication meant that no Christian was supposed to have anything to do with John: since most of his civil
servants were bishops or priests, it was an effective blow. Only
one bishop remained in England, at Winchester. The interdict of 1208 decreed that no services were to be held in the
parish churches. The Mass was allowed in monasteries – but
only behind closed doors. Infants could not be baptized except
at home or in the church porch; the dead could not be buried
in consecrated ground; the living could not receive Holy Communion except when at the point of death; church bells were
silent. King John retaliated by plundering the Church, but
when the pope threatened to authorize the French king to take
over England a shrewd deal was made. Near Dover on 15 May
1212 John resigned the kingdoms of England and Ireland to
the papacy, and received them back in return for homage and
an annual tribute, together with the promise of a restitution of
the money seized from the Church in the royal counter-attack.

On that day the submission of England to Rome which
William the Conqueror had avoided was achieved – and it remained the formal position for more than a century. However,
the most important immediate result of John's humiliation was
that Pope Innocent was now put firmly on his side in his

struggles with the barons and the French; and the pope's agents received new orders. Chief among those agents in England was the Archbishop of Canterbury.

When he had taken up his revenues and responsibilities in the settlement of 1212, the archbishop had to cope with a complicated situation. He later became famous as a leader of the barons who extracted concessions from John. The king made a temporary peace in the meadow called Runnymede on the banks of the Thames on 15 June 1215: it was the great charter, Magna Carta. Langton, indeed, is reputed to have been not only the midwife of the charter but its father; for, according to more than one chronicler of the time and to many subsequent historians, he began the idea of a great new charter by reading Henry I's coronation charter to the barons assembled in St Paul's Cathedral. Actually, the evidence is less clear cut. There can be no doubt that Langton had the intellectual equipment to influence the course of events in 1215 and that he shared the ideas from which the great charter drew its strength, but evidence that Langton produced Henry I's charter, or was always on the side of the barons against King John, is unsatisfactory. The archbishop was always prominent; Innocent III noted (with pain) that the opposition to John dated from Langton's arrival in England. But the king was never able to pin a charge of treason on him, and on the whole 'the evidence presents him as a mediator and a moderator, rather than an originator'.[19]

Stephen Langton was a mediator because he had to serve his pope and his king, as well as his fellow-barons and his conscience. And he experienced a mediator's usual lack of thanks. He was suspended from his archbishopric, and forced into another exile, by Innocent III when he delayed excommunicating the enemies of the pope's new royal protégé. He had to wait for the election of another pope before he could resume his work in England.

Thus even when the king was the notorious John, there was solid substance in the idea of the Christian monarchy of England. It should not come as a surprise when we find

---

[19] J. C. Holt, *Magna Carta* (Cambridge, 1965), p.188.

Cardinal Langton in the next reign protecting the interests of
the young king, Henry III, against the barons; at one crisis, in
1224, he ordered the bishops to take over the most important
royal castles from the barons, as trustees for the king. Nor,
indeed, should we be amazed when we find him assuring a
London congregation in 1213 that 'because you are layfolk it is
your business to believe that your prelates are men who do all
things discreetly and with wisdom'.[20] Langton was never a
democrat. He was not sent to England in order to encourage
democracy. His mission was to carry out the policy of Pope
Innocent III.

Innocent, a Roman nobleman autocratic by temperament,
was the first pope to use the title 'Vicar of Christ' (the title that
Archbishop Wulfstan two hundred years before had applied
to the King of the English), and he was the first pope to insist
that he alone in his 'plenitude of power' had the right to
authorize the veneration of a saint; to appoint to ecclesiastical
posts throughout Christendom by 'provision'; to be the universal pastor. Of course such a pope was determined to say who
should be the next Archbishop of Canterbury; he was also
determined to decide who should be the next Patriarch of
Constantinople or the next Holy Roman Emperor. What interested him was not Magna Carta but the reforming programme of the Fourth Lateran Council, held in Rome in the
same year, 1215. This was the council that defined the Faith
(against the new Albigensian heretics in France) and the Mass
(developing Lanfranc's teaching into the full doctrine of the
'transubstantiation' of bread and wine into Christ's body and
blood). The council insisted that the archbishops should hold
provincial synods every year; that the bishops should teach
regularly and reform morals; that the parish priests should
reside in their parishes, with a reasonable income and security; that the laity should be married only in church and the
clergy not at all; and, most important, that at least once a year
every lay person in Christendom should confess his or her sins
to the parish priest and receive absolution and communion. It
was a programme not of one nation's democracy but of a

[20] C. R. Cheney, *From Becket to Langton* (Manchester, 1956), p.155.

whole Christian civilization's discipline. The great pope identified with it wanted King John to support it more than he wanted anything else in England.[21]

THE CHURCH AGAINST TYRANNY

In strange company with a pope whom he regarded as a foreign enemy of 'this England', William Shakespeare cared nothing for Magna Carta; his *King John* did not mention it. Why, then, has history taken the great charter so seriously? Why has it seen King John's momentary agreement with the barons as the climax to which all events after the Norman Conquest lead? Why has the Church been praised for fighting for more than its own freedom? It was the first clause in Magna Carta, as in Henry I's coronation charter, that the English Church 'may be free and enjoy its liberties and rights unimpaired'. But why has the document thus introduced – a document full of liberties for barons, of rights already defined in feudal custom – been venerated as the English-speaking world's first charter of liberty, putting that world in debt to the English Church?

Part of the answer to these questions is the truth that the Church was the only body in England strong enough to prevent the monarchy which the Conqueror had founded from becoming a tyranny.

As we have seen, in every reign bishops and other churchmen worked hard and prayed hard as servants of the Christian monarchy. It was typical that the *Dialogus de Scaccario*, the handbook which for many years set the pattern for the working of the king's exchequer (and the efficiency of the English exchequer was the wonder and envy of all other kings), was compiled by a Bishop of London, Richard Fitz Nigel. But Thomas Becket was by no means the only servant of the king to put his loyalty to the Church above all other earthly loyalties. On innumerable occasions bishops who owed their

---

[21] See C. R. Cheney, *Pope Innocent III and England* (Stuttgart, 1976).

promotion to a king were found pursuing the Church's objectives rather than his, and even before they were rewarded with high ecclesiastical office civil servants who were clerics must always have had in mind this possible future tension in their loyalties. When a man had become a bishop a show of independence might incur the royal wrath – but not total disaster. A rebellious lay baron could be defeated, imprisoned or executed by a king. But a bishop was more of a problem. Men felt uneasy at the idea of roughing him up – was he not the priest who could 'make God' in the Mass, the tribe's chief magician? It was also out of the question for the king to risk permanently alienating the whole body of the clergy on whom he depended from his coronation onwards. In that generally illiterate age, only the clergy could propagate the sacred status of an anointed king – and only they could organize his household, gather his taxes, add up his accounts, issue his orders and conduct his diplomacy. Besides, all the kings from William the Conqueror to John (William Rufus alone excepted) seem to have been orthodox believers, convinced that the clergy held the keys to heaven or hell and that before death the God known best to them bestowed or withheld victory and wealth. The moral power of the clergy in the Middle Ages was displayed when in 1070 the pope's legate persuaded the Norman bishops to impose penances on all who had shed blood in the invasion of England. Those who had fought without pay for King William had to perform a year's penance for each life taken. Mercenaries had to do the same penance for taking part in the expedition as for homicide. So those who had conquered with the Conqueror still had to kneel before a mysteriously higher power.

Had the power of the clergy not checked the monarch's power, the course of English history might have been very different. For the monarchy fastened on England by the Norman Conquest was a tyranny in the making.

Admittedly William needed the support of other aristocrats from France to conquer England, to hold it down, and to defend his realm against external foes or internal traitors. Throughout his life he knew very little peace, and all his hopes depended on the fighting capacity of some five thousand trained troops which his English tenants-in-chief were obliged to provide at his demand. But he was determined to reduce this dependence on others to the minimum. He built on the old position of the monarchy in England, already the best administered country in eleventh-century Europe, in order to develop Europe's most united state. He inherited in England a taxation system (developed out of the need to buy off the Vikings with Danegeld) and a coinage superior to anything in Normandy. He maintained the administrative structure of shires divided into 'hundreds' (or in some regions into areas called 'weapon-takes'); and royal letters or 'writs' were for many years still sent to them in Old English. And he made one dramatic innovation.

He was the anointed king and claimed to inherit through his coronation any mystique or administrative support which had gathered around Edward the Confessor's throne. But he had not succeeded to the kingdom in peace, despite Edward the Confessor's probable wishes; he was the Conqueror. As such he claimed that the entire country was his to hold or to grant to his favourites in return for their promises. He had a power of which no Anglo-Saxon king (and no Duke of Normandy) had ever dreamed. To keep the aristocracy in personal touch with him, he turned the Anglo-Saxon *witenagemot* into a Great Council which brought the great lords to his court at least every Christmas, Easter and Whitsun. In 1086 he assembled at Salisbury all the chief landowners of England, whether or not they were directly his own tenants, and made them all do homage to him, making it clear that no loyalty owed to any other lord should be allowed to conflict with their duty to their king. During the same year the king caused Domesday Book to be compiled. The most detailed survey of any kingdom to be made in the Middle Ages, its purpose was to record the estates held by the king's chief tenants, county by county, comparing the position in 1086 with that on 'the day when King Edward was alive and dead'. Given time, it could have become the basis of a taxation far more grinding than anything achieved by William Rufus or John. Given successors of his own ability, William could have founded an absolute monarchy.

That the Great Council of the king turned out to be the

ancestor of a democratic Parliament, that some of the barons combined against the king for purposes larger than their self-enrichment, and that England learned that the king's will was not the highest law in every sphere – all this was due to the moral leadership provided by churchmen more than to any other personal influence. We know the balance of power in 1086 exactly.[22] Domesday Book showed an England of which about twenty per cent was owned directly by the king and his family. More than half was held from him by tenants-in-chief, the aristocracy, of whom only about five per cent were native English. The remaining quarter was owned by the Church. These figures matter because they show that the Church could hold the balance in politics, if strong personalities were at its head; that bishops could one day help barons to impose law on the king, as they had already helped the king to impose order on the country.

To appreciate what was involved, we need to go back over the story we have told, to get at the secrets of the fame of two celebrated archbishops, St Anselm and St Thomas.

ANSELM

Anselm was born in Italy like Lanfranc, but belonged to a noble family. His father was given up to a secular way of life (although he became a monk on his deathbed) and quarrelled with his sensitive son. The boy loved his mother and her death plunged him into such continuing unhappiness that he left home.

In his wandering Anselm came to Bec – and to Lanfranc, who became his second father. For a time he hesitated about staying at Bec, fearing that Lanfranc would become too domineering; he had not come to be bullied by a second father. But his genius was different from Lanfranc's. He was no organizer, except of thoughts; no teacher, except of

---

[22] It is well summed up by R. V. Lennard, *Rural England 1086-1135* (Oxford, 1959), pp.25-30.

friends. Where he excelled was in friendship with his fellow-monks. Through this, he had the ability to attract them into the spiritual progress he was himself making. While Abbot of Bec he was a firm but kind father of the family, and a spiritual teacher in many conversations; in the verdict of Dom David Knowles, 'perhaps the nearest approach to the ideal abbot that the Benedictine centuries ever saw'.[23] He wrote prayers which are still moving to read. He was a devotional and theological pioneer in the cult of the Virgin Mary, the heavenly mother. And in the realm of pure theology he continued to teach as he had done in conversations with his monks, for he developed a method which seemed to many contemporaries (including Lanfranc) to be too adventurous to be worthy of theology's grandeur. He would not quote authorities from the history of the Church. He would not even quote Holy Scripture itself at any length. Among friends, like a father talking at the supper table, he would rely on the warmed heart, the converted mind, to go straight to God. The courage and the energy with which he abandoned the reliance on earlier, written authorities had some precedent in the thought of Lanfranc's theological enemy Berengar of Tours, but no one could dismiss Anselm as they dismissed Berengar. Within orthodox Christian thought he made a new beginning, to which is rightly applied the adjective: revolutionary.[24]

His supreme achievement, establishing him as the first great theologian of medieval Europe, was the writing of three short books, two dating from 1077-78. In the *Monologion* he meditated on the reality of the Creator. The existence of good things required the existence of the highest good. The existence of anything required the existence of the Supreme Being. But having completed these arguments, he continued to be preoccupied. Surely there must be a simpler argument which would confirm by reasoning what was already held by

---

[23] David Knowles, *The Evolution of Medieval Thought* (revised, London, 1970), p.99.

[24] See G. R. Evans, *Anselm and Talking about God* (Oxford, 1978), with *A Companion to the Study of St Anselm*, ed. J. Hopkins (Minneapolis, Minn., 1972).

Christian faith? (For him faith came first; his was the method of *fides quaerens intellectum*, faith seeking understanding, or *credo ut intelligam*, 'I believe in order that I may understand'). At length, one night during Matins in the monastery, the argument came to him. Only a fool said there was no God: so Psalm 14:1 declared. But even the fool knew what the word 'God' meant. It meant a reality greater than any other reality which could be conceived. But to conceive of 'God' as existing only in the mind meant to conceive of a reality inferior to the 'God' who existed not only in the mind but also in fact; so that the 'God' in whom the atheist did not believe was not the real God whom Christians worshipped. The man who had a fully adequate understanding of 'God' must believe in God's full existence.

Anselm wrote the *Proslogion* in order to work out the argument that flashed into his head while his brethren sang the service that night. In Anselm's time Lanfranc, when the book was submitted to him, was distressed that it made so little use of the Scriptures or the Fathers; and in the eighteenth century the philosopher Kant demolished its logic. Its intellectual clarity, power and independence are, however, amazing when one remembers that Anselm knew the Greek philosophers only through their Christian interpreters or translators (Plato through Augustine, Aristotle through Boethius) – yet did not fall very far below their level. Whether or not the argument was faulty (and it is an extraordinarily difficult argument either to understand or to disprove in a hurry), it was the perfect reflection of the way in which Anselm's mind worked. For him, the path to religious faith began in goodness. The road ascended to God through the wisdom which, being raised above the everyday world, saw clearly what the philosophers called the 'universals'. These 'universals' were the unities of classes of things, the patterns deeper than the variety on the surface of things. And the chief of the 'universals' was God. Yet God was utterly unique, for he alone satisfied the heart's longing to worship. When another Norman monk wrote a reply to the *Proslogion*, pointing out that one could conceive of the large island of Atlantis lying out in the western seas without necessarily believing that it was really there, Anselm

calmly replied: to think about Atlantis was not the same thing
as thinking about God. He was so sure of the reality of God, so
sure that he and his friends were day by day and night by night
not addressing a void, that he never could understand the
atheistic 'fool'. His task was to think not whether, but why, the
Christian's faith in God was true.

This was the mind that had to endure contact with the mind
of William Rufus – and watch the royal body enjoying itself.
This was the mystic who had to sit listening to arguments
about the law of feudalism at the king's court. Protesting
against his appointment to Canterbury, he said that would be
like yoking an old sheep to an untamed bull. The yoke did not
leave the sheep spiritually undamaged, as we can see from the
sad record of Anselm's conscientious absorption in defending
the complete rights of his archbishopric. He was not exempt
from the general medieval obsession with the rights of an
office – 'rights' which others might describe as privilege or
pride. Courage he never lacked, nor the freedom to exercise it;
he once wrote that man's freedom lay in his ability to maintain
uprightness of will. But out of a sense of duty he became
bogged down in controversies very different from the level
where his spirit was at home. From Bec he had sent out a
stream of loving letters to other monks, guiding them in the
spiritual life; he rightly felt those letters to be edifying, and
collected them for publication. But the last letter which he
wrote before dying was to suspend the Archbishop of York
from the exercise of his office until he should have
acknowledged the supremacy of Canterbury (York's relative
status was unclear until a papal decision of 1119). It was an
attitude which fell short of the highest holiness.

Anselm was not on morally unassailable ground even in the
cause for which he defied both William Rufus and Henry I. As
if the life of the Christian Church had been at stake, he
objected to the ceremonies in which the king would hand a
new bishop his ring and staff ('crozier') and the bishop would,
in return, put his hands between the king's, as a sign of feudal
homage.

In tones of profound conviction Anselm repeated the argument he had heard in Rome, that a priest's hands which

'created' Christ afresh out of the bread and wine in the Mass should not be polluted by being placed between the blood-stained hands of a soldier-king. Yet before the decrees of the Council of Claremont and the pope settled the matter for him, he had himself consecrated bishops who had received their rings and staffs from the hands of William Rufus; he had received his own ring and staff from the royal hands, although he later protested that he had been physically forced to undergo this indignity and the details of what took place in William's sick room are obscure. In the end, although as a result of the controversy this ceremony of 'investiture' was abandoned, there was no change in the ceremony of homage to the king before a man who had been elected as bishop or abbot was allowed to assume office – as was inevitable when the bishop or abbot was a major landowner in a feudal state. And the king continued to have the decisive word in the choice of almost all the bishops.

So Anselm's years as archbishop were a prolonged martyrdom. Secular business made him weary or ill; his mind, he said, was seized by 'a horror such as an infant might feel when face to face with some terrible ghost'. He hated life at the court of William Rufus, the cruel, cynical and blaspheming lout who pawed other men in his drink. What endured from the wreck of those years was a book which he began to write in Canterbury and which he completed when exiled to an Italian mountain village in 1098: *Cur Deus Homo*.

To this little masterpiece three other short books were attached. An earlier essay entered the depths of the mystery of the Trinity, and there were two later treatises, one exploring the depths of sin and the answer to it through the Lord's birth from a virgin, another exploring man's free will and God's foreknowledge. Normally Anselm did not write for the common man. How could someone 'whose mind is so dark that it cannot distinguish between his own horse and its colour', he once asked, understand God who is three persons in One? How could a man whose very conception was due to his parents' sin of lust understand the All-Holy? But *Cur Deus Homo* was a book for its time – and for subsequent ages.

Why had God become man? Simply, because it was necessary. God was lord over all his creation, as the king was lord over England. His 'honour' had been offended by man's sin, as a king's honour would be offended by a baron's rebellion; and in heaven as on earth, discipline must be upheld. But while a baron might offer 'satisfaction' to an offended king, the offering required to satisfy God's honour must be greater than the whole of the creation. If God's honour remained unsatisfied, then man's soul must be left to the devils as a hare is left to a yelping pack of hounds. (Anselm once explained this to his companions while a hare was taking shelter under his horse.) And the offering needed to save man could be provided only by God becoming man and sacrificing himself. This was the understanding of Christ's cross in terms of feudalism that came to Anselm as he sat, alternately bored and revolted, at the feudal court of the Conqueror's son.

Anselm's secretary and biographer, the Canterbury monk Eadmer, told the story that Pope Urban II greeted him as 'one who is almost our equal, being as it were pope and patriarch of another world'. Whether or not that compliment was ever actually paid, Eadmer saw that another world than the world of William Rufus or Henry I had been brought into view by the life and thought of his master. It was the world of an invisible kingdom, the kingdom of spiritual reality; a world where what decided issues was what a pope, not a king, thought. It was a world dominated by the cross of Christ — only, this cross was no longer seen as in *The Dream of the Rood*. Here was no longer an object to be contemplated in the vision of devout ecstasy; here was a necessity in reasoning, the reasoning of the law court. The cross was not the place where Christ did battle against evil, for evil was not now thought strong enough to offer battle; it was the place where God's own justice was satisfied by God's own action in God's own way. Anselm dwelt in a world high above the devils and devil-possessed men whose hands were bloody.

The new ideals did not make for smooth co-operation between the higher clergy and the crown — as Eadmer found when he had to put his principles into practice as Bishop of St Andrews, discovering that the King of the Scots was no more amenable than the King of the English. But Eadmer — himself an Englishman, the country's best historian since Bede, a patriot who delighted to honour the Anglo-Saxon saints – was able to see that under the brutal sons of the Conqueror an Archbishop of Canterbury had made an alternative to their monarchy not only possible but also imperishably public.

After Anselm, the Church under the papacy would now always be, at least potentially, a rival to the crown in medieval England. In the nineteenth century an Anglican scholar who was no uncritical admirer of the papacy wrote that Anselm had a vision of 'a throne of judgement, different in its origin and authority from all earthly thrones; a common father and guide of Christians whom all acknowledged, and who was clothed with prerogatives which all believed to come from above; a law of high purpose and scope, embodying the greatest principles of justice and purity, and aiming, on the widest scale, at the elevation and improvement of society; an administration of this law, which regarded not persons and was not afraid of the face of man, and told the truth to ambitious emperors and adulterous kings and queens'.[25]

He died shortly before Easter 1109. He had told Eadmer to destroy the biography he was writing. Fortunately for us, the obedient monk did so only after making a copy of it. Together with his *History of Recent Events in England*, Eadmer's *Life* is the main source of our knowledge of St Anselm, the only theological genius ever to be burdened by the duties of the archbishopric of Canterbury.[26]

THOMAS BECKET

Called to Canterbury in 1162, Thomas Becket was acutely aware of the example set by Anselm. He tried to persuade the pope formally to declare his predecessor a saint (a step not

[25] R. W. Church, *St Anselm* (London, 1870), p.267.
[26] The *Life* has been translated by R. W. Southern (London, 1963) and the *History* by Geoffrey Bosanquet (London, 1964). See also R. W. Southern, *St Anselm and His Biographer* (Cambridge, 1963).

taken until the fifteenth century). Just before dying he invoked
the name of Alphege, the archbishop murdered by the
Danes — whose memory, which Lanfranc had tried to sup-
press, had been restored by Anselm. And it seems that this
heritage of the saints of Canterbury who had resisted
oppressors was the crucial factor in the transformation of
Becket's life when he had accepted election as archbishop.
Previously he had not even been ordained as a priest; instead,
during his eight brilliant years as the king's chancellor he had
lived the life of a polished gentleman, except that he had
preserved his piety and chastity. When made a priest and a
bishop, he instantly signalled his sense of entering a new
heritage by ordering that the day when he became a bishop
should be perpetually observed as Trinity Sunday. He resigned
the chancellorship and devoted himself to prayer and good
works. During a visit to the pope he also resigned his great new
ecclesiastical office, so that he could receive it back from
hands holier than any king's. Little time passed before he was
appearing in public not only as the lavish dispenser of charity
but also as the inflexible defender of the Church's rights,
expecting and even stimulating persecution by a tyrant, until
the moment came when he walked into the king's council at
Northampton clutching his tall archbishop's cross.

It seems that Henry never understood what had changed
Thomas. Although in many moods he demanded nothing less
than the traitor's ruin, the last talk which the king ever had
with his former friend was still dominated by his hurt
bewilderment at the betrayal. He then seems to have expressed
a whimsical hope that somehow the old relationship could be
restored. When the news of Becket's death was brought to him
he stayed for three days in his room, fasting, weeping or in a
stupor. Enemies such as Bishop Foliot put Becket's change in
1162 down to simple hypocrisy — or at least they made this ac-
cusation when most exasperated. But the real secret seems to
be that Becket was determined to be as magnificently the
hero-archbishop as he had been the hero-chancellor, even if
the new role involved austerity, conflict, exile and death. He
would not yield an inch of the estates of the archbishopric, not
an inch of its legal position, not an inch of the glory be-

queathed by its saints. He had only to stand firm, whatever the cost, and he would be vindicated by the applause of God and God's saints. This was an attitude far subtler and more courageous than play-acting to secure the world's cheers. One of his large staff who became one of his many biographers, Herbert of Bosham, put his finger on it: 'He was generous far beyond the demands of his high office, expansive to all, magnificent to all and beyond all, great of heart, great in height, and great in display'.

During his lifetime Thomas Becket was no saint. John of Salisbury urged him to devote his exile to the study of the psalms and of theology; but Becket, having quietened his conscience and inflamed his emotions by abasements before his God in prayer, arose from prayer to study ecclesiastical law and to argue like a lawyer. When he studied the Bible, the passages he noticed most were those when prophets or priests denounced the kings of Ancient Israel; or when Christ or St Stephen suffered persecution. He was no doubt sincere in frequently regretting his former worldliness and in constantly bemoaning his present unworthiness, but he lacked the self-forgetful love as well as the self-transcending joy of the saints. Even his most dramatic scenes – his brave inflexibility at Northampton, his last minutes in Canterbury – had to be spoiled by unsaintly remarks to his enemies, insults which betrayed how unregenerate was his temper. But he had such a respect for the saints' examples that he acted like one when he could. His heart had been so touched by the Church's spiritual glory that he was content to adorn this glory in death, even if unable to do so in life. His death could not completely vindicate his cause in politics or law; that was impossible while the English Church remained part of a country ruled by a Christian monarch. But his dealings with death did vindicate his personal reputation – and, with that, the reputation of the Church among the common folk. His posthumous career must make us remember St Paul's boast: 'dying, and behold we live'.

As early as 1173 he was formally canonized as a saint. Thus the papacy gave to him in his tomb the unqualified support which it had denied him during his conflicts. Not much longer was needed for him to become a hero in the folk religion of England. It was as if a popular referendum said an overwhelming 'yes' to Thomas Becket, the civil servant turned prelate, the churchman who had demanded that murderers should not be hanged if they were clerics, the ecclesiastical grandee who had insisted that the Archbishop of York should be punished for placing a crown on the head of the king's eldest son. People were enthusiastic about the 'holy, blissful martyr' for many reasons. He was a miracle-worker in his tomb; the doctor of the obscure, the penniless and the hopeless. Riding to his shrine through Kent made a pleasant trip. The offerings at his shrine could reconstruct and enrich Canterbury Cathedral when most of the building in which he had died, the building which had stood as a monument to Lanfranc, had been destroyed by fire. The fact that he had withstood the most powerful king of his time, an Angevin (and did not St Bernard say of the Angevins: 'from the Devil they came and to the Devil they will return'?), captured the imaginations of many of the English. So the rumour spread that he had himself been an Englishman, although in real life both his parents were solid Norman colonists. But we have also to ask why the fame of St Thomas of Canterbury spread so quickly and lasted so long throughout Christendom, from Norway to the Holy Land; and the best answer is that his story showed that the heroic days of the Catholic Church were not over. The thrill had not entirely gone from the rich, proud institution. There was still dew at noon.

It is clear from the abundant records about his death that what impressed his household and the surrounding monastery was Becket's combination of two spiritually magnificent gestures in his farewell performance. Dying without physical resistance – even if he had exchanged a few insults with the knights – he deliberately identified himself with all the universal Church's martyrs and with the crucified Christ. And when he was dead, a vermin-infested hair shirt was found beneath his official robes. So Thomas Becket proved himself to be more than Anselm's worthy successor in the struggle to impose law as the Church understood it on the king. Gladly sacrificing his life in that struggle, he joined the class of St Cuthbert in

Durham, St Edward in Westminster, and the martyrs of
England such as St Edmund and St Alban. In his tomb he
reigned, a prince of Christendom.[27]

ENGLAND IN CHRISTENDOM

Stephen Langton was one of the innumerable Englishmen
devoted to the Martyr of Canterbury, during whose lifetime he
had been born in Lincolnshire. While waiting for admission to
King John's England Langton chose to live in the Cistercian
monastery at Pontigny, where Becket had spent his exile. In
July 1220, when his troubles were over, he was the preacher at
a splendid ceremony in the rebuilt cathedral at Canterbury.
King Henry III (then aged thirteen) was present, as were many
bishops and other lords. They had assembled to honour the
removal or 'translation' of the martyr's body from his first
tomb to his new shrine, soon to become the most expensively
decorated grave in the world. This ceremony, with the lavish
hospitality around it, bankrupted Langton but ensured a rich
future for St Thomas.

Far less evidence has survived about Langton's character
than about Anselm's or Becket's; the biography written by
Matthew Paris has disappeared. But modern scholars can
study a considerable number of the lectures or sermons which
he delivered during his twenty years at the University of Paris
as student or teacher. They show a fine mind at work,
although a mind without Anselm's gift for philosophy or
Becket's for drama. Langton was a first-class scholar, one of
the pioneers in the medieval study of the Old Testament. His
division of the Bible into chapters was used when later Bibles
were being copied out in Paris or elsewhere, and was in the
end taken over when printing began; thus every copy of the
Bible became a memorial to Langton. He also wrote commen-
taries on the Bible and these books had immense influence on

---

[27] The best recent biographies of *Thomas Becket* are by Richard Winston
(New York, 1967) and David Knowles (London, 1970).

the thirteenth century. Through the Paris years he expounded the work of Israel's prophets, before he was unexpectedly challenged to become a prophet himself.[28]

Almost certainly from Langton's pen in Paris came the *Golden Sequence*. In a modern English translation of the famous hymn, this prayer to the Holy Spirit arises from Christendom in the early Middle Ages:

Heal our wounds; our strength renew;
On our dryness pour thy dew;
  Wash the stains of guilt away;
Bend the stubborn heart and will;
Melt the frozen, warm the chill;
  Guide the steps that go astray.

The finest element in the Norman achievement was the fact that they compelled England to join this civilization which had now given birth to the University of Paris. The nation hewed out by William the Conqueror, his companions and his successors, became a place where moral leadership could be given by Christians of the stature of Lanfranc, Anselm and Langton – men whose minds had been formed in France. In this England the Church for which Becket died could, for all its faults, do something to protect the life to which the *Golden Sequence* referred. This taking of England into the Christendom of Europe can be compared with the results of other amazing conquests made by the Normans: in Sicily or southern Italy, in north Africa or the area around the biblical city of Antioch in Syria. Everywhere they pulled their subjects into the mainstream of the European tradition; into what Charles Homer Haskins, in his pioneering book of 1927, taught students to call *The Renaissance of the Twelfth Century*.

The Norman adventures in the Mediterranean were Viking raids on the grandest possible scale. Their leaders – Robert Guiscard who started his Italian career as a brigand in 1047, or his brother Count Roger of Sicily, or his son Bohemund,

---

[28] There has been no biography since F. M. Powicke, *Stephen Langton* (Oxford, 1928).

Prince of Antioch – were morally and intellectually primitive while being ruthlessly efficient fighters. A characteristic Norman exploit was the sack of Rome in 1084, 173 years after the baptism of the Norwegian pirate chief Rollo before he was allowed to settle in Normandy. But the strange fact is that Rollo and the other Scandinavian settlers in the north of France, like the Danes who settled in the east of England, adopted the Christian Church – if not the Christian morality – with zest. Perhaps they were anxious to appear, although not to be, civilized; or perhaps their motive was a never satisfied religious or superstitious hunger. William the Conqueror's father, Duke Robert, surprised his contemporaries by abandoning the power struggle in Normandy to go crusading. He died during the crusade, leaving his little bastard son to begin a lifetime of battles. In the conquest of Sicily as in Duke William's conquest of England, the Normans fought under the blessing of the papacy, and they liked to be reminded by their minstrels of the heroism of Charlemagne's knights riding against the Saracens. They were devoted to St Michael, the archangel with the sword. Their piracy was now christened as a crusade.

They remained in many ways barbarous; yet they became patrons of religion and learning. In Sicily the court of Roger the Great, king 1130-54, was a cosmopolitan centre, rendering priceless services to Christian Europe by welcoming the culture of the Arabs including medicine and philosophy. It was a traffic – the word comes from the Arabic – in intellectual as well as material wealth. Adelard of Bath, who spent much of his life as a civil servant under Henry I, acquired in the Norman kingdom of Sicily most of the knowledge which enabled him to be a bravely creative figure in scientific humanism among his fellow-countrymen when he returned to England. In Sicily the feudal government, fastened on a country previously turbulent and backward, enabled an Arab-Norman civilization to flourish.

A similar verdict would be valid about England. When the Anglo-Norman kingdom was established by the slaughter of the Anglo-Saxon aristocracy, by the devastation of the north and by all the rough 'justice' which brought a Norman baron's tenants and serfs to heel, it appeared that the glory of England was over. 'To the ordinary Englishman who had lived from the accession of King Edward to the death of King William', Sir Frank Stenton wrote, 'the Conquest must have seemed an unqualified disaster'.[29] Yet without the impact of the Normans, wrote another distinguished historian, 'true medieval society is unimaginable'.[30] From the soil which the conquerors trod down there grew a civilization richly English, richly European, richly Christian.

[29] F. M. Stenton, *Anglo-Saxon England*, p.677.
[30] J. M. Wallace-Hadrill, *The Barbarian West* (London, 1946), p.146.

CHAPTER FIVE

THE AGE OF FAITH

Westminster Abbey . Choir and High Altar.

WHY THEY BUILT CHURCHES

England's cathedrals and other churches surviving from the Middle Ages have often been described as the products of the people's faith. It is a description which needs some qualification.

Medieval church-building was a more sophisticated, even commercial, business than some legends have suggested. Although the peasants of a manor might be compelled by their consciences or their lords to lend a hand when their parish church was being built or rebuilt, or to provide their carts to take stone or timber to a cathedral, much evidence survives of payments for labour and materials at the normal rates. Although a monastery's sacrist or 'warden of the works' would control a fabric fund and its disbursements, monks did not as a rule build their churches with their own hands. Before the Cistercian monks became (for a time) frequent exceptions to this rule, one Norman abbot, Hugh of Selby, was talked about as a very rare exception; in his enthusiasm for church building he wore a labourer's smock. People contributed – mainly through offerings at the shrines in the cathedral (hence the importance of inheriting, or developing, a saint's shrine), or through subscriptions in exchange for indulgences (promises of a reduction of time spent suffering in purgatory after death), or through legacies (trusting to be remembered when in purgatory). But the bishops and the monasteries also paid for building projects out of their own great wealth as landowners. And despite all this income, finance remained a problem. That is shown by the patience which bishops or monks often had to exercise before their projects reached completion. The history of almost any great church shows that it was built by stages.

The actual building was under the control of a master mason, a man who knew stone because he had himself been a stonemason but who was now a highly skilled professional. Such an expert was well equipped (and well paid) to negotiate with clients, to prepare designs reflecting current fashions, to provide materials including vast quantities of stone and timber, and to manage a large gang of masons and other craftsmen. These master masons were not anonymous. It was only accidental that not many of them were well remembered. It has been possible for modern scholars to recover many of their names, which deserve fame more than do most of the architects of later generations. And stonemasons often went from job to job in a region in order to secure a lifetime's employment, and sometimes left marks on the stone to show it. This was one of the most mobile trades in the Middle Ages, and one of the most carefully organized.[1]

---

[1] See L. F. Salzman, *Building in England down to 1540* (revised, Oxford, 1967), and John Harvey, *Medieval Craftsmen* (London, 1975).

So a little knowledge corrects the talk about medieval churches being built by the people's faith. Deeper reflection, however, shows the substantial truth in such talk. The churches were in reality the factories of the industry to which medieval England attached the greatest importance; the chief public buildings of a period which was in truth the Age of Faith, or at least the Age of Acquiescence.

The work was done with a thoroughness and speed which must suggest popular enthusiasm. No doubt there was a welcome to this provision of employment because the money might easily have been wasted on wars, knights' tournaments or rich men's feasts, but there was also a positive approval of this particular expenditure. A contemporary poem on the building of Salisbury Cathedral paid tribute to the 'workmen's faith' along with the 'king's virtue' and the 'bishop's devotion'. We also know that the canons of the cathedral agreed to contribute a quarter of their incomes for seven years. Much other evidence reminds us that in this age church-building was popular. The wealth of the estates owned by the bishops or the monasteries itself testified to this: as was often said, the land had been given in exchange for the promise of prayers. The wealth was the monastery's or the aristocracy's investment in the hope of eternal happiness according to the Church's doctrine. When objections were occasionally raised to the passion which so many kings, bishops and abbots exhibited for building, it was because an over-elaborate church might distract the worshippers from the purer type of prayer, or because an over-luxurious monastery might destroy the monastic ideal, not because the building would impoverish the people.

The fundamental truth was that a new medieval church was the creation of a whole society and therefore that society's pride. Resentful workmen could not have carved those smiles on angels' faces. A society seething with rebellion would not have made that foliage to adorn the capital of a column: on the pillars of the chapter house at Southwell Minister, the leaves of oak, hawthorn, hop, vine and ivy are as alive today as in a summer of the 1290s. The women of thirteenth-century England were famous (as those of the eleventh-century had been) for their embroidery of ecclesiastical vestments, the *opus Anglicanum* of which only fragments survive. Pope Innocent IV wrote in 1246 that the excellence of this embroidery, which he coveted for Rome, made England seem to him a 'garden of delights, an inexhaustible well'. The men who created so much beauty out of stone must have approached their work in a similar spirit. We have no reason to doubt that in the huts that surrounded a great medieval church as it was being built there existed a faith about the universe and its divine Architect, although words were not what the builders used to express that faith. It cannot be claimed that thirteenth century England was thoroughly Christian. The statistics of murder in this period would prevent such a sentimental assessment. But a great church could raise to heaven the faith of a society where daily life was often nasty and short. As André Malraux was to sum it up, 'the cathedral is the expression of man's gratitude to God: it presents to him creation turned Christian'.[2]

There were protests about Henry III's expenditure on Westminster Abbey because it was financed out of taxes, then regarded as disasters to be justified only by emergencies. But the building itself was admired as a house fit for kings and for the King of Kings. When the new abbey was consecrated on 13 October 1269, with the solemn removal or 'translation' of the bones of St Edward the Confessor to his sumptuous shrine, no one of whom we have record lamented that it would have been cheaper to repair the Confessor's own church instead of pulling it down. At one stage some eight hundred men were directly engaged on the site, in addition to all the others who quarried the stone, felled the timber, collected the jewels and rich cloth, poured out their skill on the metalwork, the mosaics and the tiles, lent money for wages or administered the special fund established by the king for the work which absorbed him over twenty-four years.

The building of Westminster Abbey was, indeed, the

---

[2] Marcel Aubert, *High Gothic Art* (London, 1964), p.58. Contrast J. B. Given, *Society and Homicide in Thirteenth-Century England* (Stanford, Cal., 1977).

climax and main justification of this reign. Henry was not a master of men. Over his tomb close to the Confessor's shrine, the first bronze effigy to be seen in England was made by William Torel in the 1290s; the face is gentle and worried. Constantly the political history of the reign shows the simplicity of his mind. He asserted himself, only to be surprised by the opposition of his barons and to be unable to hold his own. This opposition to him should not be thought of as parliamentary. The barons knew that 'in the end they depended upon the king, just as the king depended on them', Sir Maurice Powicke commented. 'They had asked for power they did not really want. As Simon de Montfort bitterly remarked, they turned tail, as Englishmen always did.' The basic problem at this stage was, it seems, the king's personality; he was 'not a big enough man to win the confidence of his barons, and so to give himself that they gave themselves to him'.[3] So politically Henry III was not a success. But he was self-giving, and therefore highly effective, as a patron of the Church and of art. His devotion was as simple as his politics. In the University of Paris and in centres of theology in Italy his contemporary, St Thomas Aquinas (who died in 1274), was in this period constructing an intellectual edifice of dazzling courage and authority, a great system which would combine the orthodoxy of the Bible and the Church with the philosophy of Aristotle; but when St Louis, King of France, asked Henry why he did not hear more sermons, he replied that he preferred the Mass (he attended at least three Masses every day whenever possible), since it was better to see his friend than to hear him spoken about. The king was charitable, with a large, systematic and personal generosity recorded in his accounts; but high in what he did for his divine friend was the creation of beauty.

Much of Henry's reign was consumed by conflicts over money and power, since he became king at the age of nine and inherited from his father John an aristocracy insistent on the charters which protected them against the crown; but in the creation of his own great church at Westminster he had his

---

[3] F. M. Powicke, *The Thirteenth Century* (revised, Oxford, 1962), p.72.

best opportunity to show what money and power under his control could achieve. Another feature of the reign was the bitter rivalry between the English barons and the French civil servants such as Peter des Roches (Bishop of Winchester) and his nephew or son Peter des Rievaux; but in the building of Westminster Abbey there was international co-operation. The king caused the latest French fashions to be copied by Henry 'de Reyns' (was this Reims in France?) and by the masons under him in enduring stone, to general admiration. Sir Maurice Powicke judged that this abbey, the tallest church yet raised in England, was 'the most strenuous and concentrated, as it was also the most gracious, expression of a rich artistic life; and this life, fanned into intensity by the king, was in its turn the outcome of a social activity which engaged the interests of thousands of people, and meant more to them than all the political and ecclesiastical issues of the day . . . Henry had a passion for metal and jewel work, for vestments and sacred vessels curiously wrought and adorned with gems, for pictures and sculpture. He knew what he wanted, he could describe it in detail, was lavish in expenditure upon it, and exacting in the performance of it. If he had concentrated his mind upon affairs of state as successfully as he did upon works of art, he might have been the greatest of our kings, though possibly not the most beneficent.'[4]

The fact that the rebuilding of Westminster Abbey evoked enthusiasm is surely significant. Here was no pyramid built by brutalized slaves for a tyrant. What, then, was the society that created the king's own abbey and the bishops' cathedrals?

PARISHES AND MONASTERIES

It is not easy to recover the history of the parishes, but we know that many parish churches received additions or other improvements in the thirteenth century. In part this was a

---

[4] F. M. Powicke, *King Henry III and the Lord Edward* (Oxford, 1947), pp.572-3.

reflection of the general rise in agricultural prosperity and the trebling of the population in the period 1050-1300 — the period in which the surnames arose which were to show future generations that their ancestors had been butchers, carpenters, clerks, cooks, masons, millers, potters, shepherds, skinners, tailors, tanners, thatchers or tylers.

'England', Graham Hutton has written, 'had been covered with new churches, big and small, mainly between 1150 and 1250, after which it was largely a matter of pulling down and rebuilding them. . . . The magnitude of both the Church's and its parishioners' offerings, converted into stone and furniture and fittings of all kinds, was colossal. Parish churches shot up almost cheek-by-jowl in town and city parishes — over a hundred in London with barely 40,000 inhabitants before 1348, over twenty-five in big towns like Norwich or York with only eight thousand to ten thousand people. As better trade, communications and agriculture brought villages nearer to each other, churches grew bigger and more imposing. Hoskins has calculated that in tiny Rutland alone there were over fifty medieval churches, one to every two hundred and fifty souls, though each capable of holding many more. Such emulation in building, out of a low standard of life, cannot have been due solely to pride, even pride in local achievement. The desire to glorify God in an age of deep belief, and in an era of short and uncertain human lives, is apparent on all sides in these new and imposing parish churches; for their naves were the people's first and only communal buildings'.[5]

There was a growing emphasis on preaching. Large churches in the towns began to be built for the Franciscan or Dominican friars whom we are about to meet and the naves of parish churches were made more spacious so that a parish priest or a visiting friar could be heard clearly — although there were as yet few pulpits from which to speak or pews or chairs on which to sit. At the same time small chapels or

---

[5] Graham Hutton, *English Parish Churches* (London, 1976), p.68. The reference is to W. G. Hoskins, *The Making of the English Landscape* (London, 1955).

'chantries' began to be set aside and staffed with their own priests (endowed with rents from property) where Mass could be sung or said until the end of time for the souls of the founder, his family and his friends. So a well-to-do merchant could now secure the services which in the previous age a baron had secured by endowing a monastery.

A network of parishes over the whole land now brought every man, woman or child in a population around 2,250,000 into the personal responsibility of a priest. More than eight thousand parishes were registered in a survey of 1291, the *Taxatio Papae Nicholai*, and later evidence adds about 1,500 more. Some of the parishes, specially in the north, were still very large, but it has been estimated that the average included some three hundred souls in the country and about two hundred in the towns. Some 23,000 priests, assisted by perhaps ten thousand clerics in the minor orders, staffed these parishes, in addition to perhaps 25,000 monks, nuns, friars and hermits. Inevitably the evidence has been lost which would enable us to do justice to the missionary and pastoral work involved in the creation and maintenance of this far-reaching system. Most of what we know of the spiritual life and work of the priests is derived from the little books of instruction compiled for them by the most pastorally minded bishops. But it is reasonable to guess that the thirteenth century saw the development of an unprecedented intimacy between priest and people, based on the new insistence on an annual confession before Easter. This confession was no hurried affair. The priest was urged to examine his parishioner in detail about the orthodoxy of his beliefs as well as about his keeping of the moral commandments. There is also evidence that the Holy Communion was now being celebrated much more frequently. The ideal was a daily Mass, supplemented by the lesser services or 'offices' said together by the parish priest and the clergy who assisted him and who were usually called chaplains. Thus, in theory at any rate, each parish church would be a little monastery.

It has been estimated that when Henry III came to throne in 1217 there were about 180 large monasteries in England, with about five hundred smaller communities, owning between them perhaps a fifth of the country's total wealth. The

monastic population, little over a thousand in 1066, was probably about 12,500 in 1217 and about 17,500 in 1340.[6] About a
quarter of the parish churches were 'appropriated' to the
monasteries. It meant that the 'tithe' (tenth) payable to the
'rector' or 'parson' on the agricultural produce of the parish
belonged to the monks although they were obliged to appoint
and pay a 'vicar' (substitute) or chaplain to undertake the
pastoral care of the parish. A major effort was made by the
bishops in the thirteenth century to improve the financial position, security and housing of these vicars; and it did not help
that the richest monasteries were exempt from the local
bishop's jurisdiction and subject only to their own abbots and
the pope. A relic of that unsatisfactory arrangement remains
to this day in medieval churches where the nave, used and
paid for by the laity of the parish, is grander than the chancel,
occupied by the clergy and paid for by the rector. Evidently
the parish church was regarded as a source of income for the
monastery, not the monastery as a source of help for the parish
church.

The bishops were not the only people to look at the monks
critically. Already in the reign of Henry II the Welsh
eloquence of an embittered Archdeacon of Oxford, Gerald,
had begun a flourishing literary tradition of attacks on the
monks' practices, although their ideals remained sacred.
When economically active, the monks were condemned for
avarice; when inactive, for idleness. When their estates provided knights to serve the king, this was regarded as worldly;
when they did not, the loss to the country was lamented. The
resentment overflowed from such grumbles into legislation. In
1259 the statute of *Mortmain* enacted that no further land was
to be given into the 'dead hand' of a monastery. No doubt
much of the criticism is unfair, and the chief effect of the
statute was that in future the king was needed to grant licences
for the further endowment of monasteries. The statistics of
monastic growth spoke louder than the critics. But the

---

[6] D. Knowles and R. N. Hadcock, *Medieval Religious Houses: England
and Wales* (revised, Cambridge, 1971), provided an annotated list.
However, all medieval statistics are uncertain.

monasteries of the thirteenth century produced no spiritual teacher able to stand comparison with the more worldly genius of Matthew Paris, the lively and widely travelled journalist and cartoonist who followed Roger of Wendover as the chronicler of St Albans Abbey in 1235. The best known abbot from the beginning of this century is Samson of Bury St Edmunds, because his life was written by his chaplain, Jocelin of Brakelond (and written up with gusto by Thomas Carlyle in *Past and Present*, 1843). And Samson, although he ruled his monks and managed his estates masterfully over almost thirty years from 1182, was no spiritual giant. Jocelin noticed that his master was happier outside than inside the monastery. Others have noticed about Jocelin – and about his brethren as they stand revealed in his artless chronicle – 'the deep essential self-satisfaction and sense of superiority, broken only at the surface by the ripples of domestic quarrel or external litigation'.[7]

In his history of *The Religious Orders of England* in the thirteenth century (1948), Dom David Knowles told of much steady discipline, of growing efficiency, of reforms to lift unsatisfactory monasteries to the level of the others; his final impression was of a 'state of equilibrium'. But he observed that the monasteries no longer resembled a tree 'white as a bride with April blossom'. He entitled only one of his chapters with the name of a leading monk – and that man was Henry of Eastry, elected prior of the cathedral monastery of Christ Church, Canterbury, in 1285. Henry was a devout monk but chiefly a superb businessman who before his death in 1331 had developed the previously insolvent monastery's estates to a level of productivity never matched before or after. It was a major contribution to the improvement of agriculture (together with the growth of the towns the most prominent feature of the economic history of the time), but we may doubt whether under such leadership Canterbury Cathedral would have been the centre of popular religious enthusiasm, had it not been for the archbishops buried in it, notably St Thomas.

---

[7] G. G. Coulton, *Five Centuries of Religion*, vol. ii (Cambridge, 1927), p.46.

Fortunately, however, the spiritual life of England no longer depended entirely on the parish priests or the old-fashioned Benedictine monks. So far the story of English Christianity had been very largely the story of heroes and their influence. Kings made the decisions nationally; more locally, landowners built and endowed monasteries and parish churches. Saints were princes in the life of the spirit, celebrated for their heroism as Beowulf and other lay heroes had been celebrated; more locally, church life was governed by bishops, abbots and the more forceful type of priest. Thomas Becket was, at least in his own eyes, one such hero. But now, as the pilgrims began to crowd into Canterbury and to seek the other saints' shrines, the people entered the story of English Christianity; for 'the great flood of devotional fervour which overwhelmed Western Europe in the late twelfth and early thirteenth centuries had as one of its springs the refusal of the laity, the Latinless, the illiterate, to be excluded from the apostolic life of the Church.'[8]

Although those who worked with their hands found their greatest opportunity in building or adorning their churches, or in the practical duties of lay officials such as churchwardens who administered the affairs of the parishes, we do know of some who gave themselves to prayer. In the twelfth century we meet, for example, St Godric – a Norfolk pedlar, sailor and merchant, who in his voyages came to know and love the holy island of Lindisfarne; who went on pilgrimages to see Rome and the Holy Land for himself; who went to school with the children of Durham in order to be able to read the psalms; and who finally settled in his own hermitage at Finchale. A contemporary wrote a biography of him, describing his extraordinarily long white beard, his skin roughened by a sailor's

---

[8] Edmund Colledge in *Pre-Reformation English Spirituality*, ed. James Walsh (London, 1966), p.29.

life, his knees hardened by a hermit's. And women could enter this life of the spirit freely. To help three noblewomen who chose a disciplined, corporate life of prayer in seclusion, a beautiful treatise was written in the English of the West Midlands around 1200 – the 'Anchoresses' Rule' or *Ancren Riwle*. With a lively use of proverbs, anecdotes and everyday illustrations to adorn its great theme, this anonymous masterpiece summoned them to spiritual adventure, not to the mere keeping of a rule.

The most popular spiritual movement of the twelfth century was more highly organized: the Cistercian Order, so named from its mother house at Cîteaux in Burgundy.

These 'White Monks' set themselves to live according to a rule more austere than the rule of the ordinary Benedictine 'Black Monks'. In the sixth century both St Gregory the Great and his ambassador St Augustine of Canterbury had been moulded by the monastic tradition which went back to St Benedict (480-550 approximately). In the eighth century the learned holiness of this Benedictine tradition had come to another climax in Bede and his brethren. In the tenth century the adoption of St Benedict's rule in English cathedrals and monasteries had been a decisive step in the recovery of discipline and moral order after the fury of the Vikings. But St Benedict himself had no intention of imposing exceptional poverty or fasting or any other form of heroism. His one aim was the recitation of the services of the 'Divine Office', the *opus Dei*, in a stable community. The spirit of the worship would spread into the common life with its ordered round of manual or intellectual work (*laborare est orare*: 'to work is to pray'). As a matter of course the monks would provide hospitality, charity and education, but that would be incidental to the worship and the common life. Since St Benedict's day many of the monasteries of his order had become the chief buildings in cities or towns, maintained by troops of servants and owning more estates than most of the neighbouring barons, each a prosperous little kingdom under its abbot's rule. They had been endowed lavishly by landowners anxious that after death their souls, and their families', should be assured of prayers. But all the time the Benedictine Order included some men who desired to escape further from the world's distractions, to sacrifice themselves more fully in order to save their own souls.

The movement for greater strictness within this great Benedictine tradition gained a centre when the abbey of Cîteaux in Burgundy was founded by some monks of Molesme in 1098. Among them was a Dorset man, St Stephen Harding, who subsequently became abbot. The movement gained a genius as its spokesman when, twenty years later, a group of young noblemen entered Cîteaux as novices; for the leader of this group was St Bernard. Bidden by Stephen Harding to found a new monastery in 1115, he established a house at Clairvaux and became its abbot. He was a spiritual pioneer who happened to be also a writer and an organizer with a capacity to mould the mind of a generation. His writings spread his mysticism; he based the soul's communion with God firmly on an exact knowledge of the Bible, on loyalty to the Church, and on a passionately personal devotion to Christ and his Mother, addressed in human terms more intimately than had been thought right for many centuries. Bernard's organizing power was soon used in the wider affairs of the Church. He upheld Pope Innocent II against rivals, was rewarded with many privileges for the Cistercian Order, and lived to see a Cistercian monk as pope (Eugenius III). This pope made another Cistercian, Henry Murdac, Archbishop of York as part of the rapid extension of the movement throughout Christendom.

The Cistercians always kept their monasteries linked as a family by an annual visit to be paid by each abbot to the mother house from which his own had derived. They built their houses right away from the towns, abandoning any attempt to run a school or a welfare centre, abandoning also the ownership of estates which were obliged to produce knights for the king's service, refusing to get entangled in the profits or responsibilities of parish churches, building their own churches with plain architecture and no painting on the walls. They dispensed with servants; instead they worked in the fields themselves and an essential role was given to the *conversi*, illiterate lay brothers who did the work on the buildings, in the fields and among the sheep. In their austere routine of life meat was as rare as heat. In their churches there was little colour but much intensity of prayer.

The first such house in England was founded very quietly in Surrey, but the movement attracted notice when White Monks went north in 1132. In York their austerity stirred the consciences of some of the monks of a very rich house, St Mary's Abbey, who left to found the abbey of Fountains, then in a remote spot. In this they were encouraged by Thurstan, who as Archbishop of York 1119-40 was a creative leader of church life in the north. Before long the York pilgrims into the wilderness raised a church of which the massively simple nave still survives, although it is now roofless. The Dean of York was among the early recruits at Fountains.[9] Soon there were many hundreds, and other Cistercian houses were built in Yorkshire, among them one at Rievaulx, in the valley of the Rye. One of the first recruits there was Ailred, who fell under Bernard's influence while they were together in Rome in 1141, and who became his English equivalent.

The descendant of a long line of married priests who had staffed St Wilfrid's church at Hexham, Ailred moved away from this comfortable heritage. First he used his education and his charm to work at the court of King David of Scotland, whose son had been sent to school at Hexham. As the king's steward he was at the centre of the whole process by which David (the son of Malcolm who had overthrown Macbeth and married St Margaret of Scotland) brought his country into the European world of Roman Catholicism and feudalism. Doubtless Ailred could have become a bishop, but he grew dissatisfied. While on a mission to the Archbishop of York he came across the new Cistercian experiment (about 1133), and throwing himself into it became its abbot in 1147. He was the warmly affectionate and spiritually encouraging father of the whole community as it struggled to grow in disciplined sanctity. His writings, and his biography by his pupil Walter

---

[9] A biography of *Thurstan* has been provided by Donald Nicholl (York, 1964), and a study of the drama in 1132 by Denis Bethell in *Journal of Ecclesiastical History* (Cambridge, 1966), pp.11-27.

Daniel, celebrate an achievement of Christian friendship – a royal court composed of mostly illiterate Cistercians in the valley of the Rye. In Ailred's leadership we can see Cicero's famous treatise on friendship quoted and practised but subordinated to the overwhelming inspiration of the New Testament. The affection which he offered drew many hearts despite his stern motto 'be still, be silent, endure'. Walter Daniel called him 'friendship's child, for his whole occupation was to love and to be loved'.

The use of many hands to make virgin soil productive corresponded with the economic reality of the time, an age of expanding food-supply and population; but inevitably the success of the Cistercians meant that they did not for long continue in the idyllic innocence which appears in everything written by, or about, Ailred. In Italy a disillusioned Cistercian monk, Joachim of Fiore, attracted much attention before his death in 1202 by prophecies that a decadent Church was about to be replaced by an 'Age of the Spirit'. It has, indeed, been suggested that not even the White Monks of Rievaulx were the totally consecrated band of brothers of whom Ailred liked to write.

Pioneering agriculture rapidly brought wealth to these men who had fled from the towns and the feudal system. The Cistercian Order became a major force in the international wool trade, and its self-discipline meant that some of its members (Ailred among them) were entrusted with affairs of state. Baldwin, the abbot of the Cistercian house at Ford in Devon, attracted the notice of Henry II and found himself first Bishop of Worcester and then, in 1184, Archbishop of Canterbury. He was a holy man and a scholar in the tradition of Lanfranc and Anselm, writing on the sacrament of the altar and on the commendation of the Christian faith. But this White Monk was involved in a bitter dispute with the Black Monks of his own cathedral, whose luxury he denounced; and involved, too, in King Richard's crusade, the reality of which broke his heart.

Other great movements arose now that the normal Black Monks no longer satisfied the spiritual ambitions of the age. There were, for example, about thirty-seven houses of the austere Carmelite Friars, originating in a union of hermits under St Berthold on Mount Carmel in the Holy Land. There were the Black (or Augustinian or Austin) Canons, brotherhoods of priests living under a semi-monastic rule of life attributed to St Augustine of Hippo but also undertaking some pastoral work in the parishes; by the end there were some three hundred such houses in medieval England, mostly small and poor. There were the White Canons, companies of austere preachers and parish priests who derived their ideals from the work of St Norbert in the valley of Prémontré; their official title was Premonstratensian Canons. In England they had some thirty houses, as did the White (or Augustinian) Friars, originating in a union of Italian hermits in 1244. But the real successors to the Black Monks as spiritual pioneers were about 180 houses of the Grey and Black Friars, as the Franciscans and Dominicans were called. Their ideal was to combine the austerity of the Cistercians and Carmelites with an involvement in the life of the people going much deeper than the Black or White Canons. For a time, these friars (brothers) seemed to be bringing back Christianity's earliest and purest days – or inaugurating at long last the Age of the Spirit of which Abbot Joachim had dreamed.

THE FRIARS

A great and shrewd pope, Innocent III, gave the Franciscan Order his blessing in 1210. At that stage the order was still in real life which it always remained in the mind of St Francis: a mainly lay fellowship, going to the extremes of a pure love of God and humanity, totally identified with the poor, delighted when it was thought foolish. Its ideals seemed completely different from those of the Dominican Order, given papal approval six years later; for the Dominicans were the Order of Preachers, attempting a reasoned defence of orthodoxy, naturally attached to the universities. Within a short period, however, before any of the friars reached England, the little brothers of St Francis had gravitated to the universities just like St Dominic's scholarly preachers.

This move is not so inexplicable as it may seem. The universities which emerged in the twelfth and thirteenth centuries were a phenomenon of the Age of Faith. They were chiefly intended to provide a general education for the clergy; theology was the 'queen of sciences' in the higher studies; and where the speciality was law or medicine that training, too, was Christian in its whole atmosphere. Yet like the friars, the universities were free and easy in comparison with earlier medieval institutions, subject neither to the discipline of a monastery nor to the supervision of a bishop. One of the reasons why universities emerged in Oxford and Cambridge was that in neither place was there a bishop. And the scholars were prepared to pay the price of this independence amid a feudal society. Most medieval scholars were always poor. They were often, as a consolation, also young; undergraduates were of an age which we should expect to find still at school. Such centres, full of unattached young men, bursting with idealism and eagerness, seemed to offer both the best sources of recruitment for the new Christian work and also the best means of training recruits. So the move to the universities is understandable. Whether or not we applaud all its consequences depends on what we make of St Francis and his extraordinary intention.

Francesco Bernadone was a charming Italian, the son of a merchant, in his youth the leader of the merry-makers in the beautiful and prosperous town of Assisi, to the end of his days a great lover and poet of humanity and of nature (whereas the founder of the Dominicans was a Spanish puritan, born of an ancient family, a scholar from boyhood). The conversion of Francis of Assisi was brought about by the direct challenge of the simplest sayings in the gospels, and it led immediately to kissing a leper. What shocked Francis was the gap between the Church of Jesus and the poor; his answer was to lead into the world an army of men as devoted to Lady Poverty as the troubadours were devoted to their mistresses (whereas Dominic found his vocation preaching against the Albigensian heretics in the south of France when the Cistercians had failed – and he organized his order to concentrate on pure doctrine, purity of life being only one of the proofs of orthodoxy). Francis appealed to romantics. He invented the Christmas crib with live animals, and was said to have preached to birds. He attracted teenagers; St Clare was only seventeen when she founded the Second Order of Franciscans. He also appealed to the mature; he won the heart of Dominic when the two saints met in Rome in 1216. He attracted and fascinated because he was supremely the 'mirror of Christ'. Before his death in 1226 the chief sign of distinction which he had received was the fruit of his identification with his Master: the stigmata, the marks of crucifixion on his own body. His last testament was a plea that no Franciscan should ever get involved in the ownership of property or in ecclesiastical politics – a plea which, after bitter controversies, the 'Spirituals' who followed his instructions failed to get established as the test of Franciscan life. The authorities declared him a saint and his successor, Brother Elias, built a very costly shrine for his body, adorned by the best art of the time.

One of the closest companions of St Francis was William the Englishman (and another Englishman, Laurence, was one of St Dominic's earliest recruits). The Franciscans first landed in England on 10 September 1224, two days before Francis received the stigmata. Their story was still fresh when it was told by Brother Thomas of Eccleston in his chronicle written in 1258-9. There were nine of them, including only one priest. Some of them were in Oxford by the end of October. That winter their joyful patience amid poverty began to win fresh converts to their way; it was noticed that their bare feet left blood on the ice as they walked on their errands of mercy. The rapid expansion of their numbers (there were 1,242 Franciscans in England by 1255) meant that Christian love was being taken into the poorer parts of the developing towns – into homes which the monks had deliberately abandoned and which most parish priests did not, it seems, visit with enough pastoral zeal. And Christian love was being made more lovable; there survives a 'Love-song of Friar Thomas of Hales', written before 1272, in which a Franciscan urges a frankly romantic love of Christ on a girl who has joined the order. But a major reason for the expansion of the English Franciscans was their appeal to Oxford men; and gradually their university links brought their aims closer to those of the Dominicans – who had landed in England three years previously and, after receiving Cardinal Langton's blessing at Canterbury, had gone straight to Oxford.

Under an Englishman, Haymo of Faversham, the international leader or Minister General of the Franciscans 1240-44, it became clear that priests, not laymen, would be dominant in the order. Under St Bonaventure, Minister-General 1257-74, himself the 'Seraphic Doctor' of Dante's *Paradiso* and the creator of a systematic theology based on the teaching of St Augustine of Hippo, it became clear that the emphasis would be upon a disciplined life within stone-built convents, with a rigorous intellectual training for all who could profit by it. The glories of the Franciscan Order came to be scholars. One such was Alexander of Hales, the Englishman who shaped the mind of Bonaventure by his lectures in Paris – and the first Christian to employ all the works of Aristotle in his exposition of the Faith. St Clare lived in seclusion for more than forty years, sleeping on the floor of her cell, eating very little, praying almost without a pause, never wasting time on a book; but now Grey Friars were to be found intellectually intoxicated in lecture halls and libraries. Franciscan missionaries took the Gospel to the slums of Europe and to the world of Islam, to China and Mongolia; but for some the most alluring country came to be the realms of the intellect, approached through the lecture halls of Paris and Oxford, and that was not the vision of St Francis. Brother Giles was a saint, the intimate friend and companion of Francis, who would go into ecstasies when the children of Perugia cried 'Paradiso!' (naturally the children would often raise the cry, to see what happened). And Brother Giles once let slip his own cry: 'Paris, Paris, why did you destroy the Order of St Francis?'

OXFORD AND GROSSETESTE

Oxford became a centre of study under circumstances which remain obscure despite all the researches of its grateful sons. It contained monasteries but in an age when men were losing their confidence that the monasteries could educate enough teachers and leaders for the Church, Oxford could offer more than a gathering of monks. The flourishing town was accessible from London, the Midlands, the west and the south. Early in the twelfth century scholars are known to have given instruction there; Robert Pullen, later a cardinal, did in 1133. When English students were recalled from Paris during the Becket dispute in 1167 they concentrated on Oxford, particularly on the church of St Mary-the-Virgin. In the 1180s we find a boastful Welshman reading aloud a book about Ireland 'before a great audience at Oxford, where of all places in England the clergy are most strong and pre-eminent in learning'.[10] By 1209 the students were sufficiently numerous to make an impact in their first fight against the townsmen. The chronicle of Matthew Paris claims that some three thousand masters and scholars left Oxford until the university was granted a fresh security by the papal legate in 1214, under its own chancellor to be appointed by the Bishop of Lincoln.

One of the early lecturers in logic at Oxford, Edmund Rich of Abingdon, was eminent in holiness as well as philosophy. There was a story of how as a boy of about twelve, walking alone in the fields, he had had a vision of Jesus as a boy walking beside him, Certainly the records indicate that in his maturity he was a man of great moral force to whom all parties instinctively turned during the political crises of the 1230s. After a spell as one of the canons of the old cathedral at Salisbury (when it was his custom to spend half the year in a

---

[10] *The Autobiography of Giraldus Cambrensis*, ed. H. E. Butler (London, 1937), p.97. The classic study of the background is H. E. Salter, *Medieval Oxford* (1936).

monastery), he was made by successive popes first Archbishop of Canterbury and then a saint. Dying on his way to a council in Rome, he was buried among the Cistercians of Pontigny where Becket and Langton had taken refuge.[11] But St Edmund was not the greatest of the founders of Oxford's fame.

Born about 1168 in a Suffolk home with no wealth, Robert Grosseteste somehow acquired an education, was ordained, and spent most of the years 1200-35 teaching in the university at Oxford. He was never an adventurous theologian; never an Anselm. Like his contemporary Langton he relied on the Bible. The morning should be given to the Bible; his other authorities – principally St Augustine of Hippo and the newly discovered works of Aristotle – could wait until the afternoon. In the exposition of such authorities he developed a massive learning. More unusual, however, was his scientific bent. He had a mathematical ability to match the far-off Arabs through whose skill the West was now learning to be numerate. As often happens with mathematicians, his love and understanding of music also went deep. He investigated many scientific problems – the reform of the calendar around the more accurate dating of Easter (he shared this interest as well as a love of the Bible with Bede), the composition of the rainbow or the stars, the whole scientific method of induction and experiment. He was particularly fascinated by light, which he regarded as a very subtle substance, analysing how it reached the human eye but also delighting to write or preach about the light of the soul. He was able to get others to share his intellectual enthusiasm, becoming the university's first chancellor and stamping on it his own emphasis on science. He has been assessed as 'the first great English scientist and philosopher of science. At a time when guidance was essential, he provided England's young university with a creative understanding of science that made it for a time the leading scientific centre in Christendom and enabled it to contribute to the modern world something entirely new'.[12]

---

[11] See C. H. Laurence, *St Edmund of Abingdon* (Oxford, 1960).
[12] A. C. Crombie in *Robert Grosseteste: Scholar and Bishop*, ed. D. A. Callus (Oxford, 1955), p.115.

But Grosseteste had one still stronger interest: the reform of the Church in the service of God and the people. When the Franciscans opened a lecture hall in Oxford, they invited the university's leading scholar to preside over it; and he accepted. Eventually he bequeathed his own books to these beloved friars. About five years later (in 1235), at an age when university teachers of later generations felt ripe for a pensioned retirement, he accepted election as Bishop of Lincoln, then the most populous diocese in the country, stretching from the Humber to the Thames. He made a point of taking Franciscans and Dominicans with him. He exercised a tireless and fearless rule over eighteen years, and no Englishman did more to follow up Cardinal Langton in enforcing the reforming programme of the Lateran Council of 1215. When resisting what he thought was wrong, he was quite willing to defy the saintly Archbishop of Canterbury or the king. When the pope attempted to intrude a nephew into a canonry of Lincoln, Grosseteste (who normally held an exalted view of the papacy as the sun of the Church, all other bishops being mere moon or stars) replied: 'as an obedient son I disobey, I contradict, I rebel.'

One of the bishop's friends was Simon de Montfort, Earl of Leicester, later to be over-praised because the enlargement of the 'parliament' (consultation) of the Great Council of the realm under his influence was thought to make him the founder of parliamentary democracy. Himself a hard man and no saint, the earl discussed Christian ideals with the bishop and their mutual friend, Adam Marsh the Franciscan leader at Oxford. He entrusted him with the education of his sons and even lent him his cook.[13] But Grosseteste was no politician. He disapproved of bishops serving as civil servants or judges, and was no more of a democrat than was Montfort himself.

His passion was to insist on the highest standards of religious discipline throughout his diocese. In his poem *Le Chasteau d'Amour* he made an elaborate comparison between Christ's

---

[13] M. W. Labarge, *Simon de Montfort* (London, 1962), pp.74-79.

Church, love's fortress, with a castle of that feudal age; and he defended it. In a single year he deposed seven abbots and four priors from their slack rule of monasteries. When the Dean of Lincoln resisted the bishop's attempt to reform the cathedral, he found himself first forbidden to enter the great church and then removed from office; and Grosseteste successfully fought the cathedral clergy's appeal to Rome. Appearing as an old man before the pope and his fellow-bishops, he declared what the work of a pastor meant to him. It must include 'the truthful teaching of the living truth, the awe-inspiring condemnation of vice and the severe punishment of it when necessary. It consists also in feeding the hungry, giving drink to the thirsty, covering the naked, receiving guests, visiting the sick and those in prison especially those who belong to the parish. . . . By the doing of these things is the people to be taught the holy duties of the active life'. And he did his utmost to make sure that every priest appointed to a church anywhere in his diocese understood these duties.

Not content with this activity, while Bishop of Lincoln Grosseteste strengthened his previous knowledge of Greek enough to devote his leisure to the work of a translator. A small library of important works in Greek was made available to Latin-readers by him or by other translators in his employment. It was his recreation. It is remarkable that a churchman so venerated by the people, the contemporary of St Edmund and spiritually his equal, was never formally canonized as a saint; and that no biography was written of him before a worthless poem of 1503. But it is not surprising, in an age when popes made saints and monks wrote biographies.

SCIENCE AND DEMOCRACY

The contrast is great between 'St Robert of Lincoln' – as Grosseteste was often called, despite the lack of official recognition – and Roger Bacon.

Bacon was a genius but spent most of his old age under suspicion and (according to tradition) under confinement, having alienated or alarmed the Church of his day by the quarrelsome freedom with which he expressed independent views on contemporary topics and personalities. He greatly admired Grossesteste, although there is no evidence that he was his pupil. Born about 1215, he devoted himself to the study of the Bible, of Greek and Hebrew (he compiled dictionaries), of Aristotle and of science, partly in Oxford but mainly in Paris. Gradually he developed an eager ambition to explore the world around him. Why should he not do for his own day what Aristotle had done for his? He would rely on experience and experiment, confident that all true knowledge, ancient or modern, would be found to confirm God's timeless revelation of himself in the scriptures. For metaphysical theologians such as his contemporary St Thomas Aquinas, he had only contempt.

He did not have the philosophical ability to construct a system of ideas to rival the new system of Aquinas. Nor was his thought fully scientific as future generations were to define science. He was always having a dialogue in his mind with Aristotle, the 'master of those who know'. He was fascinated by astrology's teaching about the influence of the stars on the destinies of men; and by alchemy's attempt to turn baser metals into gold. He was sure that Antichrist was about to appear, heralding the end of the world. One of the reasons why he urged Christians to be scientists was that the Antichrist would be one. Yet at an uncanny number of points he urged the importance of experiments which, when pursued after his time, were to shape the modern world. It may be the case that he invented the telescope, the microscope and the thermometer. He argued for the possibility of cranes, of self-propelling boats, of submarines, of flying machines, of a continent across the Atlantic, of many other marvels.

This miraculously gifted inventor had a magnificent trust in the intellect, arguing that irrationality was the essence of barbarism. He longed for the English ('who are, and have been, distinguished more than all others for their learning') to become the architects of a thoroughly reasonable civilization based on science as well as faith. And his great opportunity came when in 1265 Pope Clement IV, a scholarly Frenchman, asked him to outline an intellectual programme for the Church. Bacon told the pope that he had already spent a vast sum on 'secret books, different kinds of experiments, the acquisition of languages, instruments, tables and other things'; and with a frantic haste he attempted to survey all knowledge and to suggest all desirable reforms for the pope's benefit. Unfortunately Clement IV died in 1268 without making any response of which we have evidence.[14]

In about his fortieth year, at approximately the same time as Grosseteste's move to be Bishop of Lincoln, Bacon became a Franciscan. Exactly why he joined the friars we do not know; he was devout, but his main motive may have been to secure backing for his researches. Among the friars he would have found more than a few with intellectual interests similar to his own, as well as others shocked by his boldness. Having been for many years under suspicion and perhaps in prison, he was eventually released to write and to die in peace (in 1292). His last work was a *Compendium of Theology*.

Thus the Franciscans unexpectedly contributed to the growth of the English universities – a word which must be in the plural, since in 1209 a large number of masters and students migrated from Oxford to Cambridge after their dispute with the townsmen, and some stayed behind. The Franciscans arrived in Cambridge in 1225, a year before the first known appointment of a chancellor in the university.

The Dominicans also contributed to the growth of the universities, but it will be more interesting to glance at what they did for parliamentary democracy. In contrast with the monks who had all been placed under the benevolent despotism of abbots, the Dominicans were given by their founder a constitution which gave elected friars, gathered in chapters, the decisive say in the affairs of the order. There is evidence that Black Friars accustomed to this measure of democracy encouraged the clergy in general to demand to be consulted about taxation by pope or king: 'proctors' or elected represen-

---

[14] See S. C. Easton, *Roger Bacon and the Search for a Universal Science* (Oxford, 1952), and for the background Alexander Murray, *Reason and Society in the Middle Ages* (Oxford, 1978).

tatives of the clergy were summoned in 1256 and 1269 in accordance with the maxim that 'what touches all must be approved by all'. The Dominicans also influenced the barons and townsmen who because of their abilities wanted to secure their services; and this influence helped to popularize the idea that the king himself must consult the 'faithful men of the realm' in regular parliaments before he levied taxes.[15]

So the contributions made to the life of England by the vitality of the friars and the scholars were extremely diverse; out of their poverty they made many rich. A record of the table-talk of Robert Grosseteste gives it some unity, however. 'The Bishop said to Brother Peter that places standing over water are not healthy, unless on a lofty site. He said, moreover, that it pleased him greatly when he saw the sleeves of the Brethren patched. And he said that pure pepper was better than ginger in a sauce. He said also that he rejoiced when he saw that his scholars did not care about his lectures, so long as he had prepared them carefully, because an occasion of vainglorying was thus taken from him, and he lost nothing of his merit'.[16] Thus the great bishop, taking his ease at table, casually assembled amateur science and holy poverty, the joys of the palate and of the mind.

THE BISHOPS

Robert Grosseteste and St Edmund of Abingdon, although outstanding, did not stand in isolation among the bishops of thirteenth century England. A typical figure showing the greater strictness of the new age was Richard Poore. He was bishop and builder of Salisbury Cathedral, a much admired pastor and administrator. He faithfully carried out the

---

[15] See M. V. Clarke, *Medieval Representation and Consent* (London, 1936), and G. L. Haskins, *The Growth of English Representative Government* (Oxford, 1948).

[16] *The Coming of the Friars Minor*, ed. E. G. Salter (London, 1926), p.114.

Church's official policy of regarding the presence of a wife or
concubine in a rectory or vicarage as a major sin; this campaign, generalled by the inflexible Anselm in the 1100s, had
been led to a more or less total victory by Pope Calixtus II at
the council of Reims in 1123. Yet Richard Poore was an illegitimate son of Henry II's clerk who became Bishop of Winchester, Richard of Ilchester. His brother Herbert had been
Bishop of Salisbury before him. He may also have been
descended from Roger Poore, whom we have already met as
Bishop of Salisbury and as the father or uncle of men eminent
in Church and State in King Stephen's reign. Times were
changing.

Bishops in the Middle Ages were not, on the whole, expected to make their mark as pastors or preachers. Diocesan
bishops were not even regarded chiefly as dispensers of
sacraments: they were primarily judges, reformers of abuses,
enablers of legal transactions. A bishop did not go round
making himself popular. He expected people to come to the
manor house where he was staying at the time and there
petition for whatever favour they wanted. He employed a considerable staff of expert clerks, a vicar-general to take charge
of the administration, specially during his absence from the
diocese, and a 'suffragan' bishop (often a friar) to carry out ecclesiastical duties such as confirmations for which he had no
time. This meant that the official life of the diocese could
function smoothly while he was himself far away performing
his other duties as a counsellor to the king and perhaps also as
a hardworking head of the civil service. Yet a surprising
number of thirteenth-century bishops were admired as men of
God.

One reason was that they had a clear reforming programme
to apply to their dioceses – the decrees of the Lateran Council
of 1215 supplemented by the legislation accepted by church
councils assembling under two able and forceful legates from
Rome, Cardinal Otto (1237) and Ottobuono Fiesci who was in
England 1265-8. And they were active. One modern authority has written that 'on the whole bishops of that period were
men of ability and principle, and long vacancies and absences
from the diocese were probably rarer than in the troubled

twelfth century or in the last two centuries before the Reformation. . . . The impression of painstaking fulfilment of duty
grows upon the reader as he passes through one register after
another.'[17] Another scholar has said about these bishops that
'as leaders, administrators, visitors, builders, and patrons of
learning and the arts, they have never been excelled'.[18]

For almost twenty years two friars held the archbishopric of
Canterbury (which for almost thirty years, 1240-69, had been
in the hands of an Italian, Boniface of Savoy, appointed
because he was the queen's uncle). Robert Kilwardby, the
Dominican provincial prior, made a conscientious archbishop
between his appointment in 1273 and his removal to Italy as a
cardinal five years later — a move which stressed that no archbishop, however English, was now much more than an agent
of the pope. His successor at Canterbury, John Pecham, had
been the leader of the English Franciscans and an equally eminent scholar. In the world of theology both he and Kilwardby
did their utmost to resist the influence of their contemporary,
St Thomas Aquinas, on the ground that he was an innovator.
What had been good enough for Stephen Langton, appealing
to the plain Bible and not troubling to digest the metaphysics
of Aristotle, was good enough for these stalwart English conservatives. But as archbishop until 1292, Pecham was an
unresting reformer. Administration must be up-to-date, while
doctrine was changeless.

Since he regarded himself as a judge of abuses in church life
throughout the province of Canterbury including Wales, he
managed to hold disciplinary 'visitations' in all the dioceses
and to sweep through many monasteries, tightening up their
rule of life or reorganizing their finances. He fought particularly against pluralism, the system (or non-system) which
had allowed a single priest to be nominally the rector of many
parishes, paying only part of the income to the priest who
did the pastoral work. Bogo de Clare, a son of an Earl of
Gloucester and a notorious pluralist, was one of the wealthiest

[17] David Knowles, *The Religious Orders in England*, vol. i (Cambridge,
1948), p.111.

[18] F. M. Powicke, *The Thirteenth Century*, p.485.

men in the kingdom. His household accounts show that in a
year he was content to spend more on ginger to spice his
dinners than on paying a vicar to serve one of his parishes. The
other bishops, too, were expected to condemn pluralism, but
had often taken advantage of it on the way up. As an ex-friar,
Pecham could hit out.

As the chief officer in England of the Catholic Church
whose pope had appointed him to Canterbury after rejecting
the king's candidate, this fierce archbishop conducted another
campaign to defend and enlarge the independence of the
Church's courts. Fresh copies of Magna Carta were ordered to
be posted up in all the cathedrals each Easter. Although his
puritanism did not make him popular, neither his energy nor
his integrity could be doubted. His most lasting monument
was an outline of doctrine and morals issued in 1281 in order
to guide parish priests. The mysteries were now made clear
and numbered. Neatly listing and expounding the fourteen
articles of faith, the ten commandments, the seven deadly
sins, the seven principal virtues, the seven works of mercy, the
seven sacraments and the three persons of the Trinity, this
document was a constantly consulted authority in English
parish life up to the end of the Middle Ages. An edition was
printed at Oxford as late as 1520.[19]

Another former chancellor of Oxford who devoted himself
to the care of a diocese – in his case, Chichester 1245-53 – was
St Richard of Wych (Droitwich). He had known poverty as a
boy; it is related that he and the fellow-student with whom he
shared a room were so poor that they had only one gown (the
equivalent of the modern coat) between them. In it, one of
them at a time would go out to a lecture. Richard did not
forget the lessons of poverty when he had been taken into the
household of St Edmund of Abingdon and launched on an ecclesiastical career. This scholar who had specialized in canon
law has been remembered chiefly by his humility while a
bishop (he was a vegetarian and he walked through Sussex on
foot), and by his prayer that he might see Jesus more clearly,
love him more dearly and follow him more nearly.

[19] See D. L. Cook, *Archbishop Pecham* (Oxford, 1952).

One of the bishops who resisted Pecham's attempt to exercise jurisdiction over all the dioceses was Thomas Cantilupe, Bishop of Hereford. But he did not resist in order to cover up intellectual sloth or moral evil. He, too, had been chancellor at Oxford – and Chancellor of England during the year when Simon de Montfort and his fellow-barons were the virtual rulers of the country (1265). Pecham excommunicated Cantilupe, who was, however, such a model of holiness that after his death in 1282 his tomb became a centre of faith in miracles and he was canonized as a saint. His uncle Walter Cantilupe, Bishop of Worcester 1236-66, had been a local pastor and national figure of much the same quality in the previous generation, the friend of Robert Grosseteste and of Simon de Montfort.

Finally we can look at the strange story of St William of York, the thirteenth century's attempt to draw from the conflicts of the previous century a martyr who could be the northern equivalent of St Thomas of Canterbury.

William had been a nobleman for whom an ecclesiastical income was necessary; his father was the illegitimate son of the Count of Blois, his mother the illegitimate daughter of King Stephen. As Treasurer of York Minster he seems to have been amiable but no more. His royal grandfather secured his election as Archbishop of York in 1140, but he was accused by Bernard, Ailred and other Cistercians of having bought the appointment (simony) and of unchastity. In reply his irritated rich friends sacked Fountains Abbey. In 1147 he was deposed by the Cistercian pope in favour of Henry Murdac, Abbot of Fountains. This sordid tale now begins to reflect some of the idealism which was to shine in the next century. William withdrew to Winchester, where he lived a quiet and austere life until Henry Murdac had died and there was a new pope. In 1154 he returned to York as archbishop, only to die a month later (an archdeacon was accused of administering poison). Once dead, he was venerated as a saint so ardently that his official canonization followed in 1227.

Whatever his real character may have been, the fact that a cult flourished around St William's shrine demonstrates the eagerness of the thirteenth century to honour a bishop who could be regarded as a saint in the great church where he had been enthroned. And under Walter de Gray, Archbishop of York for forty years from 1215, the cult helped to finance the construction of the majestic transepts of York Minster. They still stand, with their climax in the Five Sisters Window, still filled with more than a hundred thousand jewel-like pieces of thirteenth-century glass.

THE CATHEDRALS

The nineteen cathedrals of medieval England were the mother churches of large numbers of parishes. Although parishioners did not attend 'diocesan services' of the modern type, their obligations to their cathedrals were brought home by the custom of bringing financial offerings on Mothering Sunday (in mid-Lent) and Whit Sunday. At all times of the year people would be found in these busy churches, praying before the saints' shrines or the altars which often contained holy relics, and unless the cathedral was also a monastery its nave was available to local people for many everyday purposes; the atmosphere in the nave of St Paul's in London, for example, was decidedly secular. The place of the cathedral in the loyalties of the people is shown by the facts that people from all over the diocese could be expected both to contribute to building projects and to leave money in their wills for the fabric.

In these limited but important senses the medieval cathedral was the people's church even if it was also a church providing incomes for many canons (Lincoln had fifty-eight) or monks. The cathedrals at Canterbury, Rochester, Winchester, Worcester, Norwich, Ely and Durham were Benedictine monasteries. Bath and Coventry were also cathedral monasteries but they shared their status in the diocese with 'secular' Wells and Lichfield; and significantly, in these two dioceses during the thirteenth century the 'secular' churches came decisively to the fore as the main cathedrals. The cathedral might be less splendid than the greatest monastic churches, Westminster or Glastonbury, St Albans or Bury St Edmunds. It might be rivalled by the large 'collegiate churches' in the towns, such as Beverley, Southwell and Ripon in the diocese of York. But it was still significant just because it was the cathedral, where the bishop's throne (*cathedra*) was. In remote Carlisle the fairly small and poor church staffed by Augustinian canons became a cathedral in 1133; and over a century and a half from 1245, its choir was rebuilt to fit this dignity.

English ecclesiastical architecture, to be seen on a sumptuous scale in these cathedrals as in the great abbeys, was marked by three styles between 1050 and 1350. The nineteenth century named these styles: Romanesque or Norman, Early English, and Decorated or Geometric Gothic. Each style had its origins in France.

The Norman conquerors were used to the idea of the grand church. St Hugh of Cluny, who ruled his abbey for sixty years and was one of the Benedictine Order's greatest reformers, taught that a very large church demonstrated, or at least encouraged, a very large piety. The abbey at Cluny set the standard by being the largest church in Christendom, with a constant round of magnificent worship. The Normans brought their own trained masons to England; when they could, they used the limestone quarried near Caen in their homeland. Already before the conquest Edward the Confessor's abbey had given a revolutionary indication of what was to come; it was over three hundred feet long, whereas the cathedral of East Anglia, then at North Elmham, was smaller by two-thirds. Now the conquerors set out to adorn England with churches which would rise to the ideal taught at Cluny and exemplified at Westminster.

The Romanesque style had originated in Lombardy around 800. The semi-circular arches, often echoed in the arcading on the walls, were inspired not only by practical considerations but also by the aqueducts and other remains of the Roman civilization in Europe. As we can still see, when St Albans Abbey was magnificently rebuilt by the Normans many thousands of Roman bricks were used from the ruins of nearby Verulamium. Battle Abbey, built where the decision of 1066

had been reached, introduced into England the French
fashion of a passage or ambulatory around the main altar of a
great church — a feature still preserved in the Norman
cathedral at Norwich and in Tewkesbury Abbey. Other
features which the Norman builders developed in England
were not so prominent in France: the large crypt beneath the
church to provide more chapels, the long nave to accom-
modate crowds or to make processions impressive, the high
lantern tower (which often collapsed). Knowing what they
wanted, they also knew that they wanted it quickly and
everywhere. William of Malmesbury wrote of Lanfranc's new
Canterbury Cathedral that its speed was as admirable as its
beauty. Almost all the monasteries were rebuilt on a grand
scale as soon as the new Norman abbot felt that he had got the
monks under his control and the neighbouring landowners on
his side. Only in Exeter and Lichfield was the old cathedral
kept — and there, only for the time being.

   The Normans came to their triumph in Durham Cathedral.
It was begun by Bishop William of St Calais, one of William
the Conqueror's clerks, who had temporarily fallen foul of the
king in 1088 for failing to provide enough knights to fight
rebels. But now in 1093 after a period of exile the bishop was
in favour again; and to celebrate he began this building,
splendidly sited above the river Wear. It was completed when
there was no bishop in the 1130s, thanks to the enthusiasm of
the monks whose church it had become. The ribbed stone
vaulting was an architectural and technical miracle; the
cheaper but less fireproof alternative, a painted wooden ceiling, can still be seen in the twelfth-century nave and transepts
at Peterborough. At Durham, however, the chief miracle was
the order of the whole building. The massive pillars and
arches were relieved by some geometric ornamentation, and
the very thick walls were made slightly less severe by two
galleries, the tribune and the clerestory; but any decoration
was subordinated to the vast building's structured lines. Any
sculpture of the human figure would be inconceivable here
(although the human figure is represented, with great dignity,
in the sixteen 'illuminated' manuscripts which are still to be
found in the cathedral's library, surviving from a larger gift by

Bishop William). This cathedral has often been called a castle of God, defending the Norman colony in England against the Scots to the north and any rebels to the south, but it might equally be called a campaign in stone, with every detail subordinated to a strict command. Here was not the ultimate advance in design and ornamentation of which the Romanesque style was capable; to find that, we must look at the two rich towers of Exeter Cathedral (about 1150), or the five-aisled Galilee which that proud prelate, Hugh de Puiset, added at the very dramatic west end of Durham (about 1180). These works — or the Durham Castle which Bishop de Puiset rebuilt as a setting for his feudal splendour — were so much more elaborate that their period within the Romanesque style is called 'transitional'. But as a proud affirmation of the Normans' faith in themselves and their God, Durham Cathedral is supreme.

The new style which came to be called 'Early English' by proud patriots originated to the south-east of Normandy, in the fertile Île de France which was at last being given peace under the immediate control of pious kings. The royal abbey of St Denis, consecrated in 1144, advertised the new style and the cathedral of Notre Dame in Paris, begun in 1163, still displays it in its full energy, while the cathedrals of Chartres and Reims, built in the first half of the thirteenth century, are probably its greatest glories. The style consisted essentially of a combination of the pointed arch and the vault ribbed with thin webs of cut stone, engineering developments which made possible a whole new architecture of variety and adventure; the great window, partitioned by tracery, to make the church radiant with light and joyously colourful with the stories of the Bible or the saints, glowing in the glass; and the 'flying buttress' outside to support the weight of stone vault as the ambition grew to raise this thin shell of stone and glass higher and higher. Nothing was at rest. On the other hand, nothing was dull or sad. The building itself was a drama, no less than was the worship which it sheltered and inspired.

The first major use of this style in England seems to have been in Malmesbury Abbey, but its most public impact came when the choir of Canterbury Cathedral was rebuilt after the

fire of 1174. It is clear from the account of the building by the
monk Gervase — the first architectural history to have survived
in England — that in Canterbury men were aware (and, to
begin with, surprised) that they were importing a revolution
from France.

The master mason of the new work was William from Sens,
where a new Gothic cathedral had just been completed. When
he fell from scaffolding, his work was carried on by William
the Englishman, with whose activity 'English Gothic architecture begins'.[20] The intention was to eclipse the memory of the
choir which had been largely destroyed, although that choir
had been a marvel when consecrated in 1130. ('Nothing like it
could be seen in England', wrote William of Malmesbury,
'either for the light of its glass windows, the gleaming of its
marble pavements, or the many coloured paintings which led
the wondering eyes to the panelled ceiling above.') Only two
chapels of that choir were left standing, with the crypt below
adorned by fabulous or grotesque figures carved on the
capitals of its columns (a reminder that cathedral-building
was not all solemn). On these foundations the new choir arose.
Pointed arches intermingled with rounded, the details were
chiselled not cut with an axe, and the vault was of stone not
wood. The windows were gradually filled with stained glass
showing biblical scenes and the miracles of St Thomas in rich
colours (mostly blue and red). Impressive steps led up to the
chapel built to glorify the saint's magnificent shrine, and the
whole effect was of soaring joy, with decoration richer than
any known in France added by the use of marble from
Purbeck in Dorset. The pilgrims coming to the new shrine of
St Thomas marvelled and told the tale.

The Gothic style spread, although few of the Canterbury
details were copied. It was to be seen in Chichester and
Glastonbury where the great churches had to be rebuilt after
fire; in the complete rebuilding of Wells Cathedral between
1175 and 1260; in the new Cistercian abbeys among which the
ruins of Roche in Yorkshire are the best. In Lincoln in 1192,
when an earthquake had shaken the hill on which his ca-

---

[20] Paul Frankl, *Gothic Architecture* (London, 1962), p.49.

thedral stood, St Hugh laid the first stone in what proved to be the very lengthy rebuilding of the great church. The brilliantly inventive Geoffrey de Noiers was his architect and gave him asymetrical vaulting, crockets growing senselessly out of pillars and staggered double arcading in the aisles – experiments which were not repeated. Further building was done at Lincoln under Bishop Grosseteste.

Gradually the Gothic style developed in daring and grace. The excitement of it proved so infectious that Bishop Richard Poore determined to have nothing less than a complete new cathedral. He abandoned the cathedral which stood next to the castle on the windy hill at Old Sarum, although that great church had been consecrated by St Osmund and enlarged as recently as the 1130s. In 1220 was begun the creation of Salisbury Cathedral on a new level site by the river Avon a couple of miles to the south. The design is attributed to Elias, one of the canons. The whole of the cathedral which we see preserves that design apart from the central tower and spire which were added (by a Wiltshire master mason, Richard Farleigh) in the middle of the next century. Apart from that, Salisbury Cathedral took only thirty-eight years to build; however, it cost as much as 42,000 marks, at a time when bishops seem to have regarded five marks a year as an adequate stipend for a priest in a parish. Undeterred by this expense, the builders added a great cloister and chapter house, unnecessary because Salisbury Cathedral was not a monastery; and when he was moved from Salisbury to be Bishop of Durham, Richard Poore planned the splendid new east end of the cathedral there – the 'chapel of the nine altars'.

The designers now felt able to give the churches more and more of the decoration which people wanted – in the stonework and the tracery of the windows as well as in the rich colouring of the painter's work added so often to the limewashed interiors. They also felt confident enough of their buttresses to reduce their walls still more drastically in favour of their windows. The new 'decorated' phase of the Gothic style was summed up for the French by the Sainte Chapelle built in Paris by Louis, king and saint – and for the English by Westminster Abbey, which Henry III raised in holy competition with his French brother-in-law. The great windows of the royal abbey's transepts and of its octagonal chapter house encouraged others to similar feats: the rose window surmounting the seven lancet windows above the high altar of St Paul's Cathedral in London, or the east window under which they reburied St Hugh at Lincoln in 1280. The wonderfully carved walls of yellow stone in the Angel Choir around the great bishop's tomb were scarcely less radiant than the glass.

Westminster Abbey was thus as challenging for architects from 1250 onwards as Canterbury Cathedral had been a century before. The king's own work was followed up by the glorious rebuilding of Exeter Cathedral to a single 'decorated' design over a hundred years from 1275, to give only one example; but 'during the early decades of the fourteenth century about every great church in England was added to or partly rebuilt in this richly ornamented style. . . . Many of the larger parish churches were rebuilt with arcades and windows of curvilinear tracery. . . . Almost all the ports and upland towns that were growing rich from the export of wool built or refashioned their churches in the new style. . . . All were decorated with the same profuse wealth of carving. . . .'[21] A special trend of the period was the building of Lady Chapels, to express the growing devotion to the Virgin Mary; the most splendid was at Ely.

Westminster Abbey did not, however, yet include a complete new nave or west front; even Henry III's tax-fed purse was not bottomless. At Westminster the nave was not finished until 1502 and the north front, then the main entrance, was modelled after the cathedral at Amiens. Breathtakingly long and elaborate west fronts, suggesting the walls of the heavenly Jerusalem, reached England elsewhere. At Peterborough a unique west front exhibited three soaring arches. At Lincoln an immensely impressive stone screen spread to right and left of the great doors admitting into the nave the people of this diocese which stretched south to the Thames. At Wells under Bishop Jocelin (1206-1244) the west front was enriched by an

---

[21] Arthur Bryant, *The Age of Chivalry* (London, 1963), p.252, with a list of some of the churches.

unrivalled series of more than three hundred and fifty life-sized statues, leading up to the resurrection of the dead, rows of angels and apostles, and Christ in majesty. Some of these statues were of biblical figures, but others portrayed the kings and saints of England, before as well as after the Conquest. This generous selection illustrated the movement, often to be seen in the thirteenth century, to honour the heroes and heroines of the Anglo-Saxon Church; England was becoming one proud nation. Lavishly painted, these statues which now look weather-beaten and venerable were then popular art. But they were probably also great art. Undismayed by the ravages of time, a modern expert is convinced that 'their faces shine with physical beauty, keen intelligence and humane benevolence not to be found again until the time of the High Renaissance'.[22]

---

[22] Peter Brieger, *English Art, 1216-1307* (Oxford, 1956), p.272.

CHAPTER SIX

REBELS AND PILGRIMS

· The Medieval Parish Church · Chipping Camden ·

THE AGE OF CHIVALRY?

The long reign of Henry III (1216-72) can be summed up with a reasonable amount of accuracy as the Age of Faith. The next period, to the end of the fourteenth century, was more complicated.

Superficially much of it makes a tale of victory and prosperity — the Age of Chivalry. It was a period when England was ruled by two military heroes, Edward I (1272-1307) and Edward III (1327-77). The feats performed under the latter were celebrated in the famous chronicle of the French priest,

Jean de Froissart, and in the still more famously patriotic Shakespearean tribute to this 'dear, dear land' which was 'this earth of majesty, this seat of Mars'. And matching the success of the English armies in Wales and France was the strength of the English Church. In 1323 Pope John XXII declared it heresy to assert that Christ and his apostles had not owned property. It was not a heresy that tempted English churchmen. In 1380 the Commons assembled in Parliament claimed that the clergy owned a third of the nation's wealth (therefore they should pay a third of the taxes). But this Age of Chivalry was also an age of rebellion. This 'land of such dear souls' witnessed the deposition and murder of two kings (Edward II in 1327 and Richard II at the end of the century) and the beheading of an Archbishop of Canterbury in the course of the Peasants' Revolt of 1381. It also saw the beginnings of a rebellion against the spiritual authority of the bishops. Mystics went on pilgrimage into a country of the soul far beyond the official routine of the Church. The leading theologian of the 1370s openly attacked the papacy.

More typical Englishmen relished stories which mocked the hypocrisy of monks and friars. Between the 1300s and the 1370s, it has been estimated, the number of monks, friars and nuns in England almost halved, falling to some eight thousand. This tendency was not due entirely to the Black Death and other plagues, although disease was an obvious enemy.

Bishops were among Edward I's most loyal servants. Robert Burnell, who had been in his employment while he was still the Lord Edward, became the mainstay of his kingdom as his chancellor for sixteen years, and the king twice nominated him for Canterbury, although each time the pope was able to insist on another man. To Burnell, who became Bishop of Bath and Wells, should be given most of the credit for the law and order long remembered as glories of a reign when the king's peace was embodied in famous statutes and shown also in the freedom which the king enjoyed to conquer Wales and Scotland. After Burnell's death his place at the right hand of Edward I was taken by another bishop, Walter Langton. So we may correctly picture this king enthroned in Westminster Abbey's coronation chair (made in 1296) and attended by loyal churchmen. However, the baronial opposition which gathered against the ageing king, and forced him to undergo the humiliation of 'confirming the charters' in 1297, had an archbishop as its leader: Robert of Winchelsea, a distinguished scholar of Paris and Oxford, elected by the monks of Canterbury in 1294. His main quarrel with Edward I was over the taxation of the clergy for the wars. Here he had to defend the refusal of Pope Boniface VIII (proclaimed in *Clericis Laicos*) to recognize any king's right to tax the clergy without papal consent – except in emergencies, as even Boniface had to add a year later. During this crisis the enraged king outlawed all the English clergy and the archbishop went into exile; but Edward I made no further attempt to tax the clergy directly.

Thus even in Edward I's time the unity of Church and State was not totally serene. However, the warrior-king was at heart a thoroughly orthodox churchman, like his father. Among the many indications of this we may notice the fact that he found time in his busy reign to visit the shrine of Our Lady at Walsingham in Norfolk (founded in the 1130s, and patronized by Henry III) ten times. The character of his son and heir was very different.

Attempting to gain the Church's favour at the beginning of his reign, Edward II recalled Archbishop Robert from exile. The king wanted to be left in peace for his favourite amusements – swimming, racing, metalwork, farmwork and dining with his men-friends. But the recall was one of his many blunders. The archbishop was no more inclined to compromise under Edward II than he had been under his more formidable father. The disputes began again and were not to end until the death in 1327 of a king who would have been far happier as a country gentleman.

Since that death had to be enveloped in the piety of the Age of Chivalry – in the incense which covered the stench – Edward II was buried close to the high altar of the great abbey at Gloucester. Abbot Thokey was resolved to pay that last tribute to the monarch who had been his guest and friend; and his courage was rewarded when the crowds began flocking to the fine, two-storied tomb. His successor, John of Wigmore, was a skilled sculptor and embroiderer and with both hands he seized the opportunity for a new architecture now presented by the people's offerings. The dark Romanesque choir which they had inherited at Gloucester was out of keeping with the spirit of the age, which loved light. It was the age when Adam of Walsingham the monastery's sacrist and William Hurley the master-carpenter built at Ely the octagonal lantern-tower (the only Gothic dome in Europe) to catch all the light over the Fens, the great sunrises and sunsets. In keeping with this desire to see the sun even while at prayer, the old Gloucester choir was partly demolished and partly modernized. Light now flooded into the choir where Edward II lay in splendour; and although most of the glass in the immense east window was white, some of it was to be filled with the heraldry of local knights who fought chivalrously for Edward III in France. But more unusual was the stonework. Slender columns now rose without interruption from the floor to the vault. Stone screens masked clumsier Norman work to add to the effect of simple elegance, elegance fit for a king.

The decoration at Gloucester was not so rich as could be seen elsewhere in fourteenth-century England; and the arches were not so pointed. If we want to see how the merchants of Bristol rejoiced in their wealth as they offered it to their God, we can look at their church of St Mary Redcliffe: at the exotic carving around the main entrance door suggesting Spanish, Arab or even Indian trade, or at the dazzling geometry of the vaults high above ('lierne' vaulting, so called because most of the ribs were not needed functionally). The new work at Gloucester seemed to be hinting that such a display of wealth was vulgar. No decoration could be as beautiful as clean lines; no sharpness of an arch as uplifting as the unity of this simple, all-embracing design. The 'Perpendicular' architecture preferred by the monks of Gloucester relied for its impact on its total composition and perfect proportions. 'For the first time', as an expert has commented, 'a rectangle of panelling is seen as the unit for the composition of a wall, whether the panel be left empty or filled with stone or with glass'.[1] And it was prob-

---

[1] Joan Evans, *English Art, 1307-1461* (Oxford, 1949), p.68.

ably no coincidence that the monks had connections with the royal household, since earlier work seems to have been done in the same style in the now vanished St Stephen's Chapel in the palace at Westminster (and in the chapter house of old St Paul's Cathedral). The simplicity of this Perpendicular style was in the course of its development to contain its own rich sophistication (a splendid example is the 'fan' vaulting of the cloisters at Gloucester); but always there was this ruling unity. Perpendicular was the only major style in architecture to be developed in England and to be almost entirely confined to the English. It is far more beautiful, the English will always think, than its less disciplined Continental contemporary, 'flamboyant' Gothic.

In 1395 Richard II sent to the pope a book about the miracles wrought at the tomb of Edward II, petitioning for his royal predecessor to be canonized as a saint. But the true story of Edward's death belongs to a world infinitely more sordid than the Perpendicular architecture at Gloucester. After completely alienating the aristocracy by his support of his arrogant and very greedy favourites, the Despensers, the king was forced to abdicate by the threat, conveyed harshly by a bishop, that he would be deposed and his children disinherited if he refused.[2] At Berkeley castle he was murdered on the orders of his queen, Isabella, and her lover, Roger Mortimer, Earl of March, who was at that time the uncrowned king. The story spread that death had been caused by an iron poker inserted into the ex-king, a reminder that one of his offences against the aristocrats' code had been his homosexuality. And although Roger Mortimer was soon hanged, the aristocracy never expressed regret that Edward had been forced to abdicate. Even Walter Reynolds, who had been the king's treasurer and chancellor and had been rewarded by him with the archbishopric of Canterbury, tried to mediate between him and his enemies. In the final crisis he became their

---

[2] The bishop was Adam Orleton. See R. M. Haines, *The Church and Politics in Fourteenth Century England* (Cambridge, 1978); Natalie Fryde, *The Tyranny and Fall of Edward II* (Cambridge, 1979); Jeffrey Denton, *Robert Winchelsey and the Crown* (Cambridge, 1980).

mouthpiece in attacking a tyrant. Celebrating the accession of a new king, the archbishop discoursed on a text with a great future before it: 'the voice of the people is the voice of God.'

EDWARD III AND HIS BISHOPS

Edward III's reign saw no repetition of that dramatic crack in the unity of England under the Christian monarchy. It was, indeed, the period when the 'Age of Chivalry' may be held to have flourished (always remembering that when that phrase came into use in the Victorian Age 'chivalry' was thought to be inferior to the higher virtues of the 'Age of Heroism' now vanished). During most of the reign Church and State seemed happily interlocked.

A working arrangement was reached between the English monarchy and the papacy on the key question of who was to appoint the Church's leadership. After 1344 it was recognized in practically all cases that the pope had the right to appoint or 'provide' bishops for the seventeen English dioceses. At the same time, however, it became normal for the king to produce his own candidate and for the pope to 'provide' him; thus the only losers were the monks or canons of the cathedral, who had enjoyed the right of 'free' election of their bishop on at least some occasions in the previous century. In 1345, when some of his cardinals complained that the king's candidate was too flippant to be a bishop, Pope Clement VI declared that if the King of England asked for an ass to be made a bishop he would grant his request. Not all popes were so complacent; they might make difficulties about 'illiterate' favourites of the king. But on the whole this arrangement between pope and king worked smoothly.[3] In the 1440s Thomas Gascoigne, a fiercely critical chancellor of Oxford University, was to complain that 'there are three things today that make a bishop in

---

[3] See J. R. L. Highfield, 'The English hierarchy in the reign of Edward III' in *Transactions of the Royal Historical Society* (London, 1956), pp.115-138.

England: the will of the king, the will of the pope or the court of Rome, and the money paid in large quantities to that court'. One factor was that the popes inherited from the days when John had surrendered to Innocent III the tradition of being the patron, or at any rate the ally, of the King of England. Not for nothing did the first two words that have survived in the handwriting of an English king refer to this relationship. *Pater sancte* ('holy father') was written on a confidential letter to the pope from Edward III when he was eighteen, in the hope that in future the recipient would recognize the king's writing.

In 1351-53 Parliament passed two statutes which later became famous: *Provisors* and *Praemunire*. On the face of them, these statutes prohibited papal appointments to English ecclesiastical posts, or appeals away from the royal judges in disputes over ecclesiastical appointments. The prohibitions were strengthened when the statutes were revised in the 1390s. The effect of these statutes was not to stop all further appointments by the pope, but they did strengthen the hands of the king or the local authority if either wished to frustrate a particular appointment. Fewer foreigners occupied English ecclesiastical posts – and the fact that any did so continued to be the subject of loudly patriotic protests in Parliament and elsewhere. Parishes to which laymen appointed priests were seldom involved in papal 'provisions'. In the cathedrals and in the growing number of well-endowed 'collegiate' churches, however, canons were often appointed by the pope. In 1398 it was agreed that one out of every three such vacancies should be filled by 'provisions'. One reason why this system was tolerated was that it provided for the promotion of graduates without powerful patrons; Pope Clement VI – again parodying the system – promised parishes to all poor clerics who would claim them from him within two months of his coronation. The main losers were the bishops, who for the rest of the Middle Ages had curiously little influence on the careers of their clergy.[4]

The role which the papacy could now play in the lives of the

---

[4] See Geoffrey Barraclough, *Papal Provisions* (Oxford, 1935).

abler clergy was illustrated in the careers of two monks who
were contemporaries in Norwich Cathedral Priory and at
Gloucester College, Oxford. In earlier days they would have
spent quiet lives in their beautiful monastery. As it was, both
were sent to represent their Benedictine order at the papal
court. As a result Thomas Brunton (or Brinton) was 'provided'
in 1366 to the bishopric of Rochester, and from this base
became the fourteenth century's outstanding preacher in
England; more than a hundred of his sermons survive.[5] He was
outspoken against the rich if these were oppressive or the poor
if these were rebellious; against the clergy if these were slack or
the laity if these were anticlerical. Preferring an international
stage, Adam Easton remained at the papal court as one of the
twenty (or so) cardinals who at that stage constituted the international Church's government. He was prolific in his scholarly
answers to contemporary attacks on the privileges of popes
and priests. He learned Hebrew in order to deal with appeals
to the Old Testament.

For most of the reign of Edward III, the government
machine was run by churchmen. The most prominent were
both humbly born but became Bishops of Winchester – now
one of the most lucrative posts in the whole medieval Church,
worth more than £3,000 a year at a time when a ploughman
earned less than £3. William of Edington, who was the king's
treasurer or chancellor 1344-63, devoted himself not only to
financing the war in France but also to increasing the beauty
of his cathedral.

William of Wykeham, Edington's pupil in the civil service
and successor at Winchester, was a leading minister, 1363-71.
His administration coincided with the recovery of the French
and he was deprived of his political office – and for a short
time of his ecclesiastical income also. At the height of his
prosperity he held a dozen ecclesiastical posts in addition to his
golden bishopric. But he, too, was a faithful Bishop of Winchester according to his own lights, dedicating much of his
wealth to the foundation of a great school (Winchester

---

[5] *The Sermons of Thomas Brinton, Bishop of Rochester*, were edited by
M. A. Davlin in 2 vols. (London, 1954).

College) and a monumental Oxford college (New College); and under his direction the Winchester nave was modernized in the new Perpendicular style. William of Wynford was his master mason in all three great works. Not for nothing had William of Wykeham made his first mark in the civil service as a manager of building projects for Edward III.[6] The last political act to which Edward III gave his assent was the restoration of his estates to his former minister. It was rumoured by the cynical that Bishop William had bribed the dying king's lively mistress. But on most occasions common sense inspired a king to keep on good terms with his bishops – as we can learn from the earlier story of Edward III's relations with John of Stratford.

Stratford was chancellor for most of the 1330s and Archbishop of Canterbury from 1333. In 1340 he was dismissed from his secular office; the king blamed him for the lack of funds for the war. His response was to preach in Canterbury Cathedral on the anniversary of Becket's martyrdom, invoking also memories of Stephen Langton and Magna Carta. He then excommunicated all who should infringe the liberties of the Church (pointedly excepting the royal family) and led the opposition to the king in the next parliament so alarmingly that he had to be restored to prominence on the king's council. The incident, with its display of ecclesiastical muscle, helps to show why a chapel in honour of St Thomas of Canterbury was endowed by this archbishop in the parish church of Stratford-on-Avon.[7]

THE FATE OF RICHARD II

The grim castle of Pontefract was one of the centres of power for Earls and Dukes of Lancaster. It was also the scene of the cult of Earl Thomas, executed here after the collapse of his rebellion against Edward II in 1322.

---

[6] See W. G. Hayter, *William of Wykeham* (London, 1970).

[7] E. F. Jacob studied his career in *Transactions of the Royal Historical Society* (London, 1962), pp.1-23.

Amid sentimentality about his death on Edward II's personal orders, people forgot that Thomas, the richest man in England after the king, had been in reality no more than an overmighty lout. Although the earl called himself 'King Arthur' in his letters, he had never let chivalry restrain his passions; he had been happy enough to gloat over the severed head of the royal favourite, Piers Gaveston, when that wretch had been dragged to his death from an Oxfordshire rectory. A modern biographer writes of Thomas: 'unscrupulous, violent and avaricious, he was not a man to convince others that he could either lead or govern'.[8] People remembered only that he had defended the charters against the king; that he had been the friend of an archbishop, Robert of Winchelsea, whose memory was already being linked with Becket's. When he had suffered 'martyrdom' outside Pontefract castle, the cult of Thomas of Lancaster as the champion of Church and people grew to the extent that Edward III had to place guards around the castle to deter pilgrims. This cult became one of the many traditions reminding aristocrats, particularly aristocrats who were bishops, that opposition to a king could be sacred.

William Courtenay, for instance, did not flinch when one evening after dinner in 1385 Richard II drew his sword on him and had to be restrained from using it. Courtenay, an earl's brother, was Edward I's great-grandson. He had been a bishop since the age of twenty-eight. As Archbishop of Canterbury 1381-96 he proved himself able and wise. Such a man could look down on an ill-tempered king even while he knelt before him. And Thomas Arundel, another earl's brother, whom the monks elected to follow Courtenay at Canterbury, was almost as impregnably aristocratic. He has been a bishop since the age of twenty. His appointments as chancellor in 1386 and Archbishop of York in 1388 were intended to conciliate the nobility. His removal from the former office signalized Richard's attempt at personal rule in 1389; his return to it two years later showed the failure of that attempt; and his banishment in 1397, when his brother was beheaded, inaugurated the final period of Richard's tyranny. Arundel

[8] J. R. Maddicott, *Thomas of Lancaster* (Oxford, 1970), p.319.

shared his exile with his cousin, Henry Bolingbroke – and shared Bolingbroke's indignation when Richard deprived him of his inheritance as Duke of Lancaster. When Henry triumphed over Richard, it was Arundel who placed him on the vacant throne, becoming his chief counsellor. Only one bishop (Carlisle) publicly denounced the usurper and privately plotted to restore Richard.

In the nave of Westminster Abbey – rebuilt in this period, but modestly in keeping with the design of the rest of the church under Henry III – can be seen a portrait of Richard II. It is the earliest surviving portrait of an English monarch. It was painted about 1390, although it has been clumsily restored since then. It shows the king with the regalia used at his coronation in 1377: the crown, the sceptre of justice, the orb displaying the cross over the globe. (The beautifully decorated *Liber Regalis*, coming from the same period and still in the library of Westminster Abbey, gives us the whole coronation service.) Under a cloak of ermine is a tunic very beautifully embroidered in gold. The king's stare is meant to be imperious. At this stare in real life, we are told, courtiers had to bend the knee. Not far away, in Westminster Hall, we can still see the walls which the king's master mason Henry Yevele (an architectural genius) adapted from the Normans' work and the immense hammer-beam roof, with thirteen arched trusses of oak and decorative angels, built under the direction of Hugh Herland the king's carpenter in 1393-1400. This hall was to be the scene of the monarch's principal feasts.

Up Whitehall, in the National Gallery, is the most exquisite painting surviving from the English Middle Ages: the Wilton Diptych (an altar-piece with two panels). The history of this diptych is mysterious until it appears in the collection of Charles I, but it seems to be one of the signs of the king's increasing obsession with his isolated dignity after the death of his queen, Anne of Bohemia, in 1394, closely followed by the death of their only son. He not only ordered the total destruction of the palace at Sheen which had been their favourite home, but also prepared his own tomb in Westminster Abbey in 1395 where he could lie alongside Anne. Like the Westminster portrait, the Wilton Diptych probably recalls the king's coronation; it shows Richard as a boy of about the appropriate age, ten. The king is being introduced into the court of heaven by three saints – St Edmund the Martyr and St Edward the Confessor who preceded him as English monarchs and his own patron, St John the Baptist, who has put a hand on his shoulder. In front of the young king is the Christ child with his mother; Christ is about to give him a standard. Attractive angels stand around, crowned with white roses, wearing above their hearts the king's badge, the white hart, together with a collar characteristic of the French court from which Richard's second queen, Isabella, came in 1396. Almost certainly this diptych was painted to adorn the king's own portable altar. Morning by morning he would draw strength from it as he received communion from his chaplain.

The colours on the diptych are delightful, suggesting that the banquets to be held in Westminster Hall would be a feast for eye as well as for palate. We cannot be surprised that Richard, who ordered the first English cookery book to be compiled, was also the first Englishman known to have used a handkerchief. But in November 1399 he was taken to spend the winter in Pontefract castle, and early in February 1400 his corpse was publicly exhibited. The new king's council had ordered that the body should be shown, whether living or dead; with that broad hint, no death warrant was needed. The body showed no sign of violence. Nor did the skeleton when it was examined in the Victorian Age. Almost certainly Richard of Bordeaux, the Black Prince's son, the splendid grandson of the splendid Edward III, had been starved to death, having been left through the winter cold and alone. The fate of this prince haunted many imaginations, until in 1595 Shakespeare made the tragedy of *Richard II* – including, however, a fight in the dungeon at the end – the summit of his dramatic achievement to that date. The summit was higher than the level reached a few years previously in Christopher Marlowe's *Edward II*; because while Marlowe had satisfied the appetite of a Tudor audience for a mixture of splendour and brutality, Shakespeare touched the heart with pity for the fallen king on whose own horse (Barbary) Bolingbroke rode 'in London streets, that coronation day'.

PLAGUE AND REVOLT

The chronicler Adam of Usk claimed that he heard Richard cry out after his deposition: 'My God! A wonderful land is this, and a fickle! Which hath exiled, slain, destroyed or ruined so many kings, rulers and great men, and is ever tainted and toileth with strife and variance and envy!' And if we look at the economic problems beneath the tensions between the king and the nobility, we find the tremors of an earthquake.

One problem was that the two warrior-kings, Edward I and III, overstrained the resources of the kingdom. Their conquests left impressive memorials behind them – Caernarvon and the other castles built by Edward I in a Wales which stayed conquered; or the tomb of Edward the Black Prince, Edward III's much acclaimed son and general, beside the shrine of St Thomas of Canterbury; or the Order of the Garter based on Windsor Castle for the leading knights in the conquest of France. But the conquests had to be financed and defended. Both in Scotland and in France this ultimately proved impossible, and the aggression which was the dark side of the Age of Chivalry (of course, a side which the chivalrous claimed not to exist) brought retribution on king and people.

At the age of sixty-eight, deep in debt, Edward I had to begin one more campaign against the Scots; he died during it, and at Bannockburn in 1314 the army he had bequeathed to his son was slaughtered. Edward III raised cash for his wars in France by loans or taxes from the wool trade, with disastrous consequences for that trade. By the 1370s, when he was senile and under the control of his mistress Alice Perrers (who robbed his corpse), almost all his conquests had melted away. The average Englishman seems to have blamed the king's ministers – hence the fall of William of Wykeham in 1371, when there was a cry from the generals and their fellow-laymen that no more bishops should be given the chief offices of state. But the real limitation on English military power was that the money ran out. The French had only to avoid major battles and victory would be theirs. In the long run it was not enough to be aggressive or to develop the longbow, the technological secret of the famous English victories at Crécy and Poitiers. One of Richard II's more sensible policies was to secure peace with France, which meant that he was solvent.

Quite apart from the difficulties in taxation, the French wars bequeathed serious problems for the future. The easiest way in which Edward III could field an army far larger than anything envisaged by the Normans was to let his generals recruit their own men by pay and by promises of ransoms or plunder. This encouraged the system which has been called 'bastard feudalism'. The successful magnate now had an army of 'retainers' who looked to him for pay and patronage. During a war they could be absorbed in France. In time of peace 'bastard feudalism' was a recipe for civil war – and locally in England the peace was now beginning to be kept by unpaid 'justices of the peace' under the influence of the local magnates, instead of by the royal justices of previous centuries.

The economic activity of England had been expanding steadily and in 1341 had supported the first gold coinage. But overpopulation had become a menace; famines had resulted from bad weather in 1314-17. Now, at the middle of the fourteenth century, the economy was very badly damaged by the Black Death, although the conclusion that one third of the population perished does not command complete acceptance among scholars.

New and deadly forms of plague – bubonic plague spread by rats, and pneumonic plague spread by person-to-person contagion – reached England in August 1348 and had caused great devastation by the end of the following year. There were other severe outbreaks in 1361, 1369 and 1379. The hundreds of thousands who died in 1349 included two Archbishops of Canterbury (Thomas Bradwardine, a mathematician and theologian of distinction, had entered into the archbishopric in the previous week), William Ramsey the greatest architect of the age, Richard Rolle the great mystic, William of Ockham the great philosopher (although he was in exile in Munich), the abbot and forty-eight monks at St Albans and the abbot and twenty-six monks at Westminster (about half these communities). People who were less well-nourished and who lived less hygienically suffered even more terribly, not only in the overcrowded towns but also deep in the countryside where fields and whole villages were abandoned because of the depopulation. In six dioceses of which we have knowledge, over forty per cent of the new parish priests appointed in 1348-9 replaced dead men.

Since agriculture and most trades depended so heavily on manual labour, it was extremely difficult to repair the ravages inflicted by the Black Death. Many modern experts believe that the economic effects of the disaster were still being felt two hundred years after 1348; and that the fascination with death, so characteristic of the later Middle Ages, was born of this plague. The Church, too, suffered very greatly from the loss of manpower. This was one of the reasons that led the Cistercian monks to abandon the system of getting their agricultural work done by lay brothers. The crisis inspired William of Wykeham to found a school and a college to train priests. On the other hand, some parts of the country escaped relatively lightly, and the nation's dependence on the labour-intensive production of raw materials (wool, hides, grain and coal) for export was anyway decreasing as manufacturing (for example, of cloth) increased; the Wife of Bath in *The Canterbury Tales* was a prosperous clothier. Moreover, the surviving peasants were in a position to demand higher wages, although at the same time the decreased demand for land also meant that tenants could force landlords to accept lower rents.

The landowners naturally fought back with all the power at their command. They did their utmost to enforce the old obligations to give manual labour to the lord of the manor, without charge where these obligations of serfs or 'villeins' had survived the growth of an economy based on rents and wages. The Statute of Labourers (1351) prohibited wages above the pre-plague rates, the movement of workmen or servants until their contracts had been fulfilled, the increase of prices on goods sold directly by their makers, and the charging of more than 'reasonable' prices on foodstuffs. Popular resentment built up over thirty years, but it is not surprising that the governing class was on the whole complacent. The social system was generally accepted as having been ordained by God and as being impregnable. England was still a land of villages, and it was assumed that any discontent would remain local. And employers and purchasers were willing to bend the laws if they needed labour or goods and were prepared to pay new prices for them: so inflation, at least in the prices of manu-factured goods, could not be prevented. But the government had grown discredited during the senility of Edward III – and was now leaderless during the minority of Richard II, since the jealousies of the aristocracy ruled out the appointment of a regent. The only thought was how to replenish the exchequer. A poll tax of a shilling a head was decreed as an emergency measure. It created a worse emergency as the poor found themselves and their families counted and made to pay no less than the rich.

Trouble over the collection of the tax broke out first in Essex and then in Kent, probably because the landowners in the south-east of England had been slower than those else-where to recognize the new facts of life for the poor. The Kentishmen elected Wat Tyler (an ex-soldier) as their leader and released a priest, John Ball, from the archbishop's prison in Canterbury. On Wednesday, 12 June 1381 rebels from the two counties were encamped outside the city of London and John Ball preached to them with a radical message of equality, quoting the contemporary catchphrase:

Whan Adam dalf and Eve span,
Who was thanne a gentilman?

On the next day they entered the city and burned down some of its most luxurious houses. The governing class was now in total disarray. It was saved only by the personal courage of King Richard, a boy not yet fifteen. On the Friday he left the Tower of London to parley with the rebels from Essex in the fields at Mile End. For some reason which has never been explained, the Tower was left feebly guarded and its drawbridge was not raised. Presumably the king hoped that the ministers he had left behind would now escape, as his mother did; but the chancellor who was also Archbishop of

Canterbury, Simon Sudbury, and the treasurer of the kingdom, Sir Robert Hales, were found and executed by the mob. A little boy, Henry Bolingbroke, who was to be Richard's successor, was rescued by a faithful servant – and, it has been suggested, never forgave Richard for leaving him to his fate. The king meanwhile pacified the rebels in the fields by promises: serfs would be released from bondage, wages would be unfrozen, traitors would be punished.

On the Saturday, after a visit to Westminster Abbey to make his confession and receive communion (while there he witnessed a lynching), Richard faced the rebels from Kent at Smithfield. Wat Tyler, still suspicious, argued with him, until the Mayor of London, losing his temper, struck down a man so impertinent. The boy-king who was the Black Prince's son retained an almost incredible presence of mind, shouting orders to the enraged mob. His words came to be reported as: 'Sirs, will you shoot your king? I am your captain, follow me'. And they followed – only to find themselves surrounded by troops summoned by the mayor. Once again Richard kept his head, insisting that the peasants should disperse peacefully with a promise of pardon. We cannot wonder that in later years he was under the illusion that political problems needed only dramatic action by him; that he had only to exert his will for the nobility to fall into line behind him; that he could even get away with the gamble of depriving Henry Bolingbroke of his inheritance as Duke of Lancaster – his last, fatal error.

Outside London there were some almost equally dramatic and revealing scenes in 1381. In St Albans the abbot, the great Thomas de la Mare, whose rule over half a century after the Black Death took the monastery to the height of its wealth and prestige, was forced to seal a charter setting free all the serfs on his estates. In Bury St Edmunds rebels beheaded the prior, the monk who controlled the monastery's estates and the chief justice of the kingdom who lived nearby. In both places the townsmen demanded more freedom from the monks who had previously controlled civic life in detail, while in Cambridge the documents setting out the university's privileges were burned amid derision in the market square. Other rebels plundered the city of Norwich and terrified Norfolk until the bishop's cavalry surrounded them and hanged their leader. Among the rebels there seems to have been some talk about a 'Great Society' but their real unity was only a hatred of the bishops, monks and scholars along with the rest of the rich – a hatred fanned by the egalitarian preaching of John Ball and (surviving sermons show) of many another village priest or poor friar, the Communists of their day.

When the rising died down all the concessions made under threat of violence were withdrawn. But in a broader perspective it cannot be said that the Peasants' Revolt was a total failure. The shock seems to have encouraged a process which might have been inevitable anyway as being in the landowners' interests: the substitution of tenants or employees for serfs, and the rise of wages to their economic level (they doubled in the period 1346-96). And there was not to be another poll tax for over a century.

THE CHURCH OF PIERS PLOWMAN

Those few violent days in June 1381 make us wonder what was going on in the fourteenth century at the levels of society beneath the kings, bishops and other aristocrats who commissioned art and architecture and who attracted the attention of the chroniclers. About any previous period we should have had to admit ignorance. But the illustrations in the Luttrell Psalter suddenly enable us to see the everyday life of the countryside in the 1330s; and some fascinating literature has survived to give us glimpses of the thinking and religion of the English people.

There were devotional books to guide English-reading Christians. The earliest to have survived is *Handlyng Synne*, based on an older book in French in 1303. Its author was Robert Mannyng, who wrote it to help his fellow-priests in Lincolnshire and then turned his hand to a history of England in more than 25,000 rhyming lines. Many sermons by English-speaking preachers have also been preserved. These preachers belonged to a tradition as vigorous and creative then as

preaching was to be in the seventeenth century. They denounced the selfishness of the rich and offered salvation to the
poor. They found mysterious or exciting symbolism in the
familiar Bible stories. They told homely stories and repeated
popular proverbs. Individually such preachers could not stand
comparison with the poets or great writers, but they had far
more influence.

The most popular poets were the authors of lyrics, for the
medieval English were well-known as a people who enjoyed
singing. Some of these lyrics had secular words. One of the
most popular lyrics was already a hundred years old in the
fourteenth century:

> Summer is icumen in
> Lhude sing! cucu.

But the natural association of spring, joy and love had already
led to many love poems addressed in English to Christ and his
mother, particularly together at Bethlehem or Calvary. These
were fresh, simple and direct in comparison with the more
carefully theological Latin hymns of the Church – although
they often kept in touch with that source by brief snatches of
Latin. And the music of the lyrics which remained secular
could be used for religious words; this was a speciality of the
Franciscan preachers, conceived of by St Francis himself as
joculatores Dei, 'God's minstrels'. The largest surviving collection of medieval English lyrics (the British Museum manuscript Harley 2253, compiled before 1315) mixes the themes of
the preacher and the minstrel. Some of the music, secular or
religious, would be dance music; the *carole* (a French word)
was any song to which men and women could dance in a ring
holding hands, for example during the festivities after
Christmas. The twelfth-century chronicler Thomas of Ely
quotes one *carole* 'to this day sung publicly in dances'. He
claims that it dated back to the time of a Danish king who had
heard the monks singing across the waters of the Fens:

> Merie sungen the muneches binnen Ely
> Tha Cnut ching reu ther by.
> 'Roweth, cnites, noer the land,
> And here we thes muneches saeng'.

So, as the fourteenth century sang and danced its way into an ever more joyful and intimate devotion, the miracle of simple grace that has become such a popular twentieth-century carol began to be possible, in praise of the Virgin Mother:

> I sing of a maiden
> That is makeles (matchless):
> King of alle kinges
> To here son she ches (chose).
>
> He cam al so stille
> There his moder was,
> As dew in Aprille
> That falleth on the grass . . .

The manuscript in which this poem was found also contains ballads, carols and Latin verse; perhaps it was the song book of a travelling minstrel. Earlier lyrics have been found containing some of the same words; even this matchless lyric sprang out of the life of the people. Fourteenth-century piety was, however, less escapist than such lyrics might suggest. It was expressed also in plays presenting biblical scenes to the people in English.

These developed out of the simpler drama which had for some time been part of the celebration of Christmas or Easter in some of the great churches (in Latin). The shepherds or Magi had come to do homage to the Christ child; the women had come weeping to Christ's empty tomb. Twelfth-century statutes of Lichfield Cathedral provide for such liturgical drama. There is a reference to 'holy dramas' representing the sufferings of martyrs being performed in London in a biography of Thomas Becket by his contemporary, William Fitzstephen. We know that clergy presented biblical plays. In 1244 Bishop Grosseteste ordered his archdeacons to put a stop to it, but the practice continued; at Christmas 1378 the minor clergy of St Paul's Cathedral presented scenes from the Old Testament. Now in the fourteenth century the laymen incorporated in craft-guilds in several towns such as Chester, York, Lincoln and Norwich took the drama out of the churches on to wagons called 'pageants' which were pulled round the streets. The clergy were, it seems, still suspicious – but the laity had lifted drama out of the moral and artistic degeneration of the public stage since Roman times. Each guild would play a separate scene. Although probably the original authors were scholars, it is clear that each scene could be adapted by local talent. The plays presented episodes in the story of man's salvation from the Fall of the Angels to the Last Judgement, but above all from the story of Christ. They were often performed at Whitsun or on the feast of Corpus Christi in the early summer; probably the combination of scenes to form a whole play on this feast was first copied from the Continent 'about the end of the first quarter of the fourteenth century at some place probably in the north of England'.[9]

At least one of these dramatists – the unknown author of the Towneley Shepherds' Play – was a major comic poet, but the most important Christian poetry about the life of the age was a poetry of protest.

Some Latin poems about fourteenth-century life survive, the most substantial being John Gower's *Vox Clamantis* which denounced rebellious peasants and greedy merchants alike, and could be dedicated to Richard II in the first edition and to Henry IV in the second. Gower also wrote in English. But a greater English poet worked many of the preachers' themes into images as vivid as those of the lyrics, in unrhymed alliterative verse. He was William Langland, and his poem – surviving in three texts showing how he revised and lengthened it again and again, from the 1360s to the 1390s – was *Piers Plowman*. Doggedly conservative while also being radical in its attacks on the new rich, and profoundly Catholic despite its many protests, it is 'the most thoroughly English of all our religious poems'.[10]

The name of the hero was traditional. One of the letters connected with the rising of 1381 that has survived to suggest a well-prepared conspiracy seems to use this name as a code-word for the rebellion itself: 'John Sheep, priest of Col-

[9] Hardin Craig, *English Religious Drama of the Middle Ages* (Oxford, 1955), p.133.

[10] R. W. Chambers, *Man's Unconquerable Mind* (London, 1939), p.90.

chester . . . greeteth well John Nameless and John the Miller,
and John Carter, and biddeth them that they . . . stand
together in God's name, and biddeth Piers Plowman go to his
work, and chastise well Hob the robber. . . .' William
Langland, however, was no advocate of armed rebellion. He
dreamed of a saintly pope, of a pure Church, of a penitent
commonwealth, of the great barn called Unity; of 'brethren of
one blood: alike beggars and earls'. Justice was to be established by the appeal of the conscience, not by force; and love
was always greater than justice. He was not afraid, any more
than the popular preachers were, any more than John Gower
was, to handle these non-violently revolutionary themes. What
defeated him was not the novelty of his essential vision but the
novelty of his attempt to turn it into a long English poem; and
the novelty of the questions that occurred to him on the way.
He felt a vocation to do in England what Dante had done in
Italy, although his questioning was more thorough and his
genius less majestic than Dante's. His success was enough to
win a public large for his time. More than fifty medieval
manuscripts of *Piers Plowman* have survived, suggesting that
the poem was read in many devout middle-class homes and
that sections of it were recited to a wider audience. Sir Adrian
Fortescue copied it all out by hand in the 1530s, and the
demand for it justified a printed edition in 1550. Its popularity may well have influenced the number of wall-paintings
surviving in churches and representing Christ as a ploughman.

To this poem he dedicated his life, as a few autobiographi-
cal references make clear. Tall and thin, he was nicknamed
'Long Will' and sometimes thought to be crazed. Born in the
1330s, in an Oxfordshire where his kind of poetry was
flourishing as a popular art, he spent much of his life in
London, living with 'Kitte my wyf and Calote my douhter' in a
cottage on Cornhill. He could not be a priest – first because
his patron died and then because, being honest, he was
officially married – but he tried to earn a living by singing
services in commemoration of the dead. At times he thought
that the praise of honest manual labour in his poem indicated
how he, too, ought to live; but he was sustained by a sense of a
vocation to be a poet. He presents himself as a dreamer, often

rebuked for his stupidity, often learning from his experience.

He divides his poem into two parts: *Vision* and *Life*. In his vision he sees the 'field full of folk' while asleep one warm morning in May among the Malvern Hills.

Some of the folk are ploughing and sowing, with no time for pleasure, producing the food which others will waste. Theirs is the common lot of poverty, cold and hunger. But most of the folk are greedy for worldly gain. The dreamer hears labourers singing bawdy songs over their shoddy work; cooks offering hot pies, and innkeepers bawling out their advertisements; Lady Mede (Money) having a grand Westminster wedding to Falsehood. Some of the folk are wandering through the countryside — tramps living by their wits, pilgrims full of lying talk, friars and pardoners deluding the people, parish priests on their way to London, pleading that since the plague their parishes have become too poor to live in. A hundred men are seen in silk gowns, making speeches. These are lawyers, as useless as the priests. Sickened by this world where everything is for sale including the law, the dreamer meets Holy Church and asks 'how I may save my soul'. Her answer is that he must find Truth, who is also Love. Piers the ploughman then appears and leads the search. He reaches Truth and is offered a pardon for sin. But when it is read out to him, this document turns out to be only the promise which is sternly moral: that those who have done well will go into eternal life and the others into eternal punishment. Knowing that this is no pardon at all, he tears it up — and quarrels with the priest who defends it. The sins of those who do *not* do well have to be forgiven as sparks from London chimneys are extinguished in the Thames. The Gospel must be about the divine compassion, which must be yet greater than the dreamer's.

The section of the poem is complex, even turgid, as the solitary poet wrestles with the mysteries of his religion. How is faith related to reason, morality to theology? Heartless learning, he sees, is as evil as covetousness. But the poem is clarified as it describes three types of a truly Christian life: Do Well, Do Bet (Better) and Do Best.

'Do Well' is the life of patient poverty, of active goodness, open to any layman or hard-working pastor: 'to see much and suffer more'. We are then shown the life of 'Do Bet' — a life in which perfect love is first contemplated and then practised, a life to be found in the best priests although not only in them. To this section belongs the famous picture of Christ dressed in the armour of Piers (for Piers is the mankind whose nature Christ took), going to joust against the Devil and Death. The conquest of hell is vividly imagined. The dreamer wakes to find that the bells are ringing on Easter morning. He calls his wife and daughter to come with him to church.

After this climax we are given a much shorter dream about 'Do Best', the mixed life of contemplation and activity characteristic of the ideal bishop. Piers is now seen as St Peter, and for him Grace builds a barn big enough to hold Christendom (and beyond Christendom, the dreamer has seen, there are Saracens who 'pray and have perfect faith in one God who is holy and mighty, and they ask for his grace'). But unlike Dante, Langland does not attempt a description of Paradise. The poem does not offer easy answers; even its end is inconclusive. Antichrist is seen coming and waging war, and Conscience who also comes to do battle doubts his own power. So Conscience sets out on one more pilgrimage, to find the perfect pope.

William Langland has rejected or ignored many of the claims of the institutional Church which he knows too well. But he does not reject any of its doctrines about God or the meaning of life. He praises true hermits and true priests. He tells us that the monk's cloister is a place for books and happiness. The revolution in which he takes part comes first by imagining the orthodox doctrines in powerfully human terms, and then by applying them without compromise to the realities of a corrupt society. So in effect he builds his own church: the poem itself. The reader of *Piers Plowman* can still explore 'the nave for the people, the choir for the clergy, yet like so many churches in the Middle Ages so crowded with tombs, rood-screens, chantries and side-altars that the total effect is a most curious blending of order and confusion.'[11]

---

[11] H. W. Wells, 'The Construction of Piers Plowman', in *Middle English Survey*, ed. E. Vasta (Notre Dame, Ind., 1975), p.168.

THE *GAWAIN* POET

An essentially similar approach is made in four poems which may all be the work of another fourteenth-century poet, more secure in his status and in the mastery of his art. His name is not known (Langland's own name is known to us only because of a scribbled note on one copy of his poem). These poems, like Langland's, are in unrhymed alliterative verse, but in the English of a district far from London: the north-west Midlands. They have survived in a single manuscript.

The longest is *Sir Gawain and the Green Knight*. On its surface it is a colourful, sometimes humorous, romance about King Arthur's knights; a poem which takes a glowing delight in aristocratic pastimes such as hunting. It seems to belong to a world entirely different from the London streets which we tread in *Piers Plowman*. But just as in Anglo-Saxon times an aristocratic entertainment such as *Beowulf* could be seen, on deeper analysis, to be a Christian poet's attempt to make his privileged listeners think out what constituted true moral or spiritual heroism, so this story told by the *Gawain*-poet was full of matters which could both attract and instruct the nobility or gentry.

King Arthur's court at its New Year festivities is startled by the appearance of the Green Knight, a figure who comes out of Celtic mythology, a vegetation-god who is now the symbol of life. The Green Knight asks that his head should be cut off and in return promises to execute his executioner: life is like that. But the Green Knight is able to ride away cheerfully, carrying the head which Sir Gawain has agreed to sever: life is like that, too. So a fearful Sir Gawain has to follow, to the Green Chapel where the second half of the bargain is to be kept. On his way he comes across a castle and the generous host offers Christmastide hospitality while he himself goes out hunting; this is the Green Knight in disguise. Sir Gawain, being no adulterer, resists the blandishments of his hostess in her lord's absence, apart from a few kisses; chivalry triumphs.

But he does accept one small gift, a girdle, without informing his host; he is not perfect. Eventually he reaches the uncanny Green Chapel, to find that the blows of the Green Knight do him no damage, except that his neck is grazed once. He must be punished to that extent because he accepted the girdle. He then returns to tell his story over dinner at Arthur's Round Table. It is a complex story on which modern literary critics, who have a strong appetite for the study of symbolism and a thirst for disputations with each other, have feasted.

We can understand more readily the Christian messages of the other three poems found in the same manuscript. *Patience* interprets the Old Testament story of Job, while *Purity* links together a dozen books of the Bible in a poet's sermon. The *Pearl* begins with the poet's loss of a pearl in the grass of a garden in August. His grief, it turns out, is really for his daughter, dead before her second birthday. But while he is asleep in his misery beside her grave in that garden he sees her in the garden of Paradise ('then saw I there my little queen'); and he talks with her. She rebukes his stubborn earthiness but when he tries to join her across the stream of death, he wakes up − to find that 'all is well with me in this dungeon of grief'. He has been to his own Green Chapel.

This poet is far less of a preacher than Langland; thus it is possible for a modern commentator on his work to reckon that he did not have any profound interest in morality or salvation, 'except insofar as they could provide a framework for the imaginative exploration of situations and feelings'.[12] But such caution is excessive. 'The pure and constant values of heaven', observes another scholar, 'are contrasted in all four poems with the tarnished standards of earth. . . . The poet consistently sees society as corrupt; even the civilization of Arthur, that golden, chivalric court in its "first age", is essentially cowardly and frivolous. . . . And the *Gawain*-poet is unyielding on this point: to accept God's appointed mission is to bring upon oneself the scorn and fury of the world. . . . Only a handful of heroes can hope for the mercy of God and for salvation in the orthodox Christian way, through the merits of Christ.

[12] W. A. Davenport, *The Art of the Gawain-Poet* (London, 1978), p.220.

Thus the father of the pearl-maiden and Gawain have in the end attained a measure of wisdom, though they are overcome by a sense of their own unworthiness and by a perception of the evil of the world in which they live'.[13]

SPIRITUAL WRITERS

During a brief lull from his duties as a statesman and general, Henry, first Duke of Lancaster, wrote down an elaborate self-examination. This was in 1354; he was to die of the plague seven years later. The duke compares himself with a sick man who needs the medicine which only Christ's atonement can provide. Like a poet he thinks in pictures and naturally we are interested in the picturesque details of his confession, revealing the home-life of an aristocrat – but there can be no doubt that his repentance was genuine. He accuses himself of exploiting the poor and of avoiding their stench. He is ashamed that he has so loved his bed, wines and sauces, the smells of flowers, fruit and women. He has taken too much pride in the strength of his arms and in the rings on his fingers. He has danced too vigorously, hoping it would lead to kisses or more. He has loved the lusty kisses of low-born women more than the restrained greetings of the aristocracy. He has bred sins as he has bred salmon. Now he needs Christ's sweat of agony as a sick man needs a broth; or Christ's mother's tears as a sick man needs to be refreshed by rosewater. Christ's body is compared with the pips of a pomegranate, then a special delicacy for the rich sick; and his blood with a hot bath, then an experience almost equally rare. Duke Henry says that he needs a priest to dig for his sins as a huntsman with a rod digs a fox out, and perhaps the manuscript that has survived was written on his chaplain's advice. But he also says that his own conscience is the terrier to sniff for the sins, and he leaves the impression that if the need arose he could sin-hunt without clerical assistance.[14]

---

[13] Charles Moorman, *The Works of the Gawain-Poet* (Jackson, Miss., 1977), pp.46-7.

This self-critical duke wrote in French but his was, it seems, the kind of household that would have enjoyed a recital of *Sir Gawain and the Green Knight*. It was a sign of the retreat of the French language in England when he apologized for his imperfect fluency '*pur ceo jeo sui englais*'. One of Richard II's courtiers, Sir John Clanvowe, became (so far as we know) the first English layman after King Alfred to write a devotional book in English, on *The Two Ways* to death and to life. And his book was part of a widespread movement to make devotion more personal. This was the age of the great mystics among the German Dominicans, Eckhart, Tauler and Suso, and of Ruysbroeck in Flanders. In Rome itself a hermit was elected pope (Celestine V in 1294 – though he abdicated after a few weeks). Far up in the north of England, one man withdrew from his comfortable life as a monk in Durham Cathedral, then at the height of its wealth and prestige about the middle of the fourteenth century. He prayed on the Farne Islands where St Cuthbert had prayed; and he wrote what he learned. He once thought he saw Christ with a smile saying: 'Love and you will be saved.'

More prolific as an author both in Latin and in English, both in verse and prose, was another hermit, Richard Rolle – and more is known about him because after his death in 1349 the Cistercian nuns of Hampole near Doncaster, whose spiritual guide he had been, collected evidence in the hope that he would be officially recognized as a saint.[15] Rolle was a Yorkshire man who when aged nineteen, in the 1320s, refused to return to the arid studies of Oxford. Instead he got his sister to give him two frocks and his father's rain-hood, which he cut up to make a hermit's dress. His sister ran away shouting 'My brother is mad!' However, the local squire, whose sons had known him at Oxford, gave him shelter. Thus Richard was able to fulfil the vocation which he later cel-

[14] *Le Livre de Sentz Medicines* by Duke Henry was edited by E. J. Arnold (Oxford, 1940) and a biography of *The King's Lieutenant* was written by Kenneth Fowler (London, 1969).

[15] See F. M. Comper, *The Life and Lyrics of Richard Rolle* (London, 1928).

ebrated in poems and almost thirty prose pieces. He wrote
with enthusiasm about the psalms (which he translated into
English) and other parts of the Bible, but his most famous
work was his *Incendium Amoris* (*The Fire of Love*) of 1343.

It began encouragingly: 'I cannot tell you how surprised I
was the first time I felt my heart begin to warm'. He recalled
that even as an adolescent he had 'ardently longed for the
pleasures of heaven more than for the delights of physical
love'. He wrote about worldly women in cruel terms, but
about prayer in the frank language of ecstasy. One day in his
hermitage he had felt an 'unusually pleasant heat' while at
prayer; one evening before supper, while reciting psalms, he
had heard heaven's song. Such pleasures had become regular
for him; and he could now promise these and greater joys to
all contemplatives who abandoned the world for the love of
God. In comparison with what he had found in this prolonged
love affair with God, he saw little merit and no attraction in
any life in the world — although he admitted that men 'unable
to persevere quietly in interior longing' might make suitable
bishops.

Such enthusiasm, warmly advertising the delights of private
prayer without too much mention of church services, was
welcomed widely, as is shown by the number of surviving
manuscripts. It is interesting today as proof that the ex-
periences known as 'Pentecostal' or 'charismatic' were not
unknown in the Middle Ages. Rolle was, however, suspected
of over-enthusiasm by maturer experts. This is shown by the
existence of two other books, which seem to have been written
partly as replies to him although each is a spiritual classic in its
own right.

The Cloud of Unknowing was written in English by an
anonymous priest, probably in the East Midlands, who was
also the author of at least four tracts with two translations of
mystical theology. He wrote *The Cloud*, he tells us, for a
friend aged twenty-four and for others 'really and wholly
determined to follow Christ perfectly'. He had nothing to offer
those merely attracted by promises of supernatural warmth
and celestial song. He wrote to stress that the contemplative
life was work ('a full great travail') and that most of the work

was God's; that memory, and even thought, must be forgotten in the 'naked intent' to love the 'unmade' God; that a 'cloud of unknowing' must be acknowledged to exist between man and his Maker; that God is No-thing, No-where; but that this cloud hiding God could be pierced by 'a sharp dart of longing love'. 'He may well be loved, but not thought. By love he may be gotten and holden, but by thought never.'[16]

The longest and most authoritative of these treatises on the hidden life of prayer comes from a canon of the small Augustinian house of Thurgaton in Nottinghamshire, Walter Hilton, who died in 1396. He had been both a doctor of theology at the University of Paris and a hermit. He wrote *The Ladder of Perfection* for a young woman who had 'forsaken the world, turning to our Lord'. She must not prize warm feelings or angelic music; 'however delightful these things may be, they are less valuable than the practice of virtue and the knowledge and love of God'. Probably because she could not understand Latin, she is told that 'you cannot very well make use of reading the scriptures'. Instead she is urged to ascend the 'degrees of contemplation' by discipline in prayer, by meditation about Jesus, by the practice of humility and charity — although neither humility nor charity is to be extended to heretics. It is all sober counsel, by a man who by climbing this long ladder himself has become very holy, very wise and rather cautious. No other English guide to mysticism has had such influence; many editions have been printed since 1494.[17]

More courageously original are *Revelations of Divine Love*, the first book to have been written in English by a woman. Some comparisons can be made between it and the teachings of two other women of the fourteenth century, the Swedish St Bridget and St Catherine of Siena, but in each case what we see is a woman teaching with authority as an advanced mystic. The anonymous author of this extraordinary English book was

---

[16] Quotations are from the translations of *The Fire of Love* and *The Cloud of Unknowing* by Clifton Wolters in the Penguin Classics (London, 1971-72).

[17] See *The Scale of Perfection*, ed. Gerald Sitwell (London, 1953).

a recluse or 'anchoress'; her cell adjoined St Julian's church in Norwich. She is therefore known as Dame or Mother Julian.

The book was based on 'showings' which came to this 'simple creature that could no letter' in her thirtieth year, 1373. After a week's sickness, she was believed to be dying. As she gazed on the crucifix held before her by her parish priest, she thought she saw Christ bleed and heard him speak. Fifteen 'showings' lasted from four to nine o'clock on the morning of 8 May, and one more came on the night of the 9th. She seems to have made a record not long afterwards; one precious copy of this document has survived. But for most of the rest of her life she pondered the meaning of those few hours, and the longer edition of her book was not completed before 1394. If she really was illiterate in 1373 she must have learned to read and write. Rightly or wrongly many echoes from other mystics — even from theologians — have been found in her own book, which shows every sign of having been written with care. Her genius was original, but not so original as to be isolated; her message was based on a direct spiritual intuition, but shaped and reshaped with a craftsman's care, as Langland shaped *Piers Plowman*.

In the very first 'showing' she saw 'a little thing, the quantity of an hazel-nut, in the palm of my hand; and it was as round as a ball. I looked thereupon with my eye of understanding and thought: *What may this be? And it was answered me generally thus: It is all that is made. . . . It lasteth, and ever shall, for that God loveth it.* And so All-thing hath the Being by the love of God'. She gradually learned to look more deeply into that mystery of God's creative goodness. It is a mystery, needing to be revealed; yet God 'will be seen and he will be sought, he will be abided and he will be trusted. . . . For he is full gracious and homely'. Christ's suffering reveals the graciousness of God; Julian dares to picture Christ as a workman in grubby clothes and even to say that 'the deep wisdom of the Trinity is our Mother'. Her thought is much more solidly Trinitarian than is most of the other piety of the period; she really does give equal glory to Father, Son and Holy Spirit. It is not that she neglects the Son, however. She hears Christ speak. 'If thou art pleased, I am pleased: it is a

joy, a bliss, an endless satisfying to me that ever suffered I passion for thee; and if I might suffer more I would suffer more.'
At the end of her book she only understands more profoundly, through her deeper understanding of Christ's cross, what was there in her early vision – the vision of the universe as small as a hazel-nut in God's hand. 'I was answered in ghostly understanding', she tells us, 'saying thus: *Would'st thou learn thy Lord's meaning in this thing? Learn it well: Love was his meaning. Who shewed it thee? Love. What shewed he thee? Love. Wherefore shewed it he? For love. Hold thee therein and thou shalt learn and know more in the same. But thou shalt never know nor learn therein other thing without end.*'

Her whole heart is given to this courteous, chivalrous Christ. 'Our Lord Jesus oftentimes said: *I it am, I it am: I it am that is highest, I it am that thou lovest, I it am that thou enjoyest, I it am that thou servest, I it am that thou longest for, I it am that thou desirest, I it am that thou meanest, I it am that is all.*' But she boldly adds that any act of love is part of Christ: 'and then I saw that each kind compassion that man hath on his even-Christians with charity, it is Christ in him'. She thinks the presence of Christ strong even in the sinner, for she has a charitable view of human nature: 'in every soul that shall be saved is a godly will that never assented to sin, nor ever shall.' And Christ prays with the sinner all the time: 'I am the Ground of thy beseeching. First it is my will that thou have it; and after, I make thee to will it; and after, I make thee to beseech it.'

Although she, too, is a recluse she has none of Rolle's contempt for mankind. She loves the people in the street outside her cell. 'The charity of God maketh in us such a unity that, when it is truly seen, no man can part himself from other.' And she is far more interested in the unchanging reality of God. 'I saw soothfastly (truly) that our Lord was never wroth, nor ever shall be. For he is God: good, life, truth, love, peace. . . .' And so hers is not the worship of a God hidden in a cloud, to be approached up a long ladder. 'God is nearer to us than our own soul: for he is the Ground in whom our soul standeth.' We begin to see in this extraordinary book the significance of the light that floods Perpendicular churches, for here is a religion of light: 'Our faith is our light in our night: which light is God, our endless day.' And here, affirmed during years of plague in a city which was for a time occupied by the rebellious peasants of 1381 before their tragedy, is an optimistic faith: 'And all shall be well, and all shall be well, and all manner of thing shall be well.'[18]

A THEOLOGICAL REVOLUTION

Contemporary with this woman mystic who saw Christ as clearly as anyone has ever seen him in England was the first Englishman to become a major heretic.

John Wyclif was born about 1330, a Yorkshireman. Up to 1378 his life was that of an Oxford theologian: the long training, the share in academic controversies, the search for sources of income so that the life of study and disputation might be maintained. In the Middle Ages unless a scholar was also a monk or a friar maintained at the university by his order this search took the form of a hunt for rich rectories and canonries in cathedrals, since there was no salary for a university lecturer as such. Wyclif was not unsuccessful as an absentee pluralist. For brief periods he was also the head of two small Oxford colleges (Balliol and Canterbury). He was a distinguished don who in an earlier age might have ended up a bishop like Robert Grosseteste or Stephen Langton; his favourite English philosopher was Grosseteste, and he was the first Englishman to lecture on the whole Bible since Langton. But in fact his employment outside Oxford was as a propagandist employed by the laymen who had been at the top in politics since the fall of Bishop William of Wykeham — most conspicuously John of Gaunt, Edward III's second son. Even that was no radical

---

[18] Quotations are from *Revelations of Divine Love*, ed. Grace Warrack (London, 1901). It was this edition that rescued this mystic from obscurity. For a commentary, see *Julian of Norwich: Showings*, ed. E. Colledge and J. Walsh (London, 1979).

departure from the Oxford tradition. Previous Oxford theologians had spoken out against the wealth of monks and friars;
for example, Richard Fitzralph had done so sensationally in
the 1350s. It is true that there had not been such an open
attack on the bishops' wealth or the pope's power before
Wyclif's zest for controversy stirred up the 1370s; Fitzralph
had himself been an Irish archbishop, and he had hoped that
the pope might reform the friars. But we may be sure that
plenty of anticlerical tongues had wagged in Oxford.

Wyclif's last appearance before parliament as a government
spokesman, in October 1378, was to defend other government
agents who had caused a scandal by killing a prisoner who had
taken refuge in Westminster Abbey. But by now he was being
taken by his own arguments into territory even more scan-
dalous to the medieval mind. If all authority or 'lordship'
depended on 'grace' or the will of God (as Archbishop Fitzralph had himself argued), was it not possible to draw more
daring conclusions? Might not the only material support to
which the clergy were entitled be the offerings of their
parishioners year by year? Might not the confiscation of the
rest of the Church's wealth be in accordance with God's will —
and save the laity from all further taxes? And if a rich bishop
such as William of Wykeham might be deprived of 'lordship',
might not a worldly pope be deposed?

During 1378 Wyclif had to appear before William
Courtenay, then Bishop of London, to defend himself against
complaints made to the pope that he was a heretic, but
escaped with a formal reproof. His escape was a reminder that
the moral authority of a pope among the English was not now
what it had been. In the 1350s King John's homage to the pope
was formally revoked by Parliament. The act symbolized a
new resentment — with new reasons. From 1309 to 1377 the
popes lived in Avignon, in the south of France. They lived in
expensive luxury (although respectably). They were the
victims of an ever-growing absorption in everyday legal
business; petitioners who got what they wanted out of them
were pleased, those who did not were resentful, and no one
thought them semi-divine priest-kings, dwelling in a spiritual
world high above criticism. Above all, they lived in Avignon.

It was beautiful, it was free of riots and plagues – but it was not Rome. This period of self-imposed exile, the 'Babylonish Captivity', created what was virtually a French papacy at a time when the French were the enemies of the English. And now in 1378 the prestige of the papacy, but not its financial appetite, was further weakened when some of the cardinals, mostly French, elected Clement VII to reside in Avignon as a rival to Urban VI in Rome, whom the English continued to recognize. The Great Schism, a scandal which was to last until 1417, had begun. These were years when it was not easy to venerate popes.

In Oxford Wyclif continued to lecture – on the Bible; on the Church; on the papacy; on the Eucharist. The delivery of the last course of lectures brought about his condemnation by a narrow majority on a committee of fellow-theologians at Oxford – a condemnation which he defied by an openly heretical *Confession* in May 1381. His chief offence was to deny that the 'substance' of bread or wine could be annihilated when the priest said the Mass. This philosophical point was of wider interest when a public figure, such as he had become, opened up a subject which had been thought closed in Lanfranc's time three centuries before. Might he not be casting doubt on the whole idea of the Mass as a miraculous new sacrifice by the priest which secured the forgiveness of sinners living and dead? The laity of England had given the monasteries and parish churches countless tithes and endowments precisely in order that thousands upon thousands of Masses should be offered every day. Wyclif's controversial view was even more noteworthy in the year when society was shaken by the peasants' revolt. Whatever its theological merit, it was a tactical mistake. Next year he was forbidden by council in London to teach in his university or to preach. He retired to his rectory at Lutterworth in Leicestershire, though he did not cease to write belligerent pamphlets, and died on the last day of 1384.

He was a great simplifier – in this, resembling Dame Julian of Norwich. But he claimed no visions. What he taught was, he argued, what had always been the essence of Christianity.

He proclaimed the Church of the 'elect', those who had

been predestined by God to be saved through true belief; the Bible, interpreted literally, as God's saving word to true believers; Christ, truly man as well as God, the brother as well as the saviour of true believers. These were not in themselves strange ideas. All who followed the doctrine of St Augustine of Hippo emphasized predestination; this had been the special emphasis of Archbishop Thomas Bradwardine. All who objected to the over-rich allegorizing which was hiding the simple message of the Bible shared Wyclif's belief that the Bible was a history of real people and of their plain teachings; this had been the special belief of the Franciscans. All who rejoiced in the divine humanity of Christ – as so many of the carols did, as Dame Julian did after the 'showings' of the divine love in her experience – shared Wyclif's insistence that Christianity was about Christ. But what was unprecedented was the defiance with which he appealed to the Bible over the heads of popes and prelates and defended his convictions when they had been condemned by ecclesiastical authority; a defiance 'increasingly dominated by his obsession with the Church's betrayal of Christ'.[19]

In his retirement at Lutterworth, he was protected by the political authority of his aristocratic patrons. But he was undeterred in pursuing a path which ultimately alienated all patrons from his followers. Determined to make available to those who read no Latin the one visible authority to which he still appealed in religion, he inspired the translation of the whole Bible from Latin into English, a task never before undertaken. At least, that is what enemies and friends agreed after his death – but the actual making of the 'Wyclif Bible' is lost in obscurity. It seems that the work was begun by Nicholas of Hereford, Wyclif's most outspoken supporter at Oxford, while still at the university before 1380 (when he conceived the

[19] See Gordon Leff, 'John Wyclif: The Path to Dissent', in *Proceedings of the British Academy* (London, 1966), pp.143-180. For the background, see the studies of Gordon Leff in *Bradwardine and the Pelagians* (Cambridge, 1957), *Richard Fitzralph* (Manchester, 1963) and *Heresy in the Later Middle Ages* (2 vols., Manchester, 1967); and J. A. Robson, *Wyclif and the Oxford Schools* (Cambridge, 1961).

crazy idea of converting the pope, and was lucky to escape from the papal prison). John Purvey, Wyclif's secretary at Lutterworth, seems to have taken the lead in completing the work after his master's death. What part, if any, was played by Wyclif himself is not known. The first translation was woodenly literal but was soon radically revised and improved, to become the parent of all the versions which were to shape the faith and language of the English.[20]

We understand more of Wyclif if we compare him with William of Ockham, who had fascinated Oxford half a century before.

Wyclif was no disciple of Ockham's; he preferred to base his mature philosophy on the work of John Duns the Scot who had studied and taught at Oxford at the turn of the thirteenth and fourteenth centuries. (John Duns was the man who most unfairly gave rise to the word 'dunce' at a time when all medieval philosophy was despised, but in fact he was a deep and subtle thinker.) In philosopy Ockham was a brilliant radical. He charged into the debate about 'universals' (for example, mankind) in relation to individuals (for example, a man). Early in the twelfth century Adelard of Bath, despite all that he did to introduce Christians to Arab science, had also taught emphatically that 'universals' were ideas in the mind of God, ideas which the human mind could abstract out of its intuition of individual things; while Anselm of Canterbury, as we have already seen, had regarded an understanding of the reality of 'universals' as any intelligent man's first step along to the road to understanding belief in God. But now William of Ockham, a young Franciscan lecturing at Oxford in the early 1320s, denied that 'universals' could be known in this way. To him, they were mere signs attached by the mind of groupings of individuals; 'no universal exists in any way at all outside the knower's mind'. In the study of the individual lay wisdom.

This Oxford radical urged his startled contemporaries to desist from exploring what was theoretically possible in metaphysics and to concentrate on what could be known through

---

[20] See Margaret Deansley, *The Lollard Bible* (Cambridge, 1920), and S. L. Fristedt, *The Wyclif Bible*, 3 vols. (Stockholm, 1953-73).

experience (or, he added, inferred from the highly individual God's self-revelation). By implication he was calling men away from speculative controversies – on these he wielded 'Occam's razor' – back to the more scientific path explored by Robert Grosseteste and Roger Bacon. He was also calling men to faith; but it seemed to be faith of a new quality. He did not deny that theology could be a science based on what God had chosen to make known. What he did deny was that truths of religion such as the existence of God or the soul could be proved by reason alone; they were matters of faith. Nor could ethics be derived from what was known to be natural. A Christian's behaviour was a response to the revealed commandments of God – a matter of the individual's will, accepting God's will which might have been very different. What mattered decisively was not therefore the calm operation of reason, but an act by the will, which could not act except in trust, in faith. Faith was a leap.

His radicalism alarmed conservatives at Oxford, who in 1324 forced William to defend himself on charges of heresy at the papal court in Avignon. There the whole luxurious atmosphere so shocked the young Franciscan that he joined himself to the party of the 'Spirituals' who within his own order were resisting Pope John XXII. Eventually he fled to join the emperor Ludwig, the papacy's chief enemy, and for twenty years deployed his logical powers in the imperial political service – where he was the colleague of an even more outspoken antipapal writer, Marsilius of Padua.

William of Ockham wielded a great influence on the history of European philosophy (where his denials were developed into the system called Nominalism, from the teaching that 'universals' were mere names). He had much less influence on the history of English religion. He was not an innovating theologian; he was interested in improving the logic by which a man could accept the unchanging Faith. A mystery such as transubstantiation in the Mass he simply accepted (or so he declared) by an act of will. And until entangled in other controversies after leaving England, he was never involved in politics. He kept his radicalism within limits – within limits which Wyclif broke. In the end he was only the forerunner of a

theological revolution, just as Wyclif was only the forerunner
of Protestantism.[21]

GEOFFREY CHAUCER'S PILGRIMAGE

It is indeed tempting to regard Wyclif as the most significant
figure in fourteenth-century England. Much of this complicated century's story – political and social disturbances, protests against the corruption of the Church, quests for a deeper
personal religion – can be told so that his brave heresy sums it
up, and we can begin to talk about 'the decline' of the Middle
Ages in Church and State. Such an interpretation would, however, not do justice to the fourteenth-century facts.

One fact was that the Christian monarchy suffered no disastrous loss of power. More significant in the long run than the
drama of the depositions and deaths of Edward II and
Richard II when they had fallen foul of the nobility was the
fact that Henry IV retained most of Richard's civil servants
and most of Richard's political policy (Richard's behaviour in
the last two years, when driven almost mad by his wife Anne's
death and by the executions of his best friends, being scarcely
a policy). The monarchy carried on. And so did the Church.

Bishop Thomas Brunton freely attacked idle parish priests;
he once complained that some clergy were entrusted with the
care of a thousand souls who would not have been given the
care of a thousand apples. But he knew he could say such
things – to attentive congregations. More significant than the
protests against the worldliness of the monks and friars was the
fact that at the end of the century people were still begging for
their prayers, still making many gifts to them, still joining
their ranks. The numbers of monks and friars seem to have
stopped falling around 1375 and (although they never returned to their thirteenth-century level) to have begun climb-

---

[21] See P. Boehner, *Ockham: Philosophical Writings* (London, 1957), and
A. S. McGrade, *The Political Thought of William of Ockham* (Cambridge, 1974).

ing to a level which fell again only during the sixteenth century. The rate of increase appears to have been higher than the growth of the population as a whole. And more significant than any appearance of heresy was the continuing strength of orthodox English piety. The rebels of 1381 wanted to deliver the Church from feudalism, just as they wanted to deliver the king from traitors; that was all. And if the peasants accepted the Church's doctrine, so did the well-to-do. During the four-teenth century England's parish churches were adorned by more than a hundred thousand monumental brasses, of which some four thousand have survived to the present day. During this century three great towers surmounted by spires crowned Lincoln Cathedral; these were the skyscrapers of the still faithful Middle Ages. Above all, the exceptionally devout and articulate, from Duke Henry of Lancaster to Dame Julian of Norwich, were pilgrims rather than rebels.

The key interpreter of the age was, it seems clear, not John Wyclif but Geoffrey Chaucer, not the rebel but the observer who was in the end happy to conform.

Chaucer's attitude can easily be misunderstood because it was a part of his sophistication to keep himself out of trouble and even out of his poetry. Unlike his Wife of Bath, he accepted 'auctoritee'. The first record about him is the expenditure of seven shillings in London on 4 April 1357 on behalf of Countess Elizabeth, whose page he was; smart shoes, red and black breeches and a short cloak were bought for him. He received his last payment from the king's exchequer on 5 June 1400, having been in the service of the royal family or the government for almost the whole of the intervening period. His wife's sister was the mistress, and then the third wife, of a king's son, John of Gaunt; and his grandson married the Countess of Suffolk. He wrote a poem exhorting Richard II to combine courage with justice, but he was not so closely identified with Richard that he lost his head when the king's enemies were in power (as did his fellow-poet, Thomas Usk). Like his friend John Gower he accepted Henry IV's patronage happily enough. He was in London for the Peasants' Revolt of 1381 but his only reference to it is humorous, in his comic masterpiece, the *Nun's Priest's Tale*. In his poems he appears either as a wooden-headed dreamer who needs to have his own visions explained to him or the 'Chaucer' on the Canterbury road who contributes a ludicrous parody of Arthurian romances (*Sir Thopas*) and, when interrupted by the host, continues with the long, edifying but dull 'tale of Melibee and Dame Prudence' in prose translated from the French. Yet the real Chaucer obviously enjoyed the skill with which he told bawdy stories through the mouths of other pilgrims. It is therefore possible to misunderstand his attitude as being morally and religiously neutral. As one scholar has said: 'For all his intelligence and piety he has no spiritual vision. He never seems angry, and rarely condemns. He is no zealous reformer; he has neither the faith nor the optimism for that; he has too subtle a mind, is too convinced of the badness of the world. He maintains a well-bred, courtly, imperturbable front which nothing can shock'.[22]

But in the last analysis this unshockability is not unlike the compassion of the Creator in whom Chaucer believed – for John Dryden spoke truly when he said that Chaucer's toleration of humanity was the provision of 'God's plenty'. 'Dryden's metaphor is so apt', writes Trevor Whittock, 'because the abundance of humanity constantly reminds us of the Creator; and while each pilgrim will differently conceive Him and the reasons for his own journey, this pilgrimage is still a common one'.[23] The climax of the *Canterbury Tales* was the *Parson's Tale*, a straightforward treatise on the seven deadly sins with a call to penitence, compiled on the basis of three works in French.

Chaucer took his own leave with an epilogue giving thanks for 'our Lord Jhesu Christ, of whom procedeth al wit and al goodnesse' and asking for the reader's prayers. He made 'retracciouns' of his worldly books including 'the tales of Caunterbury thilke that sownen into (make for) synne' with 'many a song and many a leccherous lay'. One of the books he thus retracted was 'the book of Troilus', but *Troilus and Criseyde* itself ended with a picture of its tragic hero now in

---

[22] D. S. Brewer, *Chaucer* (London, 1953), p.137.

[23] *A Reading of the Canterbury Tales* (Cambridge, 1968), p.52.

heaven looking down at 'this litel spot of earth' and laughing
at those who mourned his death. Then Chaucer had addressed
his audience, presumably at the amorous court of Richard II
in the early 1380s:

> O yonge fresshe folkes, he or she,
> In which that love up groweth with your age,
> Repeyreth hom (return home) from worldly vanyte. . . .

When he felt that his own end was near, he rented a house
in the shadow of Westminster Abbey, where he was buried in
the transept which subsequently became the Poets' Corner. So
much for his hatred of monks! But perhaps the most per-
suasive evidence of his genuine piety was supplied when he was
at the height of his powers. His poetry is thoroughly medieval,
which means that its background cannot be understood without some knowledge of theology and church art.[24] Above all,
his poetry – for all his complete and glad acceptance of life –
shows 'the acceptance of full moral responsibilities; it involves
very sensitive and sure ethical discriminations and judgements'.[25] And these are the moral verdicts of a Christian who
prays. 'In his many prayers, especially to the Virgin, Chaucer
blends a joyful lyricism with splendour of thought and of
diction, as he does nowhere else. Humility and exaltation,
simplicity and magnificence, go hand in hand'.[26]

His attitude to human frailty was as profoundly Christian as
Dame Julian's. Many will reckon that it was far more Christian
than John Wyclif's bitterly uncharitable tirades, perhaps also
more Christian than William Langland's puritanism (Langland noticed only that pilgrims told lies to each other).
Chaucer was, of course, not a theologian; he earned his living
as a courtier, soldier, diplomat, controller of customs in
London and the king's clerk of works. Nor was he a mystic;
in the year that Dame Julian saw Christ bleed on the crucifix
in Norwich he had his own life-turning experience in

---

[24] This was stressed, probably over-stressed, in D. W. Robertson's *Preface
to Chaucer* (Princeton, N.J., 1962).

[25] John Speirs, *Chaucer the Maker* (London, 1951), p.204.

[26] D. S. Brewer, *op. cit*., p.151.

Florence, where during a brief visit he began his familiarity
with the new literature of Dante, Boccaccio and Petrarch. But
when he set himself to reproduce Boccaccio in English, he did
it without the Italian's contempt for human nature. In his
Troilus and Criseyde, which was derived from Boccaccio, both
the overwhelmed lover and the pretty young widow who for a
time is faithful to him are portrayed with understanding and
respect. So far from being lewd, they have to be pushed into
bed together by Criseyde's lecherous uncle Pandarus (in Boccaccio, a mere go-between) with the plea that it is raining. So
far from being contemptibly fickle, Criseyde is allowed to
show us why life and love must go on; she needs someone else
to live with and to love during the prolonged absence of
Troilus. Troilus is a suitable mouthpiece for philosophy which
Chaucer has derived from Boethius:

> Love, that of erthe and se hath governaunce,
> Love, that his hestes (hosts) hath in hevenes hye. . . .
> Love, that knetteth (knits) lawe of compaignie,
> And couples doth in virtu for to dwelle. . . .

Chaucer wrote this long poem, which has often been called
the first English novel, using leisure from his supervision of the
collection of customs in London. He had already tried his
hand at a number of poems which show his ambition to do in
English what several poets had already done in France (most
notably those whose work he translated in his *Romaunt of the
Rose*). His own earlier poems were all in praise of love − to him
an inexhaustible theme, mostly amusing, sometimes serious,
sometimes sad. It was about love, and only by implication
about the poet's trade, that he wrote 'the lyf so short, the craft
so long to lerne'. The poems have a set pattern: the reading of
a book, the sleep, the dream, the supernatural interpreter of
the dream as a celebration of love. And they have a style: as
aristocratic as *Sir Gawain and the Green Knight* but twice as
elegant because now freed from the prison-house of alliter-
ation inherited from the Anglo-Saxons. In his *Boke of the
Duchess* he mourns for Blanche, John of Gaunt's first wife,
dead in her early twenties. It is all conventional, but even here
she is alive:

I saw hir daunce so comlily,
Carole and singe so swetely,
Laugh and pleye so womanly,
And loke so debonairly.

The *Parlement of Fowles* (probably written to celebrate the bretrothal of Richard II to Anne of Bohemia) is the most attractive work of that early period. It develops a tradition which had made a brief appearance in English under Henry II with the writing of *The Owl and the Nightingale*; there the two birds debate their rival merits and agree to submit to the judgement of 'Master Nicholas of Guildford' (probably the author). In Chaucer's mind there could be no question about the superiority of the nightingale. He was a troubadour of sweet lovers in the spring, singing as they sang in sunnier France; but he would sing in English. In 1363 English was used for the first time in the chancellor's speech opening Parliament. Chaucer would use it for a debate about humanity's most attractive theme.[27]

It seems, however, that when he moved from the city of London out to Greenwich in 1386 he resolved to write 'som comedye' about English life — and about life slightly lower in the social scale. He abandoned his collection of tales called the *Legend of Good Women* because his imagination had been fired by a more mixed group. His *Canterbury Tales* could not be about the peasants; Geoffrey Chaucer (a London wine merchant's son) did not know them. But it was about a splendid variety of middle class types — 'sondry folke, by adventure yfalle in felaweshipe'. As he watched the pilgrims to Canterbury passing near his Greenwich home, an idea caught fire in the poet's mind: the idea of the human richness of Christian England.[28]

We are struck by the number of rogues on this pilgrimage, particularly rogues in the full-time service of the Church. Prioress Eglentyne (Sweet Briar), the monk and the friar have

---

[27] See C. S. Lewis, *The Allegory of Love* (Oxford, 1936), and C. Muscatine, *Chaucer and the French Tradition* (Berkeley, Cal., 1957).

[28] See D. R. Howard, *The Idea of the Canterbury Tales* (Berkeley, Cal., 1976).

all forgotten the austere ideals of their orders. The nun is a coy, delicately living, sentimental spinster, devoted to 'smale houndes', compassionate to mice; the monk a country gentleman dressed up to look like a monk (more expensively than most laymen could afford), the bell on his bridle as loud as any chapel bell. The friar 'knew the tavernes wel in every toun' — and the women. The lesser officials of the Church, the 'summoner' to the archdeacon's court and the 'pardoner' peddling ecclesiastical indulgences and fake relics, more directly trade on people's credulity. They are almost totally repulsive; 'of his visage children were aferd'. But we should also notice the saints. There is the knight who embodies the ideals of the Age of Chivalry — true, perfect and a gentleman:

> He was a verray parfit gentil knyght.

There is the 'clerk of Oxenford' who would prefer 'at his beddes heed twenty books, clad in black or red' to a rich wardrobe. There is the 'poure persoun of a toun' who preached Christ's message 'but first he folwed it hymselve'. And there is the parson's brother the ploughman, a hero to Chaucer in common with Langland:

> Lyvynge in pees and parfit charitee,
> God loved he best with al his hoole herte.

Although medieval readers are likely to have admired the preaching, no doubt the main attraction of the *Canterbury Tales* has always lain in the tales told by the sinners — by those who would say with the Wife of Bath that Christ's message was not for them:

> He spak to them that wolde live parfitly;
> And lordlinges, by your leve, that am not I.

After the courtly tragedy of fighting over a girl in Ancient Greece told by the knight, we are all ears for the ribald anecdotes of village life exchanged (with insults) by the miller and the reve. These are some of the tales of which the dying Chaucer repented; but as soon as we meet the rich old Oxford carpenter's wife, eighteen-year-old Alisoun, we know that we are going to like her while we laugh at the bedroom farce

which results from her being 'wylde and yong'. Even more do
we relish that great lover of life, the Wife of Bath, although
she has worn down five husbands.

For Chaucer the world is no monastery. The world lives by
the interplay of the sexes and by the making of money, and the
shipman is not the only pilgrim of whom this is true:

> Of nyce conscience took he no keep.

And this is more than a chuckling matter, for Chaucer has
noticed much more than the look on the Wife of Bath as she
inspects the parish clerk's legs in the procession behind her
fourth husband's bier. He knows, as the merchant's tale
demonstrates, what is the horror of old Januarie's loveless
marriage. He knows – and gives us the pardoner's tale in order
to make sure we know – what moral degradation results from
avarice. And we have no reason to suppose that he had a
basically flippant attitude towards the public violence of his
time. On the contrary, his poem called *The Former Age* shows
his seriously conservative values:

> For in oure dayes nis (nothing) but covetyse,
> Doublenesse, and treasoun, and envye,
> Poyson, mansalughtre, and mordre in sondry wyse.

But he is not one to condemn those who share his own flesh
and blood. He does not write off the young squire who is 'as
fressh as is the month of May' merely because the boy is at
present 'a lovyere and a lusty bacheler'. He expects the boy to
marry – how many of these tales are about marriage! – and to
end up as a knight like his father; or at least like the pot-
bellied, red-faced franklin whose tale is about married bliss.

Even the pardoner's sins of hyprocrisy and deceit – which
(in accordance with the Christian tradition) Chaucer regards
as much worse than any lust of the flesh – do not finally put a
man outside the common pilgrimage. The host insults the
pardoner after the nauseating smugness of his tale (offered as
a 'moral' tale 'though myself be a ful vicious man'), but is persuaded by the knight to kiss him as a sign of peace. When the
pardoner is pardoned it may be the most Christian moment of
the fourteenth century. And so they ride on, until the sun

begins to set and the parson is persuaded to preach his sermon – for, as the host declares,

Thou shouldest knytte up wel a greet mateere.

Chaucer never described the arrival at the shrine – or the return journey, although in the prologue he had the host, Harry Bailey, ordain that each of the pilgrims is to tell two tales on the journey back as well as two on the road to Canterbury. He no doubt visited Canterbury, where in the 1390s the master mason Henry Yevele (his colleague at the court of Richard II) was building that forest of stone, the Perpendicular nave of the cathedral: 'the supreme triumph of English architecture, which is to say, of English art.'[29] But the 'greet mateere' for Chaucer was the *journey* of people; he never aspired to be a Dante, majestically eloquent about destinations. His ambition was so to describe these people's journey that the English language (which he knew to be changing rapidly in his time, as several passages of his poetry show explicitly) would make another great advance. That is why, when presenting him in a twentieth-century book, it is surely right to quote his words without modernization; it is a tribute to what he did for English. 'Chaucer', writes Ian Robinson, 'recognized the different powers of English and brought them together. He did not, as used occasionally to be thought, himself compose the English language; but he did make it, with the help of his contemporaries and his readers, the language of a great literature'. English was to be no longer the less-than-French dialect of a region, or the less-than-Latin language of sermons and private devotions. Specially in the London or court dialect which Chaucer used, it was to be the language of a great people. We owe to the *Canterbury Tales* an 'extraordinary feat of genius': the 'seeing England whole' which is also 'the creation of a national literature'.[30]

That was the advance which Chaucer most desired. He did, however, also notice that these people were on a pilgrimage.

---

[29] John Harvey, *English Cathedrals*, p.98.

[30] Ian Robinson, *Chaucer and the English Tradition* (Cambridge, 1972), pp.283-4.

He did not attribute a deeply religious motive to most of them, but he knew what such a motive might be. When his mood in contemplating the world was 'her is non hoom, her nis but wildernesse', he embodied the spirit of a sincere pilgrim's progress in his short *balade* called *Truth*:

> Forth, pilgrim, forth! Forth, beste, out of thy stal!
> Know thy contree, look up, thank God of al;
> Hold the heye (high) way, and lat thy gost (spirit) thee lede;
> And trouthe thee shal delivere, it is no drede (dread).

CHAPTER SEVEN

THE SUDDEN STORM

St. George's Chapel and the Castle at Windsor.

A SECURE CHURCH

Right up to the 1530s the Church of popes and monks, the Mass and the pilgrimage, the cathedral and the hermitage, seemed eternal in England.

In telling the history of the so-called 'decline' of the Middle Ages it is possible to put all the emphasis on the protests, taking them as preparations for Protestantism. Almost any noise can be interpreted as a rumble of the coming storm. In 1427 Pope Martin V rebuked Cardinal Henry Beaufort for the arrest of a papal tax gatherer. In 1528 Simon Fish, a London barrister who had fled to Antwerp after daring to take the leading part in an anticlerical play, wrote a much discussed pamphlet. It was entitled *A Supplication for Beggars*, and Henry VIII is said to have kept it 'in his bosom' for several days. Fish urged that the time had come to end papal taxation once and for all; to end a situation in which the English clergy, one-four-hundredth of the population, owned a third of the land. He wrote, as he acted, with gusto. From the century between these incidents in 1427 and 1528, many complaints could be gathered. Englishmen protested against papal taxation, for that took good money out of England; against papal appointments of foreigners to lucrative posts in the English Church; against priests who drew incomes from parishes where they did not reside; against the exemption of the clergy from the ordinary courts; against abuses which laymen experienced in the ecclesiastical courts; against the far too frequent use of the penalty of excommunication (a penalty which was an ecclesiastical court's only weapon when, for example, one of the parties in a dispute about a will failed to appear in court). These were complaints which the House of Commons took up when it met in November 1529, and so began the 'Reformation Parliament'.

Sometimes the complaints were bitter. Among the grumbles about the tithes due to the parish priests a particular resentment accompanied the custom by which a priest claimed a 'mortuary' or one of the possessions of a dead man in lieu of unpaid tithes. The notorious case of Richard Hunne, found hanging in the Bishop of London's prison in 1514 and subsequently burned by the Church as a suicidal heretic, had begun with a quarrel over a mortuary. This merchant tailor had refused to give the local rector the cloth under which his dead baby son had been carried to church.[1] And all the time there was, no doubt, resentment among the laity at the wealth of many ecclesiastics, who had secured to themselves possessions a great deal larger than that cloth from an infant's funeral.

But while there were all these protests at abuses, the system

---

[1] See A. Ogle, *The Tragedy of the Lollards Tower* (Oxford, 1949).

itself seemed secure, any storm remote. Among the literate,
piety was still supreme; of the 349 titles of books printed between 1468 and 1530 and now in the British Library, 176 are
religious. Among the people (who remained mostly illiterate),
the Robin Hood of the late medieval Midlands ballads was admired for his daring as he extracted money out of fat abbots –
but even this fearless anticlerical had to have his own fat
chaplain, Friar Tuck. English piety at these different social
levels was much boasted about by a nation as patriotic as it
was orthodox. In 1427 Pope Martin's letter was addressed to
one of the wealthiest men in that world, a bishop of royal
blood who was also Chancellor of England. The pope's com-
plaint was not that the ill-treatment of his representative
proved that the English were determined to ruin the Church
but that the incident had occurred in a land 'which considers
itself better than all other Christian nations in devotion, faith
and the worship of God'.[2]

A century later England was still the same, content to live
and think within the sound of church bells. Even in London,
whose citizens were often ready to believe the worst of the
clergy, many pious gifts to the Church were still being made.[3]
A recent study of the diocese of Lincoln concludes that 'few
Tudor parishioners were as anticlerical as Simon Fish' –
because according to these parishioners' complaints to bishops
or archdeacon, 'the rectors, vicars or curates who served them
seem to have exhibited few of the enormities described by
Simon Fish'.[4] Certainly the clergy were not as a class provoca-
tively rich; the average net stipend of a vicar in Lincoln
diocese in 1526 was under £7. Another study of local church
life concludes that in Essex – a county much influenced by the
lingering effects of the Lollardy started by John Wyclif,
burdened by monasteries which seemed second-rate and

---

[2] *The English Church and the Papacy in the Middle Ages*, ed. C. H.
Lawrence (London, 1965), p.235.

[3] See J. A. F. Thomson, 'Piety and Charity in Late Medieval London',
Journal of Ecclesiastical History (Cambridge, 1964), pp.178-195.

[4] Margaret Bowker, *Secular Clergy in the Diocese of Lincoln, 1495-1520*
(Cambridge, 1968), p.180.

futile, and soon to be sympathetic with the new excitements of the German Protestantism of Martin Luther – traditional piety flourished mightily in the parishes early in the sixteenth century. 'Many people were passionately devoted to religion. The parish church provided not only for the religious but also for the social life of the people, and was bound up with the day-to-day administration of the local community's life.'[5] For the more remote and conservative areas such as Lancashire, the Durham region or Cornwall, the detailed evidence to the same effect is still stronger. England was overwhelmingly Catholic.[6]

The only tax which the laity had to pay to Rome was Peter's Pence, amounting to a mere £200 a year. The clergy were indeed taxed by the papacy. The 'tenth' which they had to pay was the pioneer of the modern income tax. Bishops had to pay 'annates' equivalent to their first year's revenue. But since they professed that the papacy was essential to the Church, the clergy could not well argue that Rome had no financial needs – and anyway, they were not beggared. The annual total of all the taxes they sent to Rome came to under £5,000 – only about £1,000 more than the income of the Bishop of Winchester and some £30,000 less than the estimated income of Cardinal Thomas Wolsey. The clergy could afford to produce a large sum when in 1500 Pope Alexander VI called for one more crusade – and a much larger sum (over £100,000) when, just over thirty years later, Henry VIII threatened them with the penalties in the statute of *Praemunire* because they had received the pope's legate (Wolsey) without licence from the Crown. The real question was not about clerical taxation. It was whether, taxed or untaxed, some of the clergy were too rich. To that question the powerful laity of England in the 1530s returned a decisive

---

[5] J. E. Oxley, *The Reformation in Essex to the Death of Mary* (Manchester, 1965), p.1.

[6] See Christopher Haigh, *Reformation and Resistance in Tudor Lancashire* (Cambridge, 1975); for Durham M. E. James, *Family, Lineage and Civil Society* (Oxford, 1974); A. L. Rowse, *Tudor Cornwall* (revised, London, 1969).

yes – although this was not an answer which helped the lay 'beggars' on whose behalf Simon Fish had claimed to be writing. However, if some of the late medieval clergy prospered excessively, most of the late medieval laity were themselves neither paupers nor basically hostile to the clergy. As the Act of 1532 which threatened the pope with loss of his revenue from England declared, both the king and the people liked to think of themselves as good Catholics. They claimed to be 'as obedient, devout, catholic and humble children of God and Holy Church as any people be within any realm christened'. Basically it was because of this general acceptance of the Catholic religion that the income of the Church, surveyed in the incomplete *Valor Ecclesiasticus* of 1535, came to £320,180. Probably the complete figure was not far short of £400,000, at a time when a labourer's average annual income seems to have been about two and a half pounds.

THE LOLLARDS

The fate of the Lollards after John Wyclif's stirring protests shows both the power and the popularity of Catholicism in late medieval England. More than seventy Lollards were burned at the stake in public under the statutes of 1401 and 1414. Floggings were far more frequent; these and public penance were the normal punishments for first offenders. Such penalties must have alarmed anyone tempted to heresy who was not already terrified by the thought of the everlasting punishment widely believed to await all heretics. The persecution was particularly effective in frightening off people such as university theologians or Members of Parliament, who in the fourteenth century had been prominent supporters of Wyclif. As late as 1395 a group of knights had put their names to 'Twelve Conclusions', a Lollard manifesto. As late as 1411 Archbishop Arundel had aroused fierce opposition in Oxford when he clumsily tried to stamp out the Wyclif tradition there. But ten years later Oxford had almost forgotten its loyalty to its dead teacher and the Lollards (the word was Dutch and meant 'babblers') had gone underground. Wyclif's own secretary, John Purvey, and his Bible translator, Nicholas of Hereford, recanted. Another of his most prominent Oxford associates, Philip Repton, ended up as Bishop of Lincoln. Such leadership as the Lollards possessed was almost all uneducated; a hunted sect, they produced no system to rival either the organization or the theology of the Catholic Church. In these circumstances the courageous persistence of humble folk in their religious convictions despite the prestige and power of their persecutors is, surely, both surprising and moving.

However, modern scholars who have investigated the fragmentary records that remain conclude that one of the chief problems of the Lollards right through the fifteenth century was their unpopularity. The public seems to have been genuinely shocked by their perversity and not at all distressed by their deaths. The explanation seems to be not only that heretics might be flogged or burned but also that heretics were thought to be antisocial. Fuel for the fire of anti-Lollard panic was provided when the movement's greatest lay leader, Sir John Oldcastle (Lord Cobham), formerly a friend of the king's, was foolish enough to lead a rebellion in 1414. There were various other outbreaks, bringing back memories of the Peasants' Revolt of 1381; but like Oldcastle's crazy attempt to enter London armed one January evening, they were easily suppressed. Another conspiracy was discovered in 1431.

In August 1407 William Thorpe was brought to trial before Archbishop Arundel in Saltwood Castle. His account of the trial, no doubt edited in his own favour, survives. It contains an interesting tribute to John Wyclif. Thorpe remembered how 'he was holden of full many men the greatest clerk that they knew then living' and the archbishop admitted that he was 'a great clerk and many men held him a perfect liver'. The conversation rambled. At one stage Arundel was defending pilgrimages and the use of music during them. 'When one of them that goeth barefoot striketh his toe upon a stone and hurteth him sore and maketh him bleed, it is well done that he or his fellow begin then a song or else take out a bagpipe.' At various points this aristocratic archbishop showed that he was human, and it is possible that in the end Thorpe escaped with his life. But Arundel's sometimes patronizing, often irritated, contempt for the Lollards expressed fifteenth-century public opinion. 'Ye presume that the Lord hath chosen you only for to preach as faithful disciples and special followers of Christ.' It did not take much for such bafflement to harden into persecution.[7]

The tragedy was that this bitter atmosphere, where revolution was pitted against reaction, made reform virtually impossible. K. B. McFarlane has pointed out that in the previous age there were many signs pointing to reform. 'The chief characteristic of English religious life in the fourteenth century is the growth of moral fervour among the laity. It was inspired and whipped up by the sermons and discourses of mendicants and other poor preachers and it infected the clergy also, but its strength was derived from its success among laymen. . . . The contemporary spirit in religion was puritan, biblical, evangelical, anarchic, anti-sacerdotal, hostile to the established order in the Church. Hence there was widespread sympathy with at least the moral content of the Lollard teaching.'[8] The doctrinal content of Lollardy was of course more difficult for a conservative (or indifferent) public to swallow, but the emphasis on the simplicity and transcendence of God, the opening of the Bible to the laity and the insistence on biblical preaching were positive proposals to which the Church might have listened to its own great advantage. But because reform became branded as heretical and treasonable, the Church made none of the adjustments which might have been expected in the earlier stages of Wyclif's career. No Bible in the language of the people was authorized in England until 1537. Equivalent translations were allowed and widely used on the Continent, and Archbishop Arundel promised that

---

[7] *Fifteenth Century Prose and Verse*, ed. A. W. Pollard (London, 1903), pp.97-174. See also J. A. F. Thomson, *The Later Lollards, 1414-1520* (Oxford, 1965); A. G. Dickens, *Lollards and Protestants in the Diocese of York, 1509-1558* (Oxford, 1959); Claire Cross, *Church and People 1450-1660* (London, 1976), pp.9-52.

[8] K. B. McFarlane, *Lancastrian Kings and Lollard Knights* (Oxford, 1972), pp.224-5.

something would be done for the English. But nothing was done. No spiritual or theological renewal based on lay knowledge of the Bible was accepted. Renewal was not going to be accepted on any other intellectual basis, either. This was shown by the fate of Reginald Pecock.

This very able and eloquent Welshman formed the ambition to refute the Lollard heresies. He would do so, however, not by the exercise of ecclesiastical power, not even by an appeal to the Fathers of the Church or to texts of Holy Scripture, but – as Anselm had done in his day – by reasoned theology, by what he called the 'doom of reason'. Believing that these issues were of concern to all, he wrote mainly in English, not Latin, although his choice of language meant that he had to invent many new words to translate the Latin technical terms. His theology would take an honest account of difficulties in the orthodox positions. He admitted, for example, that Moses had been the editor rather than the sole author of the books attributed to him; that the apostles had not written the Apostles' Creed; that the Roman emperor Constantine had not given the papacy its vast estates in Italy. He expounded mysteries such as Christ's descent into hell after his crucifixion in such a way as to suggest that they were mysterious. He summed up his own doctrine in a 'new English creed', which has not survived.

To this self-imposed duty of authorship, with all the necessary study, he gave the best of his life. He was financed from a variety of sources – as a Fellow of Oriel College, Oxford; as a rector in Gloucestershire; in the mastership of a small college in London recently founded by a rich merchant, Richard Whittington of nursery rhyme fame. He continued to write books while Bishop first of St Asaph and then of Chichester. But his literary labours won him no reward. There were complaints that he neglected preaching and pastoral work – complaints which he unwisely answered by arguing in public that a bishop was not obliged to be a preacher. There was alarm because he wrote in English. Had he confined himself to Latin he might have been given the considerable liberty which scholars still enjoyed for their speculations, but by working in a language which the ordinary man might

understand he exposed himself to the charge of unsettling the
people's faith with intellectual doubts. Yet the man in the
medieval street certainly could not have understood these
books, had he ever come across them in handwritten copies.
They were far too closely argued, and far too heavily packed
with technical terms, to appeal to the laity whose ignorance of
theology was happy and whose devotional reading presup-
posed a religion of the heart not of the mind. The radical
courage of these books, the seriousness and toughness of
their argumentation, might have appealed to middle-class
Lollards — only, Pecock happened to be a bishop of a Church
which in this period was burning heretics, and his writing was
intended to help the burners rather than the burned. He was
very energetically supplying theology to a market which did
not exist; and which would have greatly disturbed his fellow-
bishops by its existence, had it existed.

He might have been dismissed as a scholar who lacked the
common touch. But his character was more controversial than
that. He was an arrogant man ('this peacock', said his critics);
perhaps he had to be, to risk so many experiments. The
habitual tone of self-praise to be found in his books, and
presumably also in his conversation, probably did as much as
any sentence in his voluminous writings to bring about a sen-
sation in 1457. He was tried for heresy by a court under the
Archbishop of Canterbury — the only English bishop to be sub-
jected to this ordeal in the Middle Ages. He apologized and
retracted. His opinions, he said, had always been tentative
and subject to the teaching of the Church, although the essential charge against him was that he had denied or ignored 'the
auctorite and determinacioun of our Mudder Holie Church'.
He thus saved himself from the stake and Pope Calixtus III
ordered his restitution to Chichester. On that pope's death he
was, however, forced to resign and was confined to a cell in a
monastery without books or writing materials. There he soon
died (in 1461), perhaps of boredom.[9]

Knowing how the sudden storm that was to break in the

---

[9] See V. H. H. Green, *Bishop Reginald Pecock* (Cambridge, 1945), and E.
F. Jacob in *Later Medieval Essays* (Manchester, 1968), pp.1-34.

1530s was to damage many things which poor Bishop Pecock, his judges and even the Lollards themselves all held sacred, we read the religious history of the fifteenth century as a tragedy – the tragedy of a wasted opportunity, in a Catholic Church hastening to catastrophe. However, that was not how things looked at the time.

A POPULAR RELIGION

Late medieval England knew a real, although patchy, prosperity. Although some of the traditional cities – York or Lincoln, Norwich or Winchester – were by now decaying, and the 'enclosures' of agricultural land to make pastures for sheep began to reduce rural employment substantially from the 1480s, it has been estimated that the wages of a builder's labourer had more purchasing power in the fifteenth century than they were to have again until the 1860s.[10] Although the population seems to have been inadequate to the economy for much of the fifteenth century (this helped to keep wages high, but more than one foreign tourist noticed the vast stretches of uncultivated land), the evidence suggests that after 1475 it began increasing – and that unemployment did not become a major problem until about 1525. In 1497 the Venetian ambassador sent home a report on the English economy. It seemed to him the richest country in Europe. He had noticed silver tankards in the inns (although admittedly without English wine to put into them) and fifty-two goldsmiths' shops in one street in London. The people, he said, were well-fed and well-dressed. With 'incredible courtesy' they kept their hats off while talking with each other, although they did not make public the 'very violent' sexual passions which they were believed to enjoy in private. They were fiercely proud of

---

[10] See R. B. Dobson, 'Urban Decline in Late Medieval England', in *Transactions of the Royal Historical Society* (London, 1977), pp.1-22. But a summary of recent research into prices and wages is provided by C. S. L. Davies, *Peace, Print and Protestantism* (London, 1976), pp.334-8.

England and if they saw a handsome foreigner would say, 'he looks like an Englishman'.[11]

The Catholic Church, triumphant over heresy, prospered with the bulk of the people. The Italian visitor just quoted was under the impression that the English attended Mass daily. That was not widely true, but a comprehensive modern survey of the clergy's life and work during the 'decline' of the Middle Ages concluded that 'the Church in England continued to pursue its old paths, an unchangeable and apparently impregnable institution, mechanical no doubt in its processes, restrained from beneficial innovations by the prevailing spirit of legalism, but presenting a calm and unruffled front to the political chaos and social change'.[12] A more recent study presents a similar picture of thousands of complacent clergy.[13]

The trouble was that most of the priests were not fully professional, for no one thought it necessary to train them for preaching or pastoral work. They were, on the whole, not unspiritual (so far as we know); but they did not produce any English equivalent to Thomas a Kempis, whose *Imitation of Christ* was beginning to cross over from the Continent into a few English hearts. They were, on the whole, not completely illiterate, and the number of graduates was steadily increasing; but the evidence surviving suggests that not many of them owned Bibles, presumably because not many of them were thoroughly at home in Latin. Many of them were to accept all the religious revolutions of the sixteenth century – much to the disgust of later Roman Catholics and Protestants. When the storm broke in the 1530s only one bishop (John Fisher) did not bend; and the most effective role in the theological defence of the Church was left to a layman, Sir Thomas More. More had once written that the clergy on his dream-island, Utopia, were elected by the citizens, were married if they so wished, and could be women. The Utopian priests were 'of exceeding holiness and therefore very few'.

---

[11] J. R. Lander, *The Wars of the Roses* (London, 1965), pp.310-313.

[12] A. H. Thompson, *The English Clergy and their Organization in the Later Middle Ages* (Oxford, 1947), p.6.

[13] Peter Heath, *The English Parish Clergy on the Eve of the Reformation* (London, 1969).

If we want to penetrate the spiritual life of this conservatively Christian England, we do not turn to its leaders or to its theologians. We have to go instead to its music, to its drama and to the churches themselves.

During the fifteenth century the most lovely poems in English were not the verbose efforts of the official poets who were, at least in their own eyes, Chaucer's successors. The best poems were the carols—no longer, it seems, usually danced but now sung by a soloist and chorus polyphonically, to tunes which for the most part seem to have been specially composed. About five hundred fifteenth-century lyrics of this sort have survived, with about a hundred and thirty musical settings.[14] We catch the reverent wonder at the heart of orthodoxy:

> A God and yet a man?
>   A mayde and yet a mother?
> Witt wonders what witt can
>   Conceave this or the other.
>
> A god, and can he die?
>   A dead man, can he live?
> What witt can well replie?
>   What reason reason give?

We are swept into the festivity:

> Nowell, nowell, nowell, nowell.
> Who is there that singeth so,
>   Nowell, nowell, nowell?
> I am here Sire Christesmasse.
> Wellcome, my Lord, Sir Christemasse,
> Wellcome to us all, both more and less.
>   Come near, nowell.

We are moved by the tenderness:

> Lullay, myn lykyng, my dere sone,
>   my swetyng,
> Lullay my dere herte, my owen
>   dere derlyng.

---

[14] See *Religious Lyrics of the Fifteenth Century*, ed. Carleton Brown (Oxford, 1939).

And we are thrilled by the optimism:

> Now is wele and all thing aright
> And Christ is come as a trew knight
>   For our broder is king of might. . . .

Music appears to have been the art in which the English most excelled. In Latin church music John Dunstable, for example, became a composer of European stature while musician to an English general, the Duke of Bedford. This was the period when organs became widely used in parishes and when the professional choirs of the great churches rose to unprecedented standards under musicians of the calibre of Robert Fairfax, organist of St Alban's Abbey and a composer used by Henry VIII. The world of church music which was to be enriched in the Elizabethan age by the genius of Tye, Tallis and Byrd was already singing.

In drama, the performances of the biblical plays developed – too far for some puritan tastes, so that the 'morality' plays such as the famous *Everyman* (itself a translation from the Dutch) were introduced, putting the ethical sermon on the stage. The earliest to have survived, *The Castle of Perseverance* written about 1425, put Man in a castle besieged by the personified vices. The clergy seem to have thought such scenes safer than popular interpretations of the Bible, but here, too, dramatists and actors could be lively. At the end of the fifteenth century a priest, Henry Medwall, who had already written a morality play (*Nature*), wrote England's first secular drama, telling of the loves of Lucres and her maid. Probably it was Christmas entertainment for the household of the Archbishop of Canterbury. From personified vices or virtues to real girls turned out to be no long step, but the road was also short if taken in the opposite direction; a non-ecclesiastical play could still be highly moral. Even in the sceptical Christopher Marlowe's *Doctor Faustus*, completed in the spring of 1589, may be heard many echoes of the spiritual drama of Everyman on his road to death and judgement a century before. The first English historical drama, John Bale's *King Johan*, was written by a Protestant (born in 1495) who also produced three plays on biblical themes and a morality play. In *King Johan* – where King John is praised as a Christian hero fighting popery – characters appear such as Sedition and Civil Order. Such was the tradition behind Shakespeare's history plays, which are always strongly moral in their plots and constitute the most memorable expression of Protestant England's sense of continuity with the English Middle Ages.

To this day, if we use our eyes in English churches we see proof of how assured and popular the Catholic Church looked as the Reformation drew near. 'In the fifteenth century,' a modern authority writes, 'hardly a parish but did something to its own church, whether by popular effort or through private enterprise of landowner or merchant. Those parts of the country which maintained a relatively high level of prosperity, particularly in Somerset and East Anglia, lavished money on fine builders' work and enrichment of every sort. . . . The screenwork, the paintings and statues, the benches – commonly in use for the first time – the stalls, the roof carvings, exist in incredible variety to tell the tale. The level of handicraft very seldom dropped below excellence: sturdy construction allied to high finish has seldom been maintained for so long on such a high plane.'[15]

Churches in the Perpendicular style such as St Mary's, Warwick (with its superb chapel memorializing the Beauchamp earls), or the churches of Chipping Campden, Fairford and Northleach in the Cotswolds, and Long Melford, Lavenham and Cavendish in East Anglia, or the chancel of Holy Trinity, Stratford-upon-Avon, where Shakespeare was to be buried, still stand and still delight. Largely paid for out of the profits of the wool and cloth trades, they are the most conspicuous achievements of a wider movement which solidly testifies to the vitality of religion in the late medieval parishes. England was, of course, already covered with churches – with too many, for during the fifteenth century many churches in abandoned villages, or in towns which had never fully recovered from the Black Death's ravages, were in ruins. The existing wealth of ecclesiastical architecture at the time is

---

[15] John Harvey, *The Perpendicular Style* (London, 1978), p.160.

suggested vividly by the notebook of a retired businessman, the first of England's enthusiastic amateur antiquarians, who between 1478 and his death in 1485 rode all over England, picking up bits of history, turning over libraries (although he had only one good eye), measuring innumerable churches by his own elderly paces.[16] But in thousands of parish churches there was new work showing the character of the English Middle Ages in their so-called 'decline' – the towers, often magnificent; the belfries, so impressive to the ear; the capacious porches where contracts were solemnized and weddings begun; the little rooms above the porches, where often boys were taught; the roofs (specially East Anglia's angel-roofs or the 'wagon' ceilings of the west country) which exhibited the carpenter's skill in an age when even rich men's houses were still being made mainly of wood; the foliage, beasts or people carved on the 'finials' at the ends of the newly introduced benches; the charming and often humorous misericords under the seats in the choir stalls; the elaborate font-covers and rood-screens; the chapels maintained competitively by rival gilds of tradesmen; the large naves, paid for by the people of the parish and used for the preaching they relished; the rood-lofts where the musicians would gather with their instruments; the many wall paintings and banners; the portrayal of prominent parishioners with a considerable naturalism on brasses, on alabaster effigies and in the picture-windows (where the invention of 'silver stain' helped the portraiture and added to the general atmosphere of a golden glory); the chantries where the really rich could be remembered by name (it seems that there were about three thousand of these endowed in parish churches or cathedrals); the great windows letting in the daylight from an England which seemed stable in its religious and social order despite the minor disorders on which historians, looking round for troublesome incidents, have concentrated too gloomily.

If we ask what inspired these men and women to lavish such wealth on their parish churches – or on the colleges of chantry priests, the hospitals and the schools which were other impor-

---

[16] See *William Worcestre: Itineraries*, ed. J. H. Harvey (Oxford, 1969).

tant foundations of this period – we can in many cases turn to their wills, reinforced by other surviving evidence of their attitudes. We find that they hoped to enter eternal bliss through the prayers of those on earth whose good will they had secured by their benefactions. In the letters of the fifteenth-century Paston family in Norfolk we meet a grasping and ruthless clan, but one which always takes it for granted that money spent on funerals and Masses is well spent. It has been truly said that 'almost all forms of medieval philanthropy had the purchase of prayers as their ultimate goal'.[17]

THE UNIVERSITIES

In 1429 the intellectual battle against heresy still seemed paramount in Oxford. Richard Fleming, Bishop of Lincoln, in that year founded Lincoln College for graduates prepared to equip themselves for this fight by the study of orthodox theology. In the previous year he had what were supposed to be John Wyclif's bones dug up and burned, and the ashes cast into a nearby river. But when Henry Chichele, Archbishop of Canterbury, founded All Souls College in Oxford nine years later, a slightly more worldly note could be struck. Although most of the forty fellows were to pursue theological studies, sixteen were to be lawyers. The doctrinal crisis had passed and in the mind of an eminently effective administrator the needs of administration on the basis of law could be given priority.

Not long after these contrasting foundations the nearby Divinity School was rebuilt; and in the 1480s Thomas Kemp, Bishop of London, paid for an appropriately elaborate vault, of an intricate pattern, under which the theological lecturers

---

[17] J. T. Rosenthal, *The Purchase of Paradise: Gift Giving and the Aristocracy, 1307-1485* (London, 1972), p.10. See also the two volumes by W. K. Jordan surveying the period 1480-1660: *The Charities of London* and *Philanthropy in England* (London, 1959-61). H. S. Bennett included a revealing chapter on religion in his *The Pastons and their England* (Cambridge, 1922).

and their students might discuss further and further refinements of orthodoxy. Although the nature of God's foreknowledge of human affairs was one of the favourite topics in the fifteenth-century university, those who lectured in that hall had not the slightest inkling of a Protestant future. Over this vault was housed Duke Humphrey's Library given in the 1440s, the nucleus of what was to grow into the assembly of the English-speaking world's learning in the Bodleian Library. Outside the city walls Magdalen College was founded by William of Waynflete, Bishop of Winchester, and built in the period 1474-1509. Between the chapel and the river lay, on one side, a cloister so impressive as to suggest that the college was going to be a monastery; on the other side a great tower, to house the bells which would summon the scholars to their devotions. Emphasizing that the aristocracy would find themselves at home in such surroundings, the founder expressly provided for the admission of twenty sons of *nobiles* who were to pay fees.

In the sixteenth century the foundation of colleges continued at Oxford. One college was deliberately conservative – Brasenose, endowed in 1508 by William Smythe, Bishop of Lincoln and a hammer of heretics, together with a devout merchant, Sir Richard Sutton. Parallel with this was the foundation of St John's College at Cambridge by Henry VII's mother Lady Margaret Beaufort, who had already virtually refounded Christ's College; these, too, were intended to be bastions of orthodoxy. Two other new Oxford colleges, however, brought the new learning of the time – Greek not Trojan, as the Oxford wits had it – into the education of men intending to be priests. Richard Foxe, Bishop of Winchester and formerly Henry VII's and Henry VIII's most trusted agent, founded Corpus Christi College in 1515, urging the study not of the medieval theologians but of the Greek and Latin classics, the Bible and the Fathers.

Ten years later Thomas Wolsey founded Cardinal College. He was influenced by the example of the founder of Magdalen College; as student, fellow, bursar and master of the grammar school he had spent all the years from 1482 to 1505 at Magdalen. But now Cardinal Wolsey was master of England

and determined that his college should eclipse all others. To endow it he secured from Rome the suppression of almost thirty small and decayed religious houses including St Frideswide's, whose fine church became its chapel (and is now Oxford Cathedral). To supply its students, this butcher's son founded a school in his native Ipswich larger than the colleges at Eton and Winchester. To staff it, he attracted the brightest teachers of the day, full of the new learning and the new hopes – and of the alarmingly new theology, as it turned out. Nothing but Latin or Greek was to be spoken within these walls. Under a dean and sub-dean Cardinal College was to house a hundred canons, with lecturers, 'censors', treasurers, stewards, domestics and a lavish chapel staff. The best musician of the day, John Taverner, was hired to take charge of the organ and the choir. The college was to train two hundred men at a time to be priests (not monks) – with more emphasis on law than on theology. 'Tom Quad' still preserves the founder's name and the dining hall is still emblazoned with his arms, although it is also still evident that the cloister he planned for it was never completed. In 1546 Cardinal College became the royal foundation of Christ Church, on a reduced but still substantial scale.

Thus the medieval system by which undergraduates were housed without much supervision in small 'halls' or private residences, and were free to attend lectures or not as they wished, was slowly being replaced by a system of colleges and tutors. A touch of luxury was reaching an Oxford which still kept most of the atmosphere of a market-town:

Towery city and branchy between towers;
Cuckoo-echoing, bell-swarmèd, lark-charmèd,
    rook-racked, river-rounded;
The dapple-eared lily below thee. . . .[18]

---

[18] Gerard Manley Hopkins, 'Dun Scotus's Oxford' (1879).

THE GREAT CHURCHES

The evidence from the monasteries is more debatable. The monastic population of England seems to have risen during the fifteenth century from about 9,500 to some twelve thousand, and in many houses this was clearly a time of secure prosperity.[19] In the next century numbers fell since many more opportunities in lay life were being opened. However, the investigations of twentieth-century scholars would not support any idea of a dramatic decay in these religious houses. On the contrary, the evidence suggests that in most of them the routine of life was kept up with no great anxiety. The main problems of the smaller houses were financial rather than religious or moral. In the greater houses the very prosperity created moral problems but their inmates seem to have been too traditionally minded to be greatly worried and in some of the favoured monasteries new building demonstrated a proud assurance in the Tudor Age. Bath Abbey was being rebuilt magnificently during the 1530s. Much of the sixteenth-century work in the monasteries was to improve the comforts of the domestic quarters, but at Sherborne, for example, or Peterborough, new fan vaulting adorned the monastic church. The king himself founded a complete new abbey as late as 1536, at Bisham; and in that year the Act of Parliament suppressing the smaller monasteries spoke of 'divers great and solemn monasteries wherein (thanks be to God) religion is right well kept and observed'.

The richest of the monasteries was Glastonbury. According to a government inquiry (the *Valor Ecclesiasticus*) in 1535 its net income was £3,311, almost a thousand pounds more than the next richest, Westminster Abbey and Canterbury Cathedral. In August 1534 its new organist contracted to serve Abbot Whiting and his successors for life (and on the basis of

---

[19] See, for example, R. B. Dobson, *Durham Cathedral Priory 1400-1450* (Cambridge, 1973).

that agreement was still drawing an annuity in 1568). During the next four years eight new monks joined the great abbey, whose accounts for 1538-39 survive. 'In them we can see the machinery of the abbey moving slowly onwards like the hands of a great clock. The enormous quantities of foodstuffs come in; the ditches and watercourses are cleansed of weeds and slime, the nettles round the chapel of St Michael on the Tor are scythed down, the abbey church is stripped of ivy, the candelabra are cleaned up, the girls' gild at St John's church receives a midsummer gift of beer; the plumber and porter between them, at considerable expense, veil the great rood in Lent. Who could know that it was for the last time? That what they and their forebears had done for centuries was never to be done again, that before the summer's foliage had withered the heart's beat of that vast body was to cease, that the weeds and nettles and ivy were to resume their kingdom, and that a silence was to fall?'[20]

Specially dramatic is the line of royal chapels raised in splendour during a period when, as we look back, we know that the medieval Church was doomed by action to be taken by the monarchy itself.

In 1441 King Henry VI, then still a teenager, having just founded at Eton a college for seventy 'poor and needy' boys and a large chapel staff, planned King's College at Cambridge. By 1445 he had decided that it should have seventy scholars. Dominating this college, which was to be recruited entirely from Eton, was a perpetual reminder of the combined authority of the monarchy and the orthodox faith: a very large chapel of which the king laid the foundation stone in 1446. His master mason was Reginald Ely. Work was interrupted when Henry was deposed in 1461, begun again when Edward IV was at peace fifteen years later, interrupted again when Richard III was killed in battle, and completed between 1508 and 1515, largely at the expense of Henry VII. The great fan

---

[20] David Knowles, *The Religious Orders in England*, vol. iii (Cambridge, 1959), pp. 348-9. See also R. W. Dunning, 'Revival at Glastonbury, 1530-39', in *Renaissance and Renewal in Christian History*, ed. D. Baker (Oxford, 1977), pp. 213-222.

vault was designed by the master mason John Wastell, but fortunately the plan to gild and paint it was never carried out. This was the chapel that moved William Wordsworth in 1820:

> Give all thou canst; high Heaven rejects the lore
> Of nicely-calculated less or more;
> So deemed the man who fashioned for the sense
> These lofty pillars, spread that branching roof
> Self-poised, and scooped into ten thousand cells,
> Where light and shade repose, where music dwells. . . .

By 1531 twenty-five vast windows in the chapel had been glazed with coloured glass mainly linking Old and New Testament scenes, the work of artists from the Low Countries. A Renaissance oak screen displayed the initials H and A tied with love-knots: it was the honeymoon period of Henry VIII and Anne Boleyn. No less splendid choir stalls housed the scholars as they meekly knelt to hear Mass. The rest of Henry VI's design, which was to have included a cloister and bell tower, was never completed; and there can be no doubt that Henry VI would not have approved of the chapel itself as completed by Henry VIII, its walls spattered with the royal insignia. A detailed document drawn up in 1448 included instructions that the architecture was to be 'clean and substantial' but not 'curious' or 'busy'.

The Yorkist king who overthrew Henry VI halted the work at Cambridge and for a time closed down the school at Eton, where the nave of the chapel was never built. He decided to leave behind a very different chapel. In Windsor Castle Edward IV caused St George's Chapel to be entirely rebuilt, with Henry Janys as his master mason. Here was to be no band of scholars; the chapel was the shrine of the king's favourites (and foreign guests) in the charmed circle of the revived Order of the Garter, modelled on the Order of the Golden Fleece at the much envied court of the dukes of Burgundy. And in Windsor, in a church to be visited between feasts, there was to be no restraint; the architecture was to take the Perpendicular style forward in luxury, and all the fittings were to be appropriately rich and royal. It was to be a setting fit for the fifty knights' stalls carved in 1478-85 around the high altar, beside which was to be found the king's own resting place. Although the elaborate instructions for a tomb in Edward IV's will were never carried out, the ironwork surrounding his grave, forged under the supervision of the Cornish John Tresilian, is the finest iron surviving from the English Middle Ages. The work at Windsor stopped not long after the king's death, to be resumed when in 1503 a Knight of the Garter, Sir Reginald Bray who had been Henry VII's chief financial agent, bequeathed a great legacy to pay for most of its completion.

In the same year a princely abbot, John Islip, laid the foundation stone of the new Lady Chapel in Westminster Abbey. It was to be built even more sumptuously, although on a smaller scale, than the chapel at Windsor. The will of Henry VII provided all the money necessary for three purposes. The king wished to honour the Virgin Mary. He wished also to erect a shrine in which Henry VI's body could be placed when it had been brought from Windsor on the completion of his official canonization as a saint (then awaited). And he wished to build a mausoleum for himself and his descendants.

This will was a classic document of the Middle Ages, combining an obviously sincere belief in the Catholic Church's doctrines about life after death with an equally sincere belief that money mattered. Ten thousand Masses were to be said for the repose of the king's soul within a month of his death; the priests were to be paid sixpence a Mass, double the standard rate. Nineteen great churches were placed under contract to remember him perpetually. Silver pyxes to hold the Body of Christ for adoration were to be placed at his expense in all parish churches which did not already possess one. A new pilgrims' road was to be built from Windsor to Canterbury. But the commemoration was to have its undying centre in Westminster, where three extra priests were to join the royal abbey in order to serve the perfectly equipped altars of the new Lady Chapel. Peter Torrigiano came from Renaissance Florence to spend six years making a tomb in bronze, marble and copper gilt for Henry VII and his queen in the centre of the chapel, and to begin a still larger tomb for Henry VIII (never completed). Statues of more than a hundred saints

looked down from the walls. The vaulting of the chapel, with
fans centred on pendants, was more intricately elaborate than
the vault at King's College and was probably designed by
William Vertue, who made the vault at Windsor and built
Bath Abbey in the same period. The glass was as fine as that at
King's, and some of the same glaziers worked at it; it was to be
destroyed by seventeenth-century Puritans. The whole building surrounded the king's body, brought here one May morning in 1509, with a traditional sanctity. The criticism that it
was extravagant had probably never entered the mind of
Henry VII. His whole purpose had been to stay on the throne
of England. Now he was resolved to purchase the kingdom of
heaven.

Thus the great chapels at Cambridge, Windsor and Westminster testified to the piety of Lancastrian, Yorkist and
Tudor kings. But the closing period of the Middle Ages also
erected a monument showing how the higher clergy could still
flourish with the support of kings.

The great central tower of Canterbury Cathedral ('Bell
Harry Tower') was raised during the 1490s, using about half a
million bricks although it was encased in stone. Although the
number of pilgrims to Canterbury had now declined, the
cathedral monastery and its archbishop could still rely on
great possessions and on royal patronage. There were now
reminders of this at either end of the nave — in the stone
Screen of the Six Kings and in the west window which
portrayed twenty-one kings, from Cnut to Henry VI. In the
north transept Edward IV and his large family looked down
from another magnificent window to the scene of Becket's
martyrdom. The new tower was commissioned by a mighty
archbishop, Cardinal John Morton, Henry VII's chancellor.
His enthusiasm for the work was matched by the prior of the
monastery, William Sellinge. Sellinge had brought back from
Italy a store of Greek and Latin manuscripts — but, so far as
we know, little trace on his mind of the turbulence of this
period when in Florence the passionately reforming friar,
Savonarola, was executed for dramatic attacks on the papacy.
At Canterbury John Wastell was master-mason for Cardinal
Morton and Prior Sellinge: his fan vault at the base of his

tower, above the six kings on their screen, was as perfect as his contemporary miracle in King's College Chapel. The tower was surmounted by a steeple and a large gilt angel.

Bell Harry Tower was not the last great work in medieval Canterbury. It is true that Canterbury's archbishop was eclipsed when the Archbishop of York, Thomas Wolsey, who was also Bishop of Durham (later of Winchester), became the king's first minister, the pope's legate and a cardinal, but there seemed no reason to believe that the English Crown had broken off its historic alliance with the Canterbury of Augustine, Dunstan and Lanfranc. John Morton, Philip Deane and William Warham had all been archbishops enjoying Henry VII's complete confidence and often employed by him in affairs of state. Why should men not expect Wolsey to contribute to the Canterbury tradition one day, if the papacy eluded his grasp? And why should his successors not continue to unite the English Church and State? The future seemed sunny. An imposing new gatehouse was ready when Henry VIII, accompanied by the Emperor Charles V and Cardinal Wolsey, rode through it to worship in Canterbury Cathedral on Whit Sunday 1520.

HENRY IV AND HENRY V

When we try to meet the people who came to parish churches or universities, monasteries or cathedrals during the 'decline' of the Middle Ages, naturally the evidence is less dramatic because it was not an age of many outstanding personalities. But the story of the kings in this period enables us to see not only the outline of the story of England but also something of the place of religion in it; to see not only why national unity was thought to be of paramount importance in Tudor England but also why obedience to the king as he maintained that unity was thought to be a religious duty.

Providing one of the rare glimpses we have into Henry IV's character, his contemporary John Capgrave tells us that the king was interested in casuistry, the science of Christian ethics;

that he delighted to dispute hypothetical moral questions with scholars at his court. Unfortunately for his peace of mind, moral problems did not remain merely hypothetical for Henry IV. Speaking in 1399 'in the name of Fadir, Son and Holy Gost' (as was solemnly recorded) he pretended that his claim to the throne was based on his royal descent; in fact, as everyone knew, it was based on a successful rebellion, and he lived to be penitent although not to make restitution. Beginning barely four months after this charade, others rebelled against him – most alarmingly, the great Percy family in the north, whose support had been indispensable during the usurpation. Combined with this threat was a rebellion in Wales led by the formidable Owen Glendower. Another conspiracy led to the execution in 1405 of Richard Scrope, Archbishop of York, although the Chief Justice resigned rather than take any part in a bishop's beheading.

It seems clear that after these rebellions which brought home to him the nature of his own, and which brought out in him a hot temper which he had not displayed in 1399, Henry IV's health collapsed. Although in his youth he had been a greatly admired soldier (he had gone on a 'crusade' with the Teutonic Knights), for months at a time he was now bedridden. The symptoms of various illnesses, so far as we can recover them, point to a neurosis. His will, dictated in 1409, began 'I Henry, sinful wretch . . .' and looked back on 'the lyffe I have mispendyd'. A modern scholar writes: 'Henry had always been a devout man, a conventionally devout man perhaps, but by contemporary standards (and they were high) above the average in punctilious devotion, a pilgrim as well as a soldier, and one who had earned widespread commendation abroad for his regularity at Mass and almsgiving. There can be little doubt that he ought to offer amends by abandoning his usurped throne, but he knew also that his sons would wish him to retain it for his dynasty and that there was therefore no release for him that way. His eldest son's obvious impatience to succeed him roused all his old tenacity and so, racked by sickness and remorse, he clung to his royal power until his death on 20 May 1413.'[21]

Henry IV died in the Jerusalem Chamber of Westminster

Abbey; then aged forty-seven, he had had a stroke while visiting the shrine of St Edward the Confessor. His heir was soon talking about his past sins and future hopes with a recluse who lived elsewhere in the abbey. There and then, at the age of twenty-five, Henry V decided to put away his boon companions, to live chastely, to be a model son of the Church. He had only nine more years to live and he never became the crusading knight of the still powerful ideal. But he made the Lancastrian dynasty undeniably respectable.

He got rid of Archbishop Arundel as chancellor because the archbishop had been too closely identified with the usurpation, and installed instead Edward III's grandson, his own uncle and tutor, Bishop Henry Beaufort. He pardoned the families of those implicated in rebellions against his father. He brought the body of Richard II to lie in Westminster Abbey near his Queen Anne and St Edward, and ordered his own tomb nearby (his father was buried beneath an unflattering alabaster effigy in Canterbury). He became the hero of his subjects, partly because he was the first medieval English king to prefer speaking and writing in English. In particular he was the hero of the clergy. Some music has survived composed by the king for the services of his chapel, which he attended with constant devotion; and his accounts show his personal interest in the members of the choir and other church musicians.[22] While briefly back in England from the war, in May 1421, he summoned all the abbots to the Chapter House of Westminster Abbey and told them roundly that his ancestors had endowed their monasteries in order to secure their prayers, and he expected them to back up the army by disciplined intercessions supported by austerity. And even the abbots seem to have been stirred by such an appeal from a great military hero. His father had felt too insecure on his own throne to be able to afford to claim anyone else's; thus the chief battles of Henry IV's reign, apart from the expeditions to

[21] K. B. McFarlane, *Lancastrian Kings and Lollard Knights*, p.104. A similar verdict was reached by J. L. Kirby, *Henry IV of England* (London, 1970).

[22] But the 'roy Henry' of the music in the Old Hall manuscript may be Henry IV.

Scotland and Wales and the repression of English revolts, had
been verbal, with Crown and Commons negotiating taxes in
exchange for satisfactory replies to petitions. Now Henry V
felt able to play a more heroic role; he conquered much of
France, no doubt deceiving himself about the justice of his
cause as his father had done when overthrowing Richard II.
He did not survive long enough to find any cause for repentance. While he lived he basked in the patriotic enthusiasm
which Shakespeare's *Henry V* was to recapture – the enthusiasm which lives for us also in the triumphant song:

> Oure kinge went forth to Normandy
> With grace and might of chivalry.
> Ther God for him wrought mervelusly:
> Wherfore Englande may call and cry,
> *Deo gracias.*

His methods of warfare were not confined to the grace of
chivalry. 'He was a hero,' as Hazlitt wrote, regretting that such
a man had appealed to Shakespeare, '– that is, he was ready
to sacrifice his own life for the pleasure of destroying
thousands of other lives.' What Henry V ordered to be done in
France brought about the macabre popularity of the horrify-
ing Dance of Death (first as an actual dance, then in paintings). No doubt he justified the ruthlessness with which he
starved out Rouen – with refugees in their thousands dying of
hunger and cold in the ditch between the city walls and the
English besiegers – by the argument that the city, although it
did not acknowledge this, was in rebellion against him as the
rightful King of France. But, as a modern biographer notes,
'even by the brutal standards of his own day there are deeds
in the record which besmirch his name. . . . The crucifying
of the gunners of Louviers, the hanging of the hostages at
Montereau, the execution of the trumpeter after the siege of
Meaux, and the fate of the unknown soldier who had insulted
him from the walls of Rouen were unworthy of any great
general in any age'.[23] An admiring chaplain who accompanied
the invasion of France recorded, among many other signs of

---

[23] H. F. Hutchinson, *Henry V* (London, 1967), p.222.

the king's piety, the fact that as he moved through the many celebrations after his victories he showed no delight. To this priest it was proof that Henry V, waging war solely for the sake of justice since France was rightfully his, ascribed his triumphs solely to God. With greater scepticism about kings' motives we may think that what was being revealed was a cold inhumanity morally inferior to the alleged warm excesses of Henry's youth — and his youth may not have been as boisterous as the chroniclers and Shakespeare depicted, since the records show that he spent much of it fighting against the Welsh or presiding at council meetings.

The invasion of France was on the whole a disaster for the English as well as for the French, although by 1420 Henry was acknowledged as regent by about half the French population, married to a daughter of the French king, and promised the throne for himself and his heirs.

The disaster was not only that as Queen of England Katherine gave birth to a son afflicted with the strange nervous disease of the French dynasty. The real tragedy was that the victory of Agincourt in 1415 deceived the English, particularly the aristocracy, into thinking that the fruits of war — or of civil war if foreign adventures were lacking — would be greater than the fruits of peace. The peace policy of Richard II, which had brought real prosperity as well as much beauty to Chaucer's England as it recovered from the scourge of the Black Death, was now abandoned with glee, but it would have been happier for England in the long run had Henry V been compelled in 1415 to conclude a treaty with the French providing only for mutual recognition and trade. Already his capture of Harfleur had been won only after the loss of thousands of English lives by dysentery and fever, and his march to Calais after that siege has been aptly called 'the most foolhardy and reckless adventure that ever an unreasoning pietist devised'.[24] At Agincourt his army of less than six thousand was outnumbered by six to one and would have lost the day had not the French generals insisted on throwing their chances away. They clumsily exposed their cavalry to the

---

[24] J. H. Wylie, *Henry V*, vol. ii (Cambridge, 1919), p.76.

English archers and failed to exert discipline as the chaos mounted. How narrow an escape it had been for Henry V and his 'happy few' is shown by their nervousness which added a grim epilogue to their victory. They butchered their prisoners towards the end of the battle, apart from a few aristocrats whose ransoms would go to the king; the arrival of further French forces had been reported mistakenly.

In Henry's later campaigning the essential picture did not change. Beyond doubt he was a courageous and tireless worker and a first-class general with eyes for finance, diplomacy, supply and public relations at home and abroad as well as for a battle or a siege; but the main causes of his success were the imbecility of the French king, the ineptitude of the French court, the readiness of many of the French to accept a conqueror, and the major error made by those who still resisted when they murdered John the Fearless, Duke of Burgundy. That murder made sure of Burgundian co-operation with the English for the time being, and Henry's only real hope of keeping two kingdoms in his hands and those of his descendants lay in this alliance to hold down France. But the alliance, although strengthened by England's link with Burgundian Flanders through the wool and cloth trades, was fragile. All the largest factors of economics, geography and language were against it.

At the time, the English invasion of France seemed to many on the Continent a nuisance because it interfered with the serious business of ending the scandal of the existence of more than one pope. The English delegation to the Council of Constance managed to get itself recognized as a 'nation' equal with the Germans, French, Italians and Spaniards; but more relevant to the work of the council was the tension between the English and the French. The hatred between the two nations proved so disturbing that the Holy Roman Emperor, Sigismund, came to England on a futile peace mission. In the end Martin V emerged as pope of a united Christendom. He was not able to secure the repeal of the anti-papal English statutes of *Provisors* and *Praemunire*; Archbishop Chichele wept as he pleaded for the pope, but the English realities remained unchanged. Nor was the new pope able to secure the acceptance

of Henry Beaufort as his legate in England with wide powers;
when Beaufort indiscreetly accepted appointment as a
cardinal without the king's permission, he had to avert his
royal nephew's wrath by a massive gift to the war finances. But
on his side, Henry V had too many distractions to be able to
achieve a permanently satisfactory settlement of the Church
while he was in a strong bargaining position. Had his mind not
been on the war, his diplomacy might have taken advantage of
a creative moment which was not to recur during the rest of
the Middle Ages: an opportunity in the 1410s for a new deal
between the pope, the council and the nations, perhaps
eventually leading to a Catholic Reformation. Probably the
hope of a 'conciliar' Church where the spiritual initiative
could come from pastorally minded bishops advised by
theologians, instead of from Italian popes immersed in the
politics and art of the Renaissance, was always illusory; but as
a 'might have been' it is interesting. Much may have been lost
because this highly effective king, who always insisted that
every major initiative must remain in his hands, saw it as his
chief Christian duty to conquer France.[25]

Whatever may have been the morality or wisdom of the
war which won such glory for Henry V, he certainly was a
'pietist'. Eminent churchmen felt able to support him wholeheartedly — and were promoted for their support. His first
chancellor, Cardinal Beaufort of Winchester, who had added
to the wealth of the see by much shrewd business in the wool
trade and other fields, was the principal source of loans to
finance the war. When the archbishopric of Canterbury was
vacant the king secured the appointment of Henry Chichele, a
quietly able lawyer, a diplomat and administrator. He also
used his father's secretary, Thomas Langley, now a cardinal
and Bishop of Durham, in many central affairs as his
chancellor, as well as in the maintenance of peace in the
north. John Kemp, who soon became Bishop of London, was
Chancellor of Normandy in the period when it was intended to

---

[25] See E. F. Jacob, *Essays in the Conciliar Epoch* (revised, Manchester,
1953).

turn it into an English colony.[26]

The best memorial of his reign was the foundation of two religious houses of strict life. His father had undertaken this work of piety when officially exonerated by the pope for the execution of Archbishop Scrope, but nothing had been done. Henry V founded two communities in 1415 before setting out for Harfleur and Agincourt, near the reconstructed palace of Sheen. One was a Charterhouse for forty Carthusian monks, and was called the House of Jesus of Bethlehem. The other was for monks, nuns and lay brothers living under an abbess according to the rule drawn up by St Bridget of Sweden; it was known as the Abbey of Mount Syon. In a hundred years of steady and strict devotion these two houses heard each other's bells ringing across the Thames. It was perhaps in reliance on such deeds that when Henry V lay dying (probably of dysentery) in the castle of Vincennes in August 1422, he shouted to the demon he thought he saw: 'Thou liest, thou liest! My portion is with the Lord Jesus Christ!'

A SAINT ON THE THRONE

Henry V died before he could see his son — and more mercifully never saw that son's future. He left Henry VI to be brought up by the old Duke of Exeter, and trusted that he would inherit two kingdoms — England over which Humphrey, Duke of Gloucester, was to be protector, and France, which meanwhile was to have John, Duke of Bedford, as its regent. It is recorded that at the age of three and a half the boy-king managed to walk from the west door to the choir of St Paul's

---

[26] There is no modern biography of Beaufort or Kemp, but there are studies of *Archbishop Henry Chichele* by E. F. Jacob (London, 1967) and *Thomas Langley and the Bishopric of Durham* by R. L. Storey (London, 1961). G. L. Harriss, 'Cardinal Beaufort — Patriot or Usurer?' in *Transactions of the Royal Historical Society* (London, 1970), concludes that the cardinal neither obtained interest on his loans — nor made them, or any other political moves, except in his own long-term self-interest.

Cathedral, with an approving Parliament around him. But he did not march on to complete the conquest of France or to rebuild the walls of Jerusalem – which is said to have been the deathbed wish of his father. Instead, the reign of Henry VI witnessed the recovery of French morale. Partly this was thanks to the peasant-girl Jeanne d'Arc who so dramatically inspired the French to relieve Orleans and to crown their own king – and whom the English cruelly and futilely burned as a witch and a heretic.

The turning point came in 1435, when the Burgundians deserted their English alliance. Some of the English still believed that greater and greater ruthlessness would bring the French back into subjection; a memorandum survives in which one particularly mercy-scorning and profit-making general, Sir John Fastolf (the name that seems to have suggested 'Falstaff' to Shakespeare), argues this case for scorching the earth. But shrewder statesmen such as Cardinal Beaufort and William de la Pole, Duke of Suffolk, saw clearly that the problem was now how to extricate England from Henry V's wildly expensive gamble. Certainly the young Henry VI, although crowned in Paris in 1431 as a counterblast to the coronation inspired by Jeanne, never showed any ambition to become a general himself. Instead he grew up to be more holy than most priests or monks. While he never renounced the claim to France, he never enforced it – or any other claim. Indeed, his only policy in the period when his reign amounted to personal rule, 1445-50, was 'peace at any price in the French war.'[27]

One of the mysteries surrounding Henry VI is how this character, so opposite to the military virtues of his father and grandfather, developed. We know that his upbringing was entrusted to a devout nobleman, the Earl of Warwick, but this is not enough to account for his virtual pacifism. Perhaps the decisive influence was that of the priest Thomas Netter, his tutor until he was ten. His meekness, his mercifulness, his reckless generosity to his friends and to the poor, his in-

---

[27] B. P. Wolffe in *Fifteenth-century England*, ed. S. B. Chrimes, C. D. Ross and R. A. Griffiths (Manchester, 1972), p.38.

difference to luxury, his support of scholars (he would tip the boys of his college at Eton when he met them), the exceptional purity of his morals (he warned the Eton boys never to go near his own court), and the monk-like strictness of his devotions: all these traits are reported as running through all the stages of his life – his boyhood, the troubled years when his minority had ended (at the age of sixteen), his five years' imprisonment. When he noticed the exposed bosoms of some girls brought in to dance at a Christmas feast, he observed: 'Fy, fy, for shame! Forsothe ye be to blame!' When he found the men bathing in the warm waters at Bath totally naked, he left immediately in indignation. And when he was wounded in the neck, he commented: 'Forsothe and forsothe ye do fouly to smyte a kynge enoynted so.' At a time when every annointed king was expected to dress splendidly, he preferred a long gown like a merchant and boots like a farmer. The principal feasts of the year he would mark by adding a hair shirt next to his skin. Sundays he devoted entirely to religion; and on a weekday he would be irritated when he was trying to read a religious book and a duke knocked on the door wanting to talk politics.

John Blacman, a Carthusian monk who was for a time his spiritual director, wrote a 'Compilation of the Meekness and Good Life of King Henry VI' containing those anecdotes. Such a character impressed contemporaries up to a point. The religion of the age was illustrated when in the year of his foundation of his college at Cambridge Henry VI was believed to be the subject of magical arts. The wife of Humphrey, Duke of Gloucester, was accused of making a wax image of the king and melting it down. Her two accomplices were executed – one by being hanged, drawn and quartered, the other by being burned – and the duchess was condemned to walk barefoot around London for three days, accompanied by the mayor, sheriffs and others, before being imprisoned for life. An age so sure about witchcraft was sensitive of the sacred aura surrounding the 'enoynted' king. But it did expect a king to rule, with the co-operation of an aristocracy which he could dominate by force of character. This came out when the Duke of Gloucester, who had exerted much influence with much irresponsibility, was himself arrested and charged with treason.

It seems that the shock brought about a fatal heart attack. In a country basically so royalist, a strong king could have done much to impose his will on affairs and if he had been devout as well that would have been to his advantage. But Henry VI did not rule – except when aroused by his wife, Margaret of Anjou. Queen at the age of fifteen, this proud and passionate Frenchwoman already possessed a personality much stronger than her husband's. She was encouraged to exert her personality (if she needed any encouragement) by observing what happened to the king's favourites who were blamed for the loss of France. Adam Moleyns, Bishop of Chichester and a leading civil servant, was murdered when he went to pay the seamen at Portsmouth; William Ayscough, Bishop of Salisbury, who had heard the king's confessions and officiated at his wedding, was killed in his own diocese; and after an attempted flight the Duke of Suffolk's headless body was thrown on the beach at Dover. In Kent a rebellion was led by a certain Jack Cade, protesting that the king's council had sanctioned misgovernment and should be renewed under the Duke of York.

With France apart from Calais gone, for any ruler of England the 1450s would have been a testing time. The glamour which had surrounded Edward III, Henry V and their generals had now come to nothing. The vast investment of blood and treasure in the conquest of France had yielded a nil return. Yet the possibility of growing rich by trade, manufacturing or agricultural improvements was largely hidden from the English aristocracy, still educated in the outdated myths of Norman feudalism and Arthurian chivalry, still living mainly off rents. Some landlords were efficient in estate management (notably Cardinal Beaufort), but the evidence of declining rents is widespread. The huge and scattered estates of the Earls of Lancaster, for example, halved in profitability, 1400-75. Industrialization on anything like the scale to be seen in Flanders seemed inconceivable in England, when the most obvious way to make a profit was to export wool or unfinished cloth to Flanders (as Beaufort had done). Trading was not for aristocrats; anyway, what with German competition and the general violence of the times, English exports slumped in the period 1425-80. Therefore to ambitious but unbusinesslike Percies, Nevilles and other aristocrats or would-be nobility, the way ahead seemed to lie through the extension of local power and its profits. A great landlord could 'maintain' his tenants, hired retainers or other dependents so as to form a private army which could terrorize a neighbourhood – and go unchecked, for the local administration of justice could itself be controlled. Although it is inaccurate to speak of the nobility as being anxious to rebel (one factor being the highly alarming penalties for treason), this was a situation where influence over a neighbourhood counted for everything and the national interest or the king's justice for very little. Characteristic of popular attitudes in the fifteenth century were the Robin Hood ballads, which projected back into the past a situation where an honest man must expect nothing from the law, where the king is far-off although good and the sheriff is a local gangster. Characteristic of more aristocratic fantasies were the Arthurian legends which Sir Thomas Malory tells us he compiled while in prison. Although attempts have been made to find an imprisoned Malory who would be more at home at Arthur's round table, and one such has been located in Yorkshire, most scholars remain fairly sure that Sir Thomas was a Warwickshire man convicted of crimes such as cattle-thieving and rape.[28]

In this national crisis Henry was fatally incompetent. He could not provide the 'good and sad' government for which the House of Commons (in a petition typical of its attitude throughout this century) had asked in 1429. A more or less complete programme for the 'governance of England' and for the defence of the laws was drawn up in books by Sir John Fortescue, who served the king as Chief Justice from 1442 until exiled in his cause in 1471. Based on the co-operation of King,

---

[28] See J. R. Lander, *Conflict and Stability in Fifteenth Century England* (London, 1969), and J. G. Bellamy, *Crime and Public Order in England in the Later Middle Ages* (London, 1973). The ballads, first mentioned in *Piers Plowman*, have been studied in R. B. Dobson and J. Taylor, *Rymes of Robyn Hood* (London, 1976). For Malory or the Malories see William Matthews, *The Ill-Framed Knight* (Berkeley, Cal., 1966), and A. B. Ferguson, *The Indian Summer of English Chivalry* (Durham, N.C., 1960).

Council, Parliament and aristocracy, the programme remained locked in books because the indispensable king lacked the political will. Indeed, his personality added to the political problems. A basic cause of the disorders which wrecked the rest of his reign was, in the judgement of a modern authority, the fact that he managed to make rebellion seem respectable 'because the nobility was unable to rescue the kingdom from Henry's inanity by any other means'.[29]

At the beginning of the disastrous 1450s Henry briefly bestirred himself to discipline Richard, Duke of York, who was now expecting the succession to the throne – and to beget a son, Edward. However, by the time this prince was born the king was not able to recognize him. In the summer of 1453 his mind gave way; for eighteen months he was unable to move or to respond to those around him. One of the many letters surviving from this period as a chronicle of a Norfolk family, the Pastons (a family as grasping and as turbulent as any in England), shows us the king at Windsor. He is being presented with his son and heir. 'The kyng yave no maner answere. . . . Alle their labour was in veyne, for they departed thens without any answere or countenaunce savyng only that ones he looked on the Prince and caste downe his eyene ayen, without any more.'

Eventually the king more or less recovered, although there was at least one relapse. Politically speaking the recovery was a pity, since it removed the competent and extremely rich Duke of York from power and made the Yorkists' forceful response inevitable.

Queen Margaret and her ally, Edmund Beaufort, Duke of Somerset, now resumed control and the Yorkists replied by open rebellion, their strongest man being the Duke of York's nephew, Richard Neville, Earl of Warwick. During a battle in the streets of St Albans, almost in the shadow of the great abbey, the Yorkists killed Somerset and captured the king. It

---

[29] K. B. McFarlane, 'The Wars of the Roses', in *Proceedings of the British Academy* (1964), pp.87-119. This judgement was developed further in the same author's lectures on *The Nobility of Later Medieval England* (Oxford, 1973).

was not long before Queen Margaret took her revenge, but the banishment of her enemies brought no lasting peace. In 1460 she had to escape with her son into Wales when the Yorkists returned in triumph, again capturing the king. This time Richard of York claimed the throne for himself, but under pressure from Warwick and others temporarily accepted the status of Prince of Wales and Protector, with the right of succession after Henry's death. To this arrangement Henry consented; but to say that his wife did not would be to put her response mildly. Queen Margaret stirred up a counterattack in the north which was temporarily successful. At the battle of Wakefield Richard of York was defeated and killed; his head was set up over the south gate of York decorated by a paper crown. It was then the turn of the Yorkists to counterattack under the leadership of their new duke (Edward) and the now unappeasable Warwick. After a slaughter of Lancastrians at Towton near York amid a snowstorm on Palm Sunday 1461, Margaret was forced to flee, with King Henry in tow; and amid the acclamations of his soldiers and of the London citizens (but no Parliament was involved) Edward IV was enthroned as the rightful king 'by descent', the entire House of Lancaster being dismissed as usurpers. After many wanderings and half-hearted attempts to arrange one more Lancastrian rally, Henry was captured and brought to the Tower of London.

That this was not the end of Henry VI was due to developments which add to the impression that the top of public life in England had gone mad. Edward IV, fancying himself for a time as another Henry V, revived the claim to the throne of France and the alliance with Burgundy. In England he so conducted himself as to alienate the people and (what mattered more) the king-maker, Warwick. Louis XI of France promptly arranged for a reconciliation between Warwick and Queen Margaret and equipped an invasion in their names. Henry VI was cleaned up and brought out of the Tower. In a dazed condition he then resumed his troubled reign for another six months. This period was ended by the return of Edward IV, the battle of Barnet, the killing of Warwick, the battle of Tewkesbury, the killing of Henry VI's son Prince Edward, and the imprisonment of the tigress-like Queen Margaret, who was eventually ransomed by the French.

On 21 May 1471 King Edward rode into London and that same night King Henry, who was now back in the Tower, died. We have no reason to doubt that he was put to death. His body – bleeding in its open coffin, or so the report went – was taken to Chertsey Abbey but reburied in 1481 in St George's Chapel, Windsor, where his tomb became the centre of devotions and healings. John Blacman quotes his Latin prayer which may be translated: 'O Lord Jesu Christ, who didst create me, redeem me, and foreordain me unto that which now I am; thou knowest what thou wilt do with me; deal with me according to thy most compassionate will.' The prayer became famous. In his will Henry VII said that he had used it from his childhood.[30]

THE YORKIST KINGS

The story of the 'Wars of the Roses' (a name given by Sir Walter Scott) has been told here – although only in outline – because of the traumatic effect which these disturbances had upon English public opinion. The actual damage done to the population or the economy does not seem to have been widespread. But great damage was done by the fact that the English nobility had been without a leader since the death of Henry V. For a time there was a cult of Henry VI as a martyred saint; but it is significant that when Henry VII had failed to persuade the papacy to proceed to an official canonization, Henry VIII, although still a devout Catholic prince, did not pursue the matter. As the nation knew, the supreme lesson of Henry VI's so-called 'reign' was that a king was of no earthly use unless he could act like a king. For a king, to be a 'good lord' was more important than being a good man.

---

[30] Bertram Wolffe has supplied a biography of *Henry VI* and Ralph Griffiths a study of *The Reign of Henry VI* (both London, 1981).

Churchmen aware of political realities were not blind to
this. Given the chance, they would have been the king's supporters and servants in strong government; in Sir John
Fortescue's ideal for the Lancastrian monarchy, as set out in
his *Governance of England*, half the king's council was to con-
sist of bishops (four) and lesser clergy (twelve). As it was,
churchmen in politics toiled away with some frustration.
Henry Chichele – a merchant's son, an industrious and highly
professional product of Winchester College and New College,
Oxford, and Archbishop of Canterbury 1414-43 – recalled in
1433 that in the previous eleven years he had missed only
thirty-three of the almost daily meetings of the king's council.
Middle-class bishops such as Chichele, who liked order in
administration as much as they liked beauty in architecture,
kept the king's government functioning during Henry VI's
minority. They had their rewards, of course: on one January
morning in 1426 the king's council, consisting of six bishops
and three secular peers, decided who should be the next Archbishop of York and the next Bishops of Lincoln, Ely, Norwich,
London, Chichester and Worcester. But they had their problems in this period when the mightiest laymen, Bedford and
Gloucester, were consumed by jealousy and the semi-royal
Cardinal Beaufort was busy enriching himself and his
nephews. One day in January 1427 Archbishop Chichele was
spokesman for the rest of the council in asking the Duke of
Bedford whether he sincerely agreed that the council, not he,
had the ultimate authority; and the next day John Kemp, now
Chancellor of England as well as Archbishop of York, put the
same awkward question to the Duke of Gloucester, who happened to be ill in bed.

However, these men who ran England kept their thoughts
about the king – and about royal dukes – well away from the
official documents which alone have survived. What did
Thomas Bekynton, who became his secretary in 1437, make of
Henry VI? We do not know; if we had known, we should not
have found him as Bishop of Bath and Wells, 1443-66.[31] We
may guess that, as he grew up, the officials had to recognize

---

[31] See Arnold Judd, *The Life of Thomas Bekynton* (Chichester, 1961).

that Henry VI was never going to be a king in the full medieval sense; that he was, as one detached observer (Pope Pius II) put it, 'a man more timorous than a woman, utterly devoid of wit or spirit, who left everything in his wife's hands'. Yet right up to the Yorkist coup, the leading churchmen considered themselves bound to Henry VI their hero's son and their own anointed king. And so did most of the nobility. As J. L. Lander points out, 'in view of Henry VI's peculiar combination of weakness and wilfulness, which very adversely affected their own interests, it is surprising how many of the aristocracy remained loyal to him for so long'.[32] What became clear during this reign was that whoever supplied strong government would earn the gratitude and prayers of a people which still expressed its gratitude most characteristically in its prayers; of a people which showed its own capacity most effectively in building and adorning its churches.

Edward IV, who for a time seemed the answer to England's prayers, did not share the profound personal religion of his predecessor on the throne or of his own mother (Duchess Cecily) and sister (Margaret, Duchess of Burgundy). When he became king at the age of nineteen the contrast between him and the bookish, sickly and shabby Henry VI must have seemed total.

Edward was tall (almost six and a half feet), handsome, charming, fashionable, clever, hard-working; a master of the art of being a king. His self-confidence was such that he thought he could afford to anger the mighty Warwick and the rest of the nobility by secretly marrying an impoverished Lancastrian widow, Elizabeth Woodville, simply because he had fallen in love with her; she is said to have been one of the few women who at first resisted his advances. When he suspected Warwick's brother George Neville, Archbishop of York and for seven years Chancellor of England, of plotting against him, he had him sent to prison in Calais. The experience so shook the princely archbishop that he died before he was forty-five. The king's own brother, George Duke of Clarence, was put to death as a traitor. Edward was a man of action, all

---

[32] J. R. Lander, *Crown and Nobility, 1450-1509* (London, 1976), p.55.

that Henry VI could never be. He was also strenuous to maintain order and to enforce the law – and shrewd enough to limit his expenditure so as to avoid direct taxation which would have been unpopular. He made a profitable peace with France when he saw that war was likely to get nowhere, and set realistic limits to his subsequent intrigues in diplomacy. He took a large share in the peacetime wool and cloth trade and levied customs on his fellow-merchants. He applied up-to-date methods to the management of the Crown's own estates and extracted forced loans or 'benevolences' from his fellow-landlords. Tightening up the central administration which he directed personally, and refraining from the feckless grants to which Henry VI had been prone, he was, it seems, the first English king since Henry II to die solvent.

He had only one major problem. He was mortal. In his early forties his lechery and gluttony seem to have caught up with him; he grew overweight and suddenly, in April 1483, died while on a fishing trip. He had been almost completely a man of the world; yet he had been happy to incur vast expenditure on St George's Chapel, Windsor, for being a successful man of the world in the last quarter of the fifteenth century still meant being a son of the Church. His deathbed was devout. During his life he arranged for members of the strictest group of the Franciscans, the 'Observants', to be brought over from the Continent to a new friary close to one of his palaces, at Greenwich. And when he boasted that he had three concubines, 'one the merriest, another the wiliest, harlot in the realm', he added that the third was among all harlots the holiest.

In Tudor history-writing (a tradition which descended from Sir Thomas More and the papal tax-collector, Polydore Vergil, through Edward Hall to William Shakespeare), Edward IV was a good king in comparison with his brother, Richard III. Richard was portrayed as a monster, physically as well as morally repulsive. The reality was, however, a more subtle tragedy, rather like *Macbeth*: the tragedy of a man fit to be a king but not born to be one.

At the time of his coronation, Richard seemed, no less than Edward, the answer to the widespread longing for strong government. The ceremony — the best attended and most sumptuous coronation of the English Middle Ages — had this very serious content. During his brother's reign Richard, then Duke of Gloucester, had been in charge of the north and of the wars against the Scots. He had shown loyalty to the king, political capacity and a sense of justice. During his short reign he seems to have continued his brother's essential policy, including at least a show of piety, to which he added abhorrence of his brother's morals and favourites. Had he lived, his act in causing the body of Henry VI to be reburied near his brother's grave at Windsor — the saint near the sinner — might have led to a more ambitious programme of religious patronage. Anyway, there appeared to be no real alternative to Richard in the eyes of most of the bishops and nobles attending the coronation. Edward IV's eldest son, whom Richard had seized, was just thirteen years of age. By medieval standards that was not particularly young, but the prince had been under the control of his mother and her rapacious family; and neither the nobility nor the people had ever taken to that family. It could well be argued — and Richard did argue — that the richly experienced royal duke who had been named 'protector' of the realm in the late king's will was forced to seize the throne in order to protect himself and his country from the Woodvilles.

The other claimant to the throne, Henry Tudor, Earl of Richmond, had been a penniless exile since 1469. For almost all this time he depended on the favour of the Duke of Brittany — and, when that failed, he threw himself on the French king's mercy. He had not yet acquired any experience of war or administration; he had been brought up in Wales, and had spent only a few weeks in England; and his right to the crown of England was obscure. The Tudor connection with the crown had begun when Owen Tudor, a Welsh adventurer, for a time butler to the Bishop of Bangor, had secured employment at the English court and made an improbable marriage with Katherine, the lonely widow of Henry V; and when the ever-generous Henry VI had made their son Edmund Earl of Richmond. Edmund had, moreover, been allowed to marry Margaret Beaufort, who could trace her descent from John of Gaunt's mistress — although when the

Beauforts had been legitimated they had also been barred from the throne. Henry Tudor was an ambitious young Welshman who made the most of these royal drops in his blood, and who now strengthened his royal connections by contracting to marry Elizabeth the eldest daughter of Edward IV; but he certainly did not seem the inevitable King of England. At the beginning of 1484 Elizabeth who was to have been his bride went to live at Richard's court – and there were rumours that Richard was about to marry her. For these reasons we can have some slight sympathy with those bishops who accepted the story put about by one of their own number (Bath and Wells) that Richard was his brother's true heir since Edward V was illegitimate. The claim, not in itself improbable, was that Edward IV had already betrothed himself to another at the time of his marriage.

What destroyed Richard III was the opposite of the carnal self-indulgence that had brought his brother to a premature grave. It was the totality of his dedication to power. The queen fled to sanctuary in Westminster Abbey before coming to terms with him, but he had Lord Hastings and Earl Rivers, two of Edward IV's leading friends and servants, executed without the formality of a trial. There is no good reason to doubt that he gave the orders which led to the murders of Edward V and his brother Richard, the 'Princes in the Tower', who were seen no more after the summer of 1483.[33] Such ruthlessness had many precedents in the history of medieval

---

[33] The princes' skeletons were almost certainly those that were discovered in 1674, examined in 1933, and reburied in Westminster Abbey. People were most unlikely to kill an ex-king without making sure of the present king's wishes. P. M. Kendall, *Richard the Third* (London, 1955), tried to incriminate Buckingham who was Constable of the Tower, but Richard himself never shifted the blame in this way. In 1502 it was put about that Sir James Tyrell had confessed to carrying out the execution, before being executed himself on another charge. However, Richard's guilt cannot be regarded as proved. Sir Thomas More's vivid narrative was written some thirty years after 1483. Henry VII never directly charged Richard. See Alison Hanham, *Richard III and His Early Historians* (Oxford, 1975); Elizabeth Jenkins, *The Princes in the Tower* (London, 1978); Charles Ross, *Richard III* (London, 1981).

England, as it was to have many sequels under the Tudors. But it enabled Tudor propaganda to depict Richard as the dragon (complete with a hunchback – one of the imaginative touches), and Henry Tudor as the knight in shining armour.

The decisive moment did not occur, however, until 22 August 1485, at Bosworth in Leicestershire. Already one revolt against Richard, led by his former accomplice the Duke of Buckingham, had failed. Now Thomas Lord Stanley arrived with a Lancastrian force and it was not clear whether he would join his king. He had been steward of Richard's household and Richard held his son as a hostage, but since 1473 he had been the third husband of Henry's formidable mother. Henry had only about five thousand troops, mostly raised in Wales. Richard's army was larger and his own courage was great. Seeing Henry, he led his household guards in a direct attack; he staked all. At this moment the Stanley forces were thrown into the battle against him; the Earl of Northumberland whom he had ordered to guard his flank stood by cynically; and he was cut down crying 'Treason!' That evening his naked corpse, with a halter round the neck, was carried to burial by the Franciscans in Leicester. Dead at the age of thirty-two, he was the last of the Plantagenet kings.

HENRY VII

The new king was crowned by Thomas Bourgchier, Archbishop of Canterbury, who in his own person symbolized the continuity of the national life through the fifteenth century despite the changing and unsatisfactory kings. Bourgchier was born about 1412, the son of a knight who had fought at Agincourt and of the immensely rich Anne Plantagenet. He began accumulating ecclesiastical offices before he went to Oxford as an undergraduate, and was made Bishop of Worcester when not yet twenty-five. As a member of the king's council he was rewarded with richer sees: first Ely and then, in 1454, Canterbury. After a year as chancellor of the realm he quarrelled with Queen Margaret and therefore lost that secular post; but he remained archbishop and enjoyed the satisfaction of crowning Edward IV. Throughout that reign he flourished, becoming a cardinal. But in his seventies things went wrong. Intending to crown Edward V, he persuaded the boy king's mother to release his brother from sanctuary in Westminster Abbey, only to find the coronation cancelled and both boys murdered. However, he unheroically proceeded to anoint and crown Richard III, as he was now performing the same office for the man for whose sake Richard had been killed. It is not altogether surprising that before his death in 1486 the old man quietly retired, without resigning the archbishopric.

His successor was John Morton, another man who served more than one master in his time. At one stage this talented lawyer was a servant of Henry VI, to the point of sharing Queen Margaret's exile; then he entered the service of Edward IV and rose in it, becoming Bishop of Ely. His practical ability was shown in his supervision of the making of a great 'cut' or drain from Wisbech to Ely, transforming much of the agriculture of his marshy diocese. Richard III, presumably feeling that the bishop had been too close to his brother, was hostile; the alarmed bishop fled into exile, while keeping his communications with the centre of politics open. He was able to warn the future Henry VII that the Duke of Brittany was about to hand him over to Richard – with the results that Henry fled in disguise to the French king and always felt that Morton had saved his life. Besides, Morton was undeniably a shrewd man capable of great toil in the new king's service. No less a judge than Sir Thomas More, who as a lad waited on him at table and listened to his conversation, has left a portrait of him in *Utopia*: 'of a mean stature. . . . In his face did shine such an amiable reverence, as was pleasant to behold. . . . In the law he had profound knowledge, in wit he was incomparable, and in memory wonderful excellent.' In 1483 Morton became the king's chancellor and Archbishop of Canterbury, and he occupied both positions until his death in 1500. He was also made a cardinal – a sign of the complete harmony in which Henry VII lived with the popes of the time, whose concentration on Renaissance politics was similar to his own. The king began the practice of appointing an Italian as

Bishop of Worcester, as a reward for services in Rome.[34]

If the ecclesiastical history of Henry's reign is almost a total blank, the political history contains some omens to indicate the future. On the surface it was largely a continuation of Yorkist policy; Henry's marriage with Edward IV's daughter was symbolic, as was the invention of a Lancastrian red rose in order that it might be married with the existing Yorkist white rose to produce the Tudor red-and-white. Henry's interest in finance, so detailed that it shocked many of those around him, was only a heightening of the interest taken by Edward IV. On the surface the reign had touches of comedy – as in the stories of the two imposters Lambert Simnel (an Oxford tradesman's son) and Perkin Warbeck (a Fleming), who claimed to be sons of the Duke of Clarence and King Edward respectively. But toughness was necessary because the situation was not comic. The rebellions around Simnel and Warbeck were supported by many, abroad and at home (including the Stanley who had saved Henry's life at Bosworth); and in 1497 other rebels were allowed to march all the way from Cornwall to London – a fact which mattered far more to the king than did John Cabot's discovery of 'New Found Land' in a voyage from Bristol in the same year. It was indeed fortunate for Henry VII that Richard III's only son and his queen had both died. Had there been a plausible Yorkist candidate at liberty, Henry's own fate might well have resembled Richard's. As it was, he kept the crown placed on his head by Thomas Bourgchier, although to do so needed all his statecraft – including his ability to derive his revenue from non-parliamentary sources.

After the death in 1502 of his fifteen-year-old son Arthur, whom he had married off to the Spanish princess Catherine of Aragon as part of his diplomacy, all the king's hopes had centred on his second son, Henry. In 1509 he left to this son a quiet country, a prosperous economy and a full treasury. He also bequeathed the conviction that a king must govern sternly if he was to survive. In Roper's *Life of Sir Thomas More* there is a story which, whether true or not, is not false to the

---

[34] Christopher Harper-Bill studied Morton's Primacy in *Journal of Ecclesiastical History* (Cambridge, 1978), pp.1-21.

atmosphere of the reign now closed. Richard Foxe, Bishop of Winchester, invited the young More to join him in the king's service. He had himself become Henry's secretary before Bosworth, and had been so busy ever since that although Bishop first of Bath and Wells and then of Durham, he had never seen those cathedrals. Now in 1504 he held glittering prizes before the young man's eyes. But Richard Whitford, then Foxe's chaplain but soon to become a monk, took More aside to warn him of the moral danger. 'For my lord, my master', he said, 'to serve the king's turn, will not stick to agree to his father's death.'

THOMAS WOLSEY

Another story is told of Thomas More and the new king, Henry VIII, whose service he had entered. The two men once walked up and down More's garden in Chelsea for an hour, deep in talk, the king's arm around his friend's neck. When congratulated later on this mark of royal favour, More observed that if his head could win the king a castle in France it would be taken off his shoulders. The story hints at the dazzling attractiveness of the young Henry — athlete, musician, inexhaustible in revelry but also well educated, able to talk with More as an intellectual equal. It also suggests his wilfulness, which had, no doubt, been increased by his father's policy of keeping him in strict seclusion, away from any young man who might have acted as his equal. Henry's accession was marked by the imprisonment, and later by the execution, of his father's chief fund-raisers, Edmund Dudley and Richard Empson. His would be the popularity not only of punishing such agents of his father's policy, but also of buying a reputation the opposite of his father's miserliness. A king of this temperament, not eighteen when he came to the throne, needed glory but needed someone to organize it for him.

The glory was to be the conquest of France, fully blessed by the pope. The minister was to be Thomas Wolsey, a member of the king's council and his chief secretary from 1509, Archbishop of York from 1513, the king's chief minister from 1514, chancellor from 1515 – an administrator of prodigious industry and decisiveness, all the more hungry for power, money and display because until he became a chaplain to the aged Archbishop Deane at Canterbury in 1501 at the age of thirty he had had a stage no bigger than the Oxford college where he was bursar and schoolmaster. The king's servant whom Wolsey had first served and then displaced, Richard Foxe, retreated to his work as the bishop of a diocese ('to do some satisfaction', as he confessed, 'for eighteen years' negligence'). William Warham, Archbishop of Canterbury, also went into semi-retirement, timidly resentful of his fellow-archbishop's pre-eminence in Church and State.

Wolsey was showered with favours from a somewhat reluctant Rome at the king's request. He was made a cardinal and given the extraordinary position of *legatus a latere* (in 1518, extended for his life in 1524). This meant that he exercised most of the papacy's legal functions and rights of appointment in relation to the English Church; no resident Englishman had ever before wielded such ecclesiastical power. His opportunity to reform the Church – the reason given by the papacy for this power – was, however, wasted apart from minor affairs. He never visited his diocese of York until he had fallen from political power. Since he also drew the revenues of Durham or Winchester, and administered other dioceses which were either vacant or occupied by Italians, the cardinal's mockery of a bishop's proper work was blatant. He accepted election as Abbot of St Albans (the monks had yielded to the king's pressure) merely in order to add one more income to his amazing wealth. His illegitimate son, Thomas Wynter, was loaded with ecclesiastical offices. Being a cardinal seemed to be for him essentially an occasion for pomp glorifying his person – pomp which survives for us in the biography written after his fall by the still loyal George Cavendish, the assistant or 'usher' who arranged much of the display. The cardinal's own energy, with an eye for a thousand details, was devoted most wholeheartedly to building palaces for himself: York Place in Westminster (later the palace of Whitehall) was next to the royal court, and Hampton Court was also on the

Thames but healthily in the country. Such a man appeared to his resentful fellow-bishops to be really interested only in the profits of ecclesiastical jurisdiction, not in righting abuses; and when he lectured monks or friars he succeeded merely in giving reform a bad name. This wasted opportunity was, it seems, on his conscience when he remarked to Sir William Kingston shortly before his death in November 1530: 'If I had served God as diligently as I have done the king, he would not have given me over in my grey hairs.'

Wolsey did not serve the king by supervising any radically new programme in domestic politics. The extension of the legal activity of the king's council into a regular court called after the 'star chamber' in which it met to hear complaints of violence was his main achievement, but high-sounding proclamations about meeting economic problems seem to have produced little effective action. One reason was his unwillingness to face the House of Commons; during the fourteen years of his ascendancy only one Parliament was summoned. All this was in contrast with the approach to be made by Thomas Cromwell, who became his chief assistant (Cromwell was used, for example, in the suppression of decayed monasteries in order to endow the college at Oxford and the school at Ipswich with a minimum of expense to their founder). Cromwell, when national power came to him, pursued a systematic policy of radical reform in Church and State — and rose to his position as Henry's chief minister by his ability to manage, or at least to understand, the House of Commons. Wolsey's capacious mind no doubt included some ideals about the enforcement of justice against 'overmighty' men; but he had too much petty business on hand to be the creator of the new England. The most important effect of his administration of Church and State was to show Henry VIII what power over both institutions could be held by the king's man — and to raise the question: why should not the king's man be the king? The most widespread reputation which Wolsey left behind was that of a tyrant, acting as if he had been begotten by a king instead of by a butcher. Dying on his way south to the Tower of London, the shattered cardinal was buried in Leicester, like Richard III. It took the mature, compassionate genius of

Shakespeare (in *Henry VIII*, the last play in which he had a major share) to see that Wolsey, like Richard III, had talents greater than those of any rightful king; so that both men, as they fall in defeat, worthily arouse our admiration.[35]

THE BREAK WITH ROME

The tragedy of the 1520s was that this superbly able minister and his king were fascinated chiefly by the chance of winning a European reputation in foreign affairs, and principally by the old dream of the conquest of France. Finding the revival of the Hundred Years' War no easy matter despite large expenditure, Wolsey organized instead the glory of spectacular, but temporary, peacemaking. The Treaty of London in 1518 and the Field of Cloth of Gold two years later provided what turned out to be the last great public pageants of the European Middle Ages. And in search of further European glory, Henry VIII put his name to a book in 1521: a *Defence of the Seven Sacraments* against the new German heretic, Martin Luther. A delighted pope, Leo X, took the occasion to pay him the compliment for which he had been angling: the royal defender of the Catholic faith and his successors were to be known for ever as *Fidei Defensores*. The title still appears on the coins of the United Kingdom.

The irony of this 'Defender of the Faith' title, however, is that within four years of its award Henry had taken the path which eventually led to his break with Rome. He had ceased to sleep with his queen (seven years his senior) and had fallen in love with Anne Boleyn, an eighteen-year-old brunette at court. Her elder sister, Mary, had already been his mistress. Anne, seeing how easily Henry had discarded Mary, refused to yield to him until she was sure of becoming his wife; and such surprising obstinacy made Henry all the more resolved to have

---

[35] Because in the end Wolsey mattered so little to England, no scholar has yet felt stimulated to replace A. F. Pollard's *Wolsey* (London, 1929). But see Charles Ferguson, *Naked to Mine Enemies* (London, 1958).

his marriage with Catherine declared no marriage at all. What was needed, then called a divorce, would nowadays be a decree of nullity. And since the pope would not agree, out of Henry's resolve to marry Anne arose the abolition of the jurisdiction of the papacy in England.

Historians as well as innumerable dramatists and film-makers have reckoned Henry's psychology to have been a major factor in this crisis. The prince whom all had ap-plauded in 1509 had grown into a handsome monster, an egotist whose assurance that his will (for the moment) was the will of God was equalled only by his cruelty in destroying any whose existence stood in his way. It is very difficult for us to see his conduct in the 1520s in any more favourable light when we have noted how heartless his behaviour became when the con-straints of medieval convention were finally abandoned and the mature man was free to reveal himself. Dressed all in yellow, he celebrated Catherine's death (from cancer) in January 1536 with a Mass of thanksgiving and a banquet – and four months later had Anne Boleyn executed, betrothing himself the next day to Jane Seymour. Nor is it possible to take with complete seriousness those who advised Henry in matters of conscience. Thomas Cranmer, the Cambridge theologian and chaplain to the Boleyns who was made Archbishop of Canterbury in 1533 in order that he might annul the marriage with Catherine, six years later declared the marriage with Anne null, in order to add to her griefs before her execution. The ground alleged was, it seems, that Henry had already en-joyed a sexual relationship with his bride's sister.

There were, however, complications. However repulsive may have been the behaviour of Henry VIII and of his clerical toadies, almost all historians believe that Henry and church-men such as Cranmer were convinced of the righteousness of their case. It is at least certain that Henry did not take one way out of his dilemma; although his reign was to be soaked in the blood of men and women executed as traitors, he did not arrange for his first wife's death. It is also clear that the king and his assistants could produce substantial arguments both in ethics and in politics.

Catherine of Aragon's marriage with Henry had taken place

in the 'observant' Franciscans' church at Greenwich in June
1509. It had been validated in the eyes of ecclesiastical lawyers
by a papal dispensation from the obstacle arising from the fact
of her previous marriage with Arthur, Prince of Wales.
Although one passage in the Old Testament (Deuteronomy
25:5) commanded an Israelite to marry his brother's widow in
order to raise children, there were other laws from another
period in Ancient Israel's history (Leviticus 18:16, 20:21)
which prohibited the practice. Accordingly this papal dispensation had been thought necessary, and had been obtained in
1503, before Henry and Catherine were betrothed. It could
now be argued that the pope had been mistaken to set aside a
moral command in the law of Moses. (Indeed, during the
delay between betrothal and marriage, in 1505, Henry had
sworn before Bishop Foxe that he had not consented to the
betrothal and would never ratify it by marriage; presumably
this secret oath had been part of his father's devious
diplomacy.) Pursuing this line, it was in the 1520s possible for
Cardinal Wolsey to be confident that he could arrange
matters – and for an academic body as orthodox as the University of Paris to agree with the English universities that
Catherine had not been free to marry Henry. It is true that
Catherine consistently denied that her marriage with Arthur
had been consummated, but because her Spanish advisers
were anxious to get her married to Henry while retaining the
small financial advantages of being Arthur's widow, she made
the fatal mistake of agreeing not to have her virginity recorded
in a papal document at the time of the dispensation of 1503.
Indeed, because the papacy had not then noted this all-
important fact about Catherine's first marriage the dispensation for her second could be held to be invalid; a point
which the sharp-witted Wolsey saw, but which later got
obscured. More relevant than his bride's virginity to Henry's
conscience was the succession of miscarriages and mishaps
(five infants failed to survive) which had been the tragedy of
their marriage. Only one child, and that a sickly girl (Mary),
had been spared to live; and Henry did not find it impossible
to persuade himself that this was a sign of the wrath of God on
incest. Leviticus 20:21 decreed the punishment of childlessness

on a man who had taken his brother's wife. Or it did so in the Latin version known to Henry; the translation of the New English Bible (1970) reads simply: 'they shall be proscribed.'[36]

When we turn to the political aspects of the problem, we enter a less shadowy world. It was not unknown for decrees of nullity to be granted by the papacy to royal and noble petitioners. In 1491 Louis XII of France had arranged one in order to marry Anne the heiress of Brittany (his brother's widow). In 1527-28 the existing marriages both of Henry's sister (Queen Margaret of Scotland) and of his future brother-in-law (the Duke of Suffolk) were annulled. Over many years signs came from Rome, holding out hopes of a similar concession to the English king. It seems probable that Pope Clement VII would have made the concession, had Catherine not been exceptionally obstinate in sticking to her marriage and had she not been the aunt of the emperor Charles V – whose troops, having crushed the French, sacked Rome in 1527 and thereafter held the pope a virtual prisoner. It is even possible that Charles V would have withdrawn his objections had he been persuaded that Henry VIII would be a reliable and effective ally in the struggle against France for the control of Italy. As it was, however, during tortuous negotiations leading to a great variety of schemes and experiments (at one stage Henry proposed that he might be licensed to commit bigamy), it slowly became clear that the emperor was adamant. It followed that the pope, although he was always eager to evade and to procrastinate, and although privately he urged Henry to go ahead and marry leaving others to sort out the legalities, was not going to oblige with a formal pronouncement.

To Henry's mind this attitude in Rome was a political disaster as well as a personal affront. He needed an heir – and one whose title could not be questioned. He could not be sure that his daughter would live to inherit the throne or that, if she did, she would escape the fates of Edward II, Richard II

---

[36] The best short treatment of the legal problems is to be found in J. J. Scarisbrick, *Henry VIII* (London, 1968), Chapter 7. The negotiations were studied by G. de C. Parmiter, *The King's Great Matter* (London, 1967).

and Edward V. The anarchy in England in the time of the last
reigning queen, Matilda, was not a good precedent. Like his
father Henry was conscious of the fragility of the Tudor claim
to the thone; England's leading nobleman, the Duke of Buckingham, was executed in 1521 for this reason. Henry was also
afraid that whoever married Mary might be the effective ruler
of England, and that such a man might have to be a
foreigner – a fear which was by no means groundless, as the
unpopularity of Mary's marriage with Philip of Spain showed
in the 1550s. Before his legitimate son Edward was born (and
survived infancy) in 1537, Henry even nursed the hope that his
bastard, Henry Fitzroy, might be acknowledged as king one
day. Accordingly the boy was made Duke of Richmond, Lord
Admiral and Lord Lieutenant in Ireland, with precedence
over Mary. But he died in 1536.

Henry's campaign to marry Anne began in the middle of
1525. It did not end until their secret wedding in January
1533; the previous month she had become pregnant, presumably consenting at long last because she was by now absolutely
sure of Henry's determination and their joint hopes had been
briefly raised by the promise of French support at Rome. The
delay of seven years is to be explained partly by Henry's extraordinary character. Although he was always devoted to his
pleasures he was also a political realist; in his heart he must
have known that his heir would have to be legitimate.
Although always ruthless he was also always self-righteous, so
that he wished still to be in a position to play the preacher
when his matrimonial problems had been settled. Although he
was often impatient, he kept hoping that this cause, so
obviously wise and right, would prevail in Rome, resulting in a
boy's birth which would be honourable and majestic in the
eyes of the world. Although he was morally indignant when
frustrated, he could be diverted from his anger by the almost
endless round of sport and feasts in which he indulged; and
although he was on occasion brutally decisive he was reluctant
to do routine work, with the result that much was left to his
ministers. Wolsey tried method after method, delay after
delay, in order to avert a fatal conflict between his position as
the king's chief minister and his position as the Englishman to

whom the pope had delegated most of his powers. When Wolsey fell in 1529, he was replaced by a group of aristocrats with little to contribute to policy-formation. Sir Thomas More, who made no secret of his disapproval of the king's matrimonial plans, acted as chancellor. Although Edward Foxe (later Bishop of Hereford) was a radical close to the king, it was not until 1533 that Henry had as chief minister a man who could suggest and superintend a creatively radical policy, in the person of Thomas Cromwell.

The fundamental cause of the delay, however, was the enormity of the step necessary if the papacy were to be ignored in the 'great matter' of the king's marriage. Until this problem arose the English monarchy and the papacy seemed to be allied for ever, in the control of the Church as well as in European diplomacy. Not many Englishmen went to Rome; Cardinal Wolsey never did, although when the papacy was vacant there was some thought that he might sacrifice his many English incomes in order to accept it. But those few who spent five weeks or so on the journey to Rome were not often morally outraged at the end of it. A typical Englishman was Christopher Bainbridge, Wolsey's predecessor as Archbishop of York, who had fitted into Renaissance Rome, its splendours and its wars, very happily as Henry's ambassador and a resident cardinal.[37] In England the unity of Christendom under the pope had been damaged by the Lollards and by the parliamentary statutes, *Provisors* and *Praemunire*, and had not been articulated in any very definite way by theologians. But it had been for many centuries a theme of religion — and the theme was still there. The only man of unblemished integrity and theological stature among Henry's bishops, John Fisher of Rochester, wrote no fewer than seven learned and acute books in his support of Queen Catherine and of the papacy. Even old William Warham at Canterbury (a Fellow of New College, Oxford, a lawyer and a diplomat, who found himself made Bishop of London in 1501 and Archbishop two years later) once went through a short period when he

---

[37] See D. S. Chambers, *Cardinal Bainbridge in the Court of Rome, 1509-14* (Oxford, 1965).

recalled Becket's example, before adding his silence to his clergy's. Thomas Cranmer, chosen archbishop by the king on Warham's convenient death, still used the seal of his predecessors at Canterbury: a representation of Thomas Becket.

In order to break this traditional acceptance of the papacy, a large array of arguments had to be assembled. The chronicles of England as well as the archives in Rome were quarries for Henry's agents. The ghost of King Arthur, whose conquests were believed to have reached Rome, was invoked in order to justify the claim that Britain had always been an 'empire'. The submission of King John to Pope Innocent had to be interpreted as a brief surrender to foreign aggression – and it had to be stressed that the fourteenth-century antipapal statutes of *Praemunire* cancelled out any other precedents. This assembly of authorities was an important task for those now serving the king. But it also seems clear that their supreme task was stiffening their king's courage to break with Rome – until the January night in 1547 when Archbishop Cranmer, summoned to his master's deathbed, found him already speechless; whereupon Henry, 'holding him with his hand, did wring his hand in his as hard as he could'.

Not even a politician as clever as Thomas Cromwell, or a theologian as loyal and as conveniently learned as Thomas Cranmer, could give Henry all the support needed for the essential step. To secure this, Henry summoned the 'Reformation Parliament' which enacted nothing less than a revolution during its seven sessions from November 1529 to July 1536 – exalting the Crown over the Church as it had never been exalted before, but also exalting itself as the sovereign 'King in Parliament'.[38]

The anticlericalism voiced in the House of Commons was now used to frighten the clergy into buying Henry's good will and into acceptance of the king's claim to be 'protector and only supreme head of the English Church' – although in a motion moved by Bishop John Fisher the clergy in the Convocation of Canterbury added 'as far as the law of Christ allows' and in the smaller Convocation of York Cuthbert Tunstall,

---

[38] See S. E. Lehmberg, *The Reformation Parliament* (Cambridge, 1970).

Bishop of Durham, added a protest even to this qualified title. In 1532 a 'supplication' came from the Commons against the workings of the ecclesiastical courts (and against tithes too, although this was soon forgotten). It, too, was used as a stick to beat the priests. On 15 May a cowed and small meeting of the Convocation of the clergy of the Canterbury province submitted to the Crown for fear of the Commons. In future no convocation was to be summoned without a royal writ, no 'canon' law was to be enacted in future without the royal assent, and the existing laws of the Church were to be revised without reference to Rome by a committee appointed by the king. In August William Warham, who had presided over this surrender, found a merciful release through death.

Thus was the way prepared for the decisive moves of 1533 – the appointment of Cranmer to Canterbury (with the pope's feeble consent); the Act to 'restrain' or forbid appeals to Rome; the declaration by the subservient Convocation of Canterbury that Henry's marriage with Catherine was invalid; Cranmer's formal judgement to the same effect; Anne's sumptuous coronation; Henry's excommunication by Rome. Only one matter could not be controlled by the king: Anne's child was a girl.

In the next year the Act of Succession provided for an oath to be taken throughout the kingdom acknowledging the new marriage and its offspring. Other Acts accompanied it. All payments to, and legal business in, Rome were forbidden, and it was no longer heresy to deny the pope's primacy. The king alone was to appoint bishops and was to receive a tenth of all clerical incomes. The earlier submission of the clergy to the king as their 'Supreme Head' was turned into English law without any reference to the saving clause about the 'law of Christ'. It was made treason even to speak (let alone act) against the king as a 'heretic, schismatic, tyrant, infidel, or usurper of the crown'. The Preamble to the Statute of Appeals in 1533 declared that, on the contrary, 'by divers sundry old authentic histories and chronicles it is manifestly declared . . . that this realm of England is an empire . . . governed by one supreme head and king . . . unto whom a body politic, compact of all sorts and degrees of people, divided in terms and by names of spirituality and temporality, be bounded and owe to bear next to God a natural and humble obedience . . .'

Those who regard this break with Rome in 1533-34 as deeply tragic have understandably been among those who have stressed that the treason laws under Henry VIII constituted a reign of terror. Yet the comparison with Hitler or Stalin should not be pressed too far. Henry had no large police force and no standing army; on the contrary, weapons were widely distributed in the homes of the people. The executions of traitors in his reign, however frightening or sickening, stopped far short of a massacre. The truth seems to be that what he did was generally accepted; or at least, that enough people who disagreed with what he did were terrified of the disorder that would result from disobeying the consecrated king. The effective terror was that exercised in their own minds by this prospect. To later generations the 'natural and humble obedience' of sixteenth-century Englishmen – who customarily protested their loyalty immediately before they were executed as traitors – has been a loyalty beyond comprehension, an abasement before monarchs who with the exception of the first Elizabeth did not deserve such flattery. But we must understand this emotion if we are to understand the best, as well as the average, of the period. A horror of rebellion was an emotion felt deeply by the mind that created the Church of England's Book of Common Prayer and by William Shakespeare. At any rate, in 1534 almost all the clergy of England signed, or otherwise accepted, a declaration that the Bishop of Rome had no greater jurisdiction in the realm of England than any other foreign bishop – which meant: none at all. Reproducing the signatures of sixty-six bishops, abbots or other dignitaries to one such document, a modern Roman Catholic history of the English Reformation gives this caption to the picture: 'The Fort is Betrayed.'[39] And the fort which the clergy surrendered was not defended heroically by the laity.

One explanation is that it was possible to accept an argument which Henry VIII put forward when it suited him (for example, in a letter to Cuthbert Tunstall, Bishop of Durham):

---

[39] Philip Hughes, *The Reformation in England*, vol. i (London, 1950).

to make the king supreme over 'the Church' or 'the spirituality'
meant no more than acknowledging power over the clergy
which he already had clearly over the laity. Another factor is
that even after all this legislation many refused to believe that
the break with Rome could be final; and that is another explanation of the willingness to surrender. Lorenzo Campeggio
was the cardinal who had been sent to England in the course
of the long farce of examining Henry's petition to the pope.
When Catherine had died and Anne had been executed in
1536, Campeggio once again prepared to visit England in
order to reconcile Henry to the Church – and to recover his
own bishopric of Salisbury. The pope and the emperor both
hailed the two women's deaths as providential. Within
England many who took the new oath may have done so in the
belief that within a short time the king and the pope wuld
once more reach agreement. And once the oath had been
taken, it was hard to develop a conscientious scruple which
would destroy one's chances of remaining a prosperous citizen,
or the pastor of a parish, or a bishop. Tunstall, for example,
who had already been Bishop of London from 1522 to 1530,
retained the ample revenues and performed the useful duties
of the bishopric of Durham from 1530 to 1552, and lost them
then only because the Duke of Northumberland coveted the
estates. He recovered the bishopric in 1554, for another five
years, until finally conscience drove him to refuse to accept the
supremacy of Elizabeth, in his eighty-fifth year.[40] No doubt
the fear of being branded – more literally, of being hanged
and, while still half-alive, disembowelled – as a traitor influenced the secret struggles of many consciences; but we have
to account for the ease with which so many assented in public
to acts which their consciences must often have rejected or
questioned. It seems reasonable to suppose that they told
themselves that their assent would be temporary.

However, any optimists who believed that the *status quo*
would soon be restored misjudged Henry. Even now that the
immediate cause of his break with Rome had been removed,
he liked being the English Church's 'Supreme Head'; it suited

---

[40] See Charles Sturge, *Cuthbert Tunstall* (London, 1938).

his consummate vanity. As teacher of his people he issued Ten Articles of Faith, mainly conservative but in places agreeing with the new Lutheran theology and defending only three, not seven, sacraments (Baptism, the Mass and Penance). And having tasted blood when he asserted this legal and theological supremacy, Henry now began to move against the English Church's fattest and softest piece of flesh: the monasteries.

In 1534 there were very few convinced Protestants in England, but when the monastic estates had been distributed to the laity the king was only one in a large number of influential Englishmen with a vested interest in opposing any idea of a return to the religion of the Middle Ages. When in the 1550s Henry's daughter Mary — a fanatical Catholic as a result of the humiliating injustice done to her mother and herself — was on the throne and determined to restore the old religion, the one piece of wisdom agreed on by almost all her advisors, and even accepted by herself, was not to touch the gentry's possession of the lands which had belonged to the monasteries. Cardinal Pole was not allowed into the country to reconcile England to Rome until he had very reluctantly accepted this condition. If the clergy's cowardice betrayed the fort, the laity's greed took the fort over; for many hundreds of religious houses now provided either a nucleus for a gentleman's handsome manor house or building materials for humbler men. The betrayed castle became the Englishman's home.

THE END OF THE MONASTERIES

When in 1537 Robert Aske was a prisoner in the Tower of London, condemned for treason with no hope of life, he wrote for Thomas Cromwell and his agents a statement of his cause. 'The abbeys in the north parts', he affirmed, 'gave great alms to poor men and laudably served God.' But now he saw only desolation: 'the blessed consecration of the sacrament now not used, the ornaments and relics of the Church irreverently used the tombs and sepulchres of honourable and noble men pulled down and sold, none hospitality now in those places kept. . . .

Also the abbeys were one of the beauties of this realm to all men and strangers passing through the same. . . .' And in 1593, clothing Robert Aske's nostalgia in local detail, a former lay official looked back at the life of the cathedral monastery in Durham. He could recall from his boyhood exactly what the routine had been and what had been the ornaments of the great church, now desolate for him. He wished to write it all down before he, too, died.[41]

Yet what is most surprising about the end of the 825 religious houses in England and Wales is not how much, but how little, opposition it aroused. The monasteries were not occupied by armed force; they surrendered to the king. Only the comparatively recent foundations of the London Carthusians, the Bridgettines and the 'observant' Franciscans refused to take the 1534 oath to the king or put up anything like a united front against the secular aggression; in almost all the houses, the superiors were able to obtain the consent of the inmates to the oath and later to the surrender. Many tens of thousands of laymen were intimately involved in the fortunes of these houses as the descendants of their founders, as their tenants or neighbours, as lodgers or employees, or simply as tradesmen; and most of those so involved seem to have kept silent apart from petitioning for their share in the loot.

The explanation cannot be that there were precedents for the destruction which began in 1536. The nearest precedents were three. The Knights Templar had been an order both military and religious until suppressed by Pope Clement V in 1312 (with greater brutality than Henry VIII ever had to show towards the monks); but almost all their lands had been transferred to the Order of St John of Jerusalem. The 'alien priories' (small houses controlled by Norman and other foreign monasteries) had been suppressed by kings from Edward I to Henry V; but almost all their estates had been used for the endowment of chapels, colleges, schools and the Carthusian monastery at Sheen. Wolsey had secured the transfer of the incomes of some small and decayed religious

---

[41] David Knowles, *The Religious Orders in England*, vol. iii (Cambridge, 1959), pp.129-137, 328.

houses to his colleges in Oxford and Ipswich; but the austere and orthodox Bishop Fisher had done the same for education in Cambridge. The destruction of the English and Welsh religious houses was a sudden and major revolution not only in economics but also in politics and religion.

The explanation of the quietness of this revolution cannot be that these houses were notorious for their moral or financial disorder. Historians have the advantage of being able to study the records of the 'visitations' by the bishops or the bishops' officials. These documents record in detail some scandals and much slackness, but the picture as a whole is certainly not one of gross immorality. The least viable houses were, it is obvious, the smallest, and even historians who lament the destruction of the greater houses with all their treasures in the spiritual life and in art agree that it would have been sensible to effect a radical reduction in the numbers of houses. But the surviving accounts do not suggest that there was widespread dishonesty or insolvency. We can also read the reports of the coarse Richard Layton and the other commissioners who were hurriedly sent in 1535 to extract evidence of corruption, to announce an austere future and to invite desertions from the monastic vows. But not even these reports persuade historians that the monastic system as a whole was seriously beyond reform.

What is clear is that by 1535 in most monasteries the old fire was burning low. The services in church, and no doubt also the prayers in private, were maintained as they had been for centuries and as they seemed certain to be for centuries to come; but in return the monks, nuns and friars expected a life as comfortable as that of the nearby gentry, apart from marriage. There was little sense of flight from the world in order to gain eternal salvation. The religious houses no longer harboured many who wished to climb the ladder of spiritual perfection or to devote themselves to scholarship and education. They were no longer unique as places where the dead could be prayed for; chantries existed for this purpose in many parish churches. They no longer contributed much to the administration, agriculture or trade of the kingdom; laymen such as Thomas More, or priests as secular-minded as Thomas

Wolsey, or the landowners whom Wolsey had tried to discipline, or the merchants who were growing into substantial capitalists (specially in London), had taken away all these roles in which monks had for long been conspicuous. They no longer copied out manuscripts; the printers had taken over.

Yet while the fire burned low, the immense rewards which had come to the monasteries for their past political and economic contributions continued. That was shown to the government by the mouth-watering financial statistics of the *Valor Ecclesiasticus*, gathered in 1535. Indeed, wealth – its advantages as well as its worries – had choked the growth of that spiritual harvest which, far more than any secular contribution, had been the passionate concern of every one of the founders of these religious orders. It was assumed, and rightly, that the monks, nuns and friars would not continue to offer to God ordered prayer and fervent charity as consecrated communities once their lavish buildings and endowments had been surrendered. A return to the simplicity of the origins of monasticism – to the poverty of the Irish monks recorded by Bede, for example – would have been extremely difficult and was never contemplated. It is also revealing how few of those who had been monks before 1540 wished to resume the life when that became possible, although difficult, in 1555 under the Catholic Queen Mary. Had these religious orders retained more of their original ideals they would have been respected more deeply both by the laity and by themselves, and might have been defended so vigorously that they would have been allowed to keep some of their property by a king whose own anxiety to seem respectable had just been laboriously demonstrated.

Another reason why the monasteries closed quietly was that the move against them, like the break with Rome, was made little by little, so that not until towards the end was any religious radicalism undeniable.

In 1533 there was a rumble of the coming storm when John Leland was commissioned to investigate the monastic libraries – a task which enabled him to save countless volumes as the storm broke, although much of the medieval legacy was then lost for ever, in literature as in art. In 1536 an Act was passed to provide for the dissolution of religious houses whose lands did not yield more than £200 a year. Although the previous year's visitation had yielded no proof that all such houses were undisciplined, the suppression of about two hundred small communities could be presented as a rationalization acceptable to all reformers, and the government propaganda machine managed by Thomas Cromwell was busy manufacturing or encouraging talk of the good purposes to which the revenues would be put. Education and charity were stressed, but the defence and administration of the realm without taxes also seemed a charitable purpose, and a 'Court of Augmentations of the King's Revenue' was established with regional officers to receive the surrendered buildings and estates. The inmates of the suppressed houses were given the choice of moving to the surviving monasteries or becoming parish priests.

Even this limited measure contributed to the rebellion known as the Pilgrimage of Grace. This broke out in Lincolnshire and Yorkshire in the autumn of 1536. It spread into Lancashire and elsewhere, but by March it was over. Essentially it seems to have been a rebellion organized by conservative gentry who vainly hoped for intervention by the emperor Charles V, but like the Peasants' Revolt of 1381 this one was fed by many local grievances against landlords; and as in 1381 this 'pilgrimage' was encouraged by priests who preached religious idealism to the excited people. In some places—particularly in Lancashire and in the mind of Robert Aske the most eloquent rebel – the suppression of the smaller religious houses was a particular grievance in a general reaction against social and religious change. And since abbots and monks were involved in such treason, this provided firm ground for the assault on the remaining religious houses.

During the period 1537-40 there was frantic activity in these houses. Many tried to buy good will by paying for licences of exemption from the existing Parliamentary Act, by bribing the royal officials, or by pensioning strong laymen in the neighbourhood. Many decided that the time had come to secure employment or pensions for themselves (the average after tax was £6 a year for an ex-monk, but there was more generous provision for superiors). But the storm raged on. In 1538 Richard Ingworth, formerly the provincial prior of the Dominicans but now Bishop of Dover, 'visited' all the friars and within little more than twelve months had obtained the surrender of the great majority. In the same year the chief pilgrims' shrines were demolished; wagonloads of treasure came to the king from the shrine of St Thomas of Canterbury. In 1539 a new Act of Parliament gave security both to the king and to almost all lay tenants or purchasers of monastic lands which had been surrendered, thus encouraging a fresh wave of surrenders into the hands of commissioners sent to sweep through the country. Where there was unwillingness to surrender, impatient methods were used towards the end. Abbot Whiting of Glastonbury was hanged – it was claimed, for concealing some of the treasures of his church. Similar fates, for alleged treason, overtook the heads of other rich Benedictine houses at Reading and Colchester before Christmas 1539. When Evesham Abbey was suppressed on 30 January 1540, the monks in the choir were not allowed to complete the psalm they were singing at Evensong. In March of that year the cathedral monasteries at Canterbury and Rochester, which had been obstinate, were dissolved; and Waltham Abbey was the last to surrender.

The Order of St John of Jerusalem was dissolved by another Act later in 1540. Apart from a few conventual hospitals (mopped up in 1545), no religious house was now left. Between eight and nine thousand monks, nuns and friars, with an unknown number of lay servants, had to find new homes.

The surrender of the larger houses was accompanied by more talk about colleges, schools, hospitals and the pastoral care of the people. Eventually the eight cathedrals which had been staffed by monks or canons were, with Westminster Abbey, entrusted to Deans and Chapters. Six new dioceses were created with cathedrals' and bishops' incomes derived from the former monasteries: Westminster (until 1550), Gloucester, Bristol, Oxford, Peterborough and Chester. At Canterbury Cranmer dreamed of a substantial college in the cathedral, but what happened was the endowment of a grammar school – as in ten other cathedral cities. Fortunately

Cranmer was able to secure that the King's Scholars at Canterbury as elsewhere should be 'poor' boys, while others argued that such a good education ought to be reserved for the sons of the gentry. Ten 'Regius' professorships were endowed by the king at Oxford and Cambridge along with his great foundations of Christ Church, Oxford (the former Cardinal College), and Trinity College, Cambridge. All this was excellent but it was less than the dream, and the expenditure which was authorized for other edifying purposes accounted for only a small part of the wealth which passed through the Court of Augmentations.

More of the profit from the religious houses was devoted to the fortification of the coasts against threatened invasion and still more to the other current needs of the government. The fall of the efficient Cromwell in 1540 increased both those needs and the appetites of buyers. Before the death of Henry VIII over half of the former monastic estates had been granted away or (and this was far more usual) sold off – normally at a price twenty times the annual rent which the land would fetch on the open market. In 1540 Henry was trying to persuade James V of Scotland that if he, too, would end the 'untruth and beastly living of those monks', then he, too, would be able to 'live like a king'.[42] But in real life what Henry's government needed was cash – and taking it from the sale of monastic lands was far more popular than asking Parliament for taxation. Still greater was the need of those who governed England during the minority of Henry's son; the Court of Augmentations had to finance the Duke of Somerset's wars in Scotland and France. By the accession of Elizabeth I, over three-quarters of these vast estates had gone. Much of the land was resold fairly quickly, and most of it ended up in small or medium-sized holdings. This was, of course, a decisive shift of power in English society – away from the Church, not to the Crown but to the gentry.

In the 1530s the Crown's own lands were worth less than a third of the net income of the monasteries according to the

---

[42] This splendid example of royal self-congratulation is printed in *The Letters of Henry VIII*, ed. M. St. C. Byrne (London, 1936), pp.288-9.

Valor Ecclesiasticus (£131,361). Had the Crown kept the monasteries' estates and exploited them, its ultimate dependence on the gentry represented in Parliament would have been far less and the whole course of English history might have been different. But there is no evidence that this was ever a serious intention. Nor does it seem probable that the authorities were ever really determined to pursue the much-advertised vision of a massive new endowment for education and other forms of charity.[43]

SPIRITUAL UNDERCURRENTS

One of the arguments used to encourage the surrender of the monasteries was that English kings had endowed many of them. The monks were merely handing back to Henry VIII what was rightfully his own. Innumerable other signs were given that Henry wished to minimize any impression that the break with Rome meant any break with the religion accepted by King Ethelbert from St Augustine and defended in the British 'empire' (the Tudors loved the word) by King Arthur. Up to the death of Henry VIII it is fair to describe the English Reformation as an essentially political and economic change, dictated by two needs which were scarcely theological – the need felt by the king to beget a legitimate male heir, and the need felt by the gentry to get hold of the monastic lands. The religion of the bulk of the people remained Catholic. This continuity was shown by the rapturous welcome to a Catholic princess, Mary, when she inherited the throne in 1553 – and further illustrated by the Duke of Northumberland, who had tried to stop Mary but who now returned to the Catholic faith before being executed for treason. Probably Protestants were still in the minority in the 1570s and 1580s under Elizabeth I.

---

[43] In addition to the masterly volume by David Knowles quoted on p.296, see *Letters to Cromwell and Others on the Suppression of the Monasteries* edited by G. H. Cook (London, 1965), and Joyce Youings, *The Dissolution of the Monasteries* (London, 1971).

But the denial of the authority of the pope and the drastic reduction in the authority and wealth of the clergy made, or at least uncovered, a vacuum which was in the end largely filled by the most vigorous variety of contemporary Christianity: Protestantism.

Late medieval Catholicism, for all its popularity, was a standing invitation to reform. In the fifteenth century and again in 1512-17, great Councils of the Church said so; and in Spain something was actually done. In the early sixteenth century, 'everyone wanted reform, or professed to want reform' – although 'when churchmen spoke of reformation, they were almost always thinking of administrative, legal or moral reformation; hardly ever of doctrinal reformation'.[44]

We have already seen some of the administrative and legal changes which in England the laity desired and achieved. But we ought also to notice that popular piety often spoke in a new way about the aspiration or hunger or suffering of the troubled individual; late medieval loyalty to the doctrine of the Catholic Church had this element of tension in it. The most popular devotions of the fifteenth century centred on the suffering of the incarnate Christ (this was the time when the devotion of 'the stations of the cross' developed); and on the humble purity of the mother of Christ (this was the century in which it became customary to recite the *Angelus* and rosary prayers in honour of Our Lady). Above all there was the emphasis on the power of the sacrifice of Christ, and of the intercession of his mother, to free the souls of the living and the dead from the pains of purgatory. Running through such devotions there was an individualism which had not been nearly so widespread in previous ages. The devotion was paid to the human Christ and Mary, remembering the dead by name, and it was stressed what ordinary people could do for their own salvation and that of their families and friends by the recital of prayers and by hiring priests to offer many Masses. Even the 'primers' or prayer books which were now being printed in abundance never suggested that the laity should corporately follow the priest's Latin words (often

---

[44] Owen Chadwick, *The Reformation* (London, 1964), pp.12-13.

spoken softly) in the liturgy of the Mass; prayers in English were given for them to say privately although they were all in church. Laymen did not receive communion together except on a few occasions in the year when they were 'houselled' or given the consecrated bread, the wine always being kept for the priest alone.

All this made for a powerful religion, powerful because it was popular. For the time being, enough individuals found their spiritual food within the inherited system after these relatively minor developments. Modern talk suggesting that 'the Church anticipated in discipline the Soviet-Nazi theory of Totalitarianism'[45] does not take account of the fact that to the end, despite the Inquisition abroad and the persecution of the Lollards in England, the medieval Church had no police. And the dismissal of medieval religion as 'magic' does not take account of the fact that the Church fought many popular superstitions. The great time for magic was when the Catholic Church had been brought low.[46] But after the religious changes of the sixteenth century – changes which transformed Catholicism in addition to creating Protestantism – it was possible to look back and see that the power of the Gospel as God's gracious answer to human needs and aspirations, producing assurance and joy in the believer, had previously been deficient.

Professor A. G. Dickens, who has examined countless printed and unprinted records of popular and conventional religion in late medieval England, has stressed these characteristics: 'its effort to attain salvation through devout observances, its fantastic emphasis on saints, relics and pilgrimages, its tendency to allow the personality and teaching of Jesus to recede from the focus of the picture. That the connection of such writings with the Christianity of the Gospel is rather tenuous could be demonstrated with almost mathematical precision'. And although it was a popular religion, fear was very prominent. Devotional manuals and people's wills,

---

[45] G. G. Coulton, *Medieval Panorama* (Cambridge, 1938), p.458.
[46] See Keith Thomas, *Religion and the Decline of Magic* (revised, Harmondsworth, Middx., 1971).

the echoes we have of popular preaching and the more elevated defence put up for Catholicism by, for example, Sir Thomas More — all this evidence points to 'a dogmatic and detailed emphasis upon the horrors of purgatory and the means whereby sinners could mitigate them. . . . Medieval men were faced by quite terrifying views of punishment in the life to come; it was small wonder that they felt more comfortable with the saints than with God, or that they came to regard the Blessed Virgin as a merciful mediatrix for ever seeking to placate the divine wrath of the Son as Judge'.[47]

Professor Dickens is also one of the modern scholars, of various religious persuasions, who make the point that not enough pastoral work was being done to commend this faith to any of the English who may have had secret hesitations over it. The pope seemed to be an Italian politician, not a spiritual leader. The bishops had for long been in most cases ecclesiastical lawyers and civil servants rather than preachers or pastors, and this tendency was stronger in England than in most of the rest of late medieval Europe. There were plenty of clergy, but far too many of them were chantry priests whose duty was to pray for the souls of the dead, not to be pastors of the living; and astonishingly little was done throughout the Middle Ages to train parish priests, to encourage their pastoral work, or to take pastoral care of them in their own problems and griefs. It was not until 1555, under Queen Mary, that a council of the Catholic Church in England set up seminaries to train priests. And the use of parish churches to swell the incomes of often distant monasteries cannot have added to an Englishman's sense that his own priest was his pastor and friend. For all its popularity, late medieval religion was becoming vulnerable as Catholicism in England had not been since the conversion of the invading Danes.

It is, of course, impossible to know how many individuals were dissatisfied amid all the evident success of late medieval religion. Very few people wrote anything that gives a real clue. Few Englishmen read anything at all; Thomas More guessed

---

[47] A. G. Dickens, *The English Reformation* (revised, London, 1967), pp.17-20.

that only four out of every ten of his contemporaries could read English, Stephen Gardiner guessed only one out of every hundred. What we do know is that a few academic radicals, unusually sensitive and intellectual, were for a time attracted by the possibility that the philosophy of Plato might help to turn late medieval Catholicism into the 'philosophy of Christ'.

Such Christian Platonists did not realize how far Platonism was from the religion of Jesus or St Paul, but one explanation of this failure was the tradition that Dionysius, St Paul's leading convert in Athens, had as a Christian written a Platonic book. In 1455 an Italian scholar, Lorenzo Valla, exposed the falsity of this tradition, and about 1501 an Oxford scholar, William Grocyn, brought Valla's arguments to England; but even then the appeal of Plato to devout Catholics was great. Thomas More's *Utopia* was, in a sense, an adaptation of Plato's *Republic*. This appeal was not only a reaction against the philosophical authority of Aristotle in the medieval universities, or an excitement that more Latin translations of Plato and the Platonists were becoming widely known. Because Plato had written about a republic, he helped a few in the late Middle Ages to explore in their minds the possibility of a society wider than the Church they knew, a society where reason rather than dogma and precedent decided issues and where wise men rather than bishops trained as lawyers governed. Because Plato had written about love, he now helped some who were dissatisfied both by the selfish materialism of everyday life and by the Church's traditional contempt for the world. Christian Platonists began to suggest (with greater or less caution) that nature's deepest instincts would, if trusted, lead to God, because there was in every man's soul a spark of divinity descended from God. And because Plato had written about God's eternity and beauty, about God as most desirable rather than most terrible, he now fed some souls starved by the normal diet in late medieval religion.

A churchman influenced by Platonism was John Colet, Dean of St Paul's in London, 1505-19. When he died, only one work of his had been published: a sermon to the clergy of Canterbury Convocation in 1511, pleading for moral reform.

'Truly ye are gathered often times together,' he declared, 'but, by your favour to speak the truth, yet I see not what fruit cometh of your assembling, namely to the Church.' Some of his own papers, and tributes paid to him by others, have, however, enabled modern scholars to study more of his life and thought.

In 1492 he went from Oxford to Italy for four years, studying both in Rome and in Florence, then the centre of interest in Plato. On his return to his university he delivered public lectures on the Bible. Notes of what he said on Genesis, Romans and 1 Corinthians have survived, showing that he had moved from the elaborate medieval method of analysing the possible (or impossible) meanings of a scriptural text, back to the simple meaning of a teacher – Moses (as he thought) or Paul – who belonged to history. In Colet's exposition this simple meaning of the Bible often turned out to be close to Plato, but the method was one which was to have very different results in different hands.

While Dean of St Paul's, Colet continued to expound St Paul's thought and found many listeners. Although the canons of his cathedral claimed that he treated them like monks, and his bishop suspected him of heresy, he charmed his fellow-Londoners by many edifying conversations over simple meals. His father had twice been Lord Mayor of London, and when the dean was left a fortune he devoted it to the foundation of St Paul's School. He chose William Lily as its head because he could teach Greek and was generally progressive, and he entrusted its management to the married laymen of the Mercers' Company. His sermon rebuking the clergy assembled in the Convocation of Canterbury in 1511 was bold and unpopular, but another incident is reported from Good Friday two years later. This much admired and beloved dean was summoned to preach before the king at Greenwich, and preached a pacifist sermon. Unfortunately Henry was just about to send his fleet, anchored nearby, to what he hoped would be the conquest of France. After the sermon, having been summoned by his monarch, the preacher so explained himself that Henry called for wine, exclaiming 'this is the doctor for me!' Two years later Colet had a still more difficult task. He preached at the great

service in Westminster Abbey when Cardinal Wolsey's red hat
was received from Rome. His theme was a call to humility,
holiness and devotion to pastoral work. These virtues, so uncharacteristic of the cardinal, were necessary in the leaders of
Christ's Church.[48]

THE REFORMATION

A man similarly charming (at least to other men), although a
far greater scholar and more prolific author, was Desiderius
Erasmus.

When this Dutchman visited Oxford in 1499, he was probably about thirty years old and beginning to shake off the
disadvantages of his illegitimate birth and a spell in a
monastery for which he had no vocation. He had been invited
to England by a young nobleman to whom he had acted as
tutor, but had gravitated to the university (it was the year
when Vasco da Gama sailed back from India). While in
Oxford the visitor made friends with Colet, who urged him to
lecture on the Bible, as he did. Firmly but politely Erasmus
replied that he must first gain a complete mastery of Greek,
which Colet had never attained. By the time of his next
appearance in England, in 1505, he had conquered this
language (his India); so he was able to present Archbishop
Warham with a Latin version of a Greek play by Euripides,
and to work with Thomas More on translation of the satires of
Lucian.

Four years later he was back again, hoping for effective
patronage from Warham, staying with More, writing a prayer
and a summary of Christianity for Colet's new school, before
going on to spend thirty months in a tower-study overlooking
the town and river at Queens' College, Cambridge. While
there he was absorbed in editing Greek and Latin classics and
the letters of St Jerome – and in grumbles about the small

[48] See Leland Miles, *John Colet and the Platonic Tradition* (London,
1962), and Sears Jayne, *John Colet and Marsilio Ficino* (Oxford, 1963).

audiences at his lectures on Greek, about the climate and about the beer. But it was in Cambridge that he resolved to do for his time what St Jerome's Latin version (the 'Vulgate') had done for Christendom since the end of the fourth century. He began a fresh translation of the New Testament into classical Latin direct from the Greek, and when he returned to the Continent where he belonged he knew the need which scholars now had for a printed Greek New Testament based on the manuscripts. Both works, in Latin and Greek, appeared in Basel in 1516 and aroused a storm of protest by conservatives convinced that the Vulgate had alone been given authority by the Holy Spirit and the Catholic Church. Together with much other writing which taught the message of the Bible as he understood it, these publications put Erasmus at the head of the reforming liberals of Europe. Both the emperor, Charles V, and the pope, Leo X, pledged support.

But on the eve of All Saints' Day 1517 a far more obscure theologian, Martin Luther, nailed his ninety-five 'theses' (arguments inviting disputation) to the door of the church in the little town of Wittenberg in Saxony. Their most dramatic feature was an attack on the granting of 'indulgences' (remissions from periods in purgatory) in return for a confession of sins and a gift to papal funds. The attack had a double significance. Within Germany it could be used as a theological blessing on the desire of princes to throw off the authority of an Italian pope, to bring local churchmen to heel and to loot church lands; in England Henry VIII and his supporters bestowed their own blessing on such actions without the aid of any major theologian. But in the Christian world as a whole, Luther's attack of 1517 announced the total dissatisfaction of a religious genius with late medieval piety. As a student of theology he had failed to find food for his mind. As a monk he had failed to find peace for his conscience. As a pilgrim to Rome he had been dismayed. As a professor he had not even tried to fit the Old Testament or the letters of St Paul into the categories of Platonism, as Colet had cautiously done in Oxford. Pursuing the 'theology of the cross' which had already been developed in later medieval German mysticism (and by Dame Julian in England), he had broken through to the insight that a Christian was declared righteous before God not because of his devotions or works or merits but because of God's own righteousness revealed upon Christ's cross — the righteousness in which that Christian must put his entire trust. By 1513 in his own style (which was very German, often coarse and almost always still in dialogue with the academic theology and popular religion of the Middle Ages), Luther had redis- covered the Gospel of God's grace. This he now taught in lec- tures on the psalms, in lectures on *Romans*, and in declar- ations to all who would listen.

In a short history of Christian England there is no need to retell the story of Protestant Europe, a separate entity once Luther had been condemned by the pope in 1520 and by the emperor in 1521. Nor is there any need to recount the history of the Counter-Reformation, the profoundly renewed Cath- olicism which gradually arose in response. Nor need we survey in full the tragedy that had overwhelmed the hopes of academic radicalism and liberal reform by the death of Erasmus in 1536. What is vital here may be said briefly.

Erasmus was very reluctant to get involved in controversy with Luther, whose freedom as a theologian he defended. Even more was he reluctant to risk being identified with the peasants' revolt and the extremist religious movements which erupted in Germany once Luther had broken the spell cast by the authority of the medieval Church. When he did tackle Luther after many entreaties from fellow-Catholics, it was on the subject of the dignity of man. Luther, he declared in a famous pamphlet of 1524, had underestimated both the freedom and the power of the human will to respond to God's grace. Luther replied vitriolically, asserting the helplessness of sinful man as St Augustine had asserted it against the British heretic Pelagius more than eleven hundred years previously. But the real conflict between the two men in religion was not completely covered by this controversy. The real contrast between Luther and Erasmus — as between Augustine and Pelagius — was that the former, despite his pessimism, was the prophet, with the stronger will to mould the Christian world's religion since he had a stronger experience of the mastering and dynamic will of God. Like Pelagius, Erasmus appealed to his fellow-men to be as reasonable, as self-controlled and as helpful as he was. To such a man, Christ was the great example – and when Erasmus grew serious or at any rate sentimental (towards the end of *The Praise of Folly*, for example, or when he was writing to educate the young) it was the gentleness of Christ that he most stressed. Like Augustine, Luther spoke alongside men and women who were swayed by their passions and depressed by guilt and the sense of total futility; and so he spoke to them. To a Luther, surrounded and invaded by coarse evil, Christ was the hero and the saviour, bringing near the God who previously had been far-off and hostile. Salvation by Christ alone, and 'justification' by faith in him alone, offered the one key needed to the Bible – and to the knowledge and love of God. Luther complained that Erasmus spoke about God in an ice-cold way. God to him was 'a glowing furnace full of love'.

The contrast between liberal reform and Protestant reformation helps us to understand what happened when a religious vacuum had been created in England by the policy of Henry VIII (who disgusted both Erasmus and Luther). The gap was not filled by the kind of reform of which John Colet would have approved. It was filled by a religion which often damaged or destroyed what the academic radicals and liberal reformers held dear: peace, internationalism, the calm consideration of the Bible, the constructive improvement of institutions, the charitable appeal to people's own ideals, pastoral love.

The new version of Christianity, Protestantism, was so named from the protest of the minority against the majority of German princes gathered at Speyer in 1529; but in some nations, including England, it was destined to become the religion of the majority. It had power; it exerted a fascination in people's hearts, and wielded an influence over their lives, not often to be seen in liberal Catholicism. It seemed to be the living voice of the Bible and the vital truth about God and man in their eternity-deciding relationship. And so it seemed to be the answer to the problem which Thomas Linacre, physician to Henry VIII and founder of the Royal College of Surgeons, a devout Catholic and a good scholar, is said to have put to himself when, towards the end of his life, he read the gospels in Greek for the first time. It is reported that on so doing he exclaimed: 'Either this is not the Gospel or we are not Christians.'[49]

ENGLAND'S FIRST PROTESTANTS

The new theology attracted a little group of Cambridge men who gathered in an inn which although officially called the White Horse (it stood next to King's College) was nicknamed 'Little Germany'.

Among the many who observed this group with suspicion was Thomas Cranmer, the son of a Nottinghamshire squire who had in 1503 entered Jesus College, Cambridge (founded six years before in a former nunnery). With uncharacteristic bravado Cranmer had married soon after becoming a Master of Arts, sacrificing his hopes of a life as a priest, but after less than a year this first wife and their infant child had died and he had resumed his advanced studies in theology. Now in the 1520s he studied the Bible and the theologians all the more intensively, pen in hand, trying to decide what to make of Luther's challenge. This in itself showed a rare independence and caution; on the other hand, he was not in any other way distinguished. During a residence in Cambridge of more than twenty-five years he wrote no book and held no important office.

The turning-point of Cranmer's life came at a supper party on an August evening in 1529. The other guests at the table were two of the king's leading officials, Stephen Gardiner and Edward Foxe. Cranmer suggested that they should seek the opinion of theologians about the king's matrimonial prob-

[49] The best introductions are R. H. Bainton, *Erasmus of Christendom* (London, 1969); George Faludy, *Erasmus of Rotterdam* (London, 1970); James Atkinson, *Martin Luther and the Birth of Protestantism* (London, 1968); Gerhard Ebeling, *Luther: An Introduction to His Thought* (London, 1970).

lems. The suggestion was not novel. What was novel was the thought emerging as the evening wore on that Cranmer himself might write a theological book advocating the king's cause. He did so, satisfactorily, and was sent to repeat his arguments in papal Rome and in Italian universities. The book was written in the London house of Anne Boleyn's father; and when the time came for Henry to appoint a new Archbishop of Canterbury in January 1533, the Boleyn family successfully urged the recall of Thomas Cranmer, then on an embassy to the emperor. It was therefore as Archbishop of Canterbury that Cranmer further pursued his studies of the theology of the Continental Reformation, in the intervals of attending to the dangers of politics such as the fate of Anne Boleyn (whose final confession he heard in prison, with what effects on his own conscience we do not know). It seems clear that he gradually became convinced of the validity of almost the whole of the Lutheran case, but that his instincts were all for caution and above all for the need to retain his king's benevolence. Such instincts were not inappropriate; without Henry's favour he would almost certainly have been executed during the reaction against Protestantism in the 1540s. He did not really come into his own until Henry was dead – perhaps not until he himself had been burned by Queen Mary in 1556, leaving behind him the memory of the Protestant martyr whose great theological learning and mastery of English had been deployed in his editorship of the Book of Common Prayer, beginning with the English Litany of 1545. Perhaps his experience of moral surrender under Henry VIII had been necessary for the expressions of penitence in that Prayer Book to be so eloquent.[50]

Other Cambridge men were more quickly courageous.[51]

One of them, Thomas Bilney, had been absorbed in legal and theological studies until he got hold of the translation of the New Testament by Erasmus; he would afterwards explain that he had been interested in its Latin. He had found in it the

[50] See Jasper Ridley, *Thomas Cranmer* (Oxford, 1962).

[51] See W. Clebsch, *England's Earliest Protestants, 1520-1535* (New Haven, N.J., 1964).

sentence about Christ Jesus coming into the world to save sinners, and it had converted him to seriousness in practising and preaching a Gospel based entirely on this New Testament, with this as the key text. He threw himself into the service of the poorest, becoming in John Foxe's words 'laborious and painful to the desperates; a preacher to the prisoners and comfortless; a great doer in Cambridge'. The change in him had led to charges of heresy, although he was no Lutheran; and he had recanted. But he could find no peace of mind when he resumed his academic life. One evening he told his colleagues in Trinity Hall that he must 'go up to Jerusalem' as a simple Bible-preacher, saving the sinners of his native county, Norfolk. He was soon in trouble with the Bishop of Norwich and in 1531 was burned. One of those who watched him die was Matthew Parker, then a boy but to become Archbishop of Canterbury under Elizabeth I.

Another future bishop deeply impressed by Bilney's holiness was a Cambridge colleague, Hugh Latimer, who had been stiff in a conservative Catholicism. Bilney reached him by making his confession to him as a priest, and years later Latimer was still extolling 'little Bilney, that blessed martyr of God'. Bilney's example strengthened Latimer to preach as a Protestant and to die as a martyr (in 1555).

Another martyr, urged by William Tyndale to 'remember Bilney', was John Frith, a product of Henry VI's two colleges at Eton and Cambridge. Because of his brilliant promise he was recruited by Wolsey for the staff of Cardinal College but, being suspected of Lutheran leanings, found himself imprisoned in its fish cellar. Others died there, but Frith escaped to become a Protestant propagandist, living in poverty, moving obscurely among the people. When arrested as a vagrant, he escaped again by talking Latin and Greek with the local schoolmaster. Imprisoned in the Tower of London, he still pamphleteered against Sir Thomas More in controversy about purgatory and the Mass, the manuscripts being smuggled for printing in Antwerp. He was burned for heresy in 1533 at the age of thirty, alongside a tailor's apprentice. His writings suggest that had he lived he would have become an intellectual, as well as a moral, leader of the English Reformation.

When Cardinal Wolsey presided at a great burning of Lutheran books one day in February 1526 an Augustinian friar, Robert Barnes, threw a faggot on the bonfire. He was attempting to satisfy the authorities, for in the little Cambridge church of St Edward on Christmas Eve he had preached a sermon against the worldliness of churchmen – a discourse which was not unnaturally interpreted as an attack on the cardinal; hence his penitence that February morning. But now the printing press was making Protestantism more than a matter of moral indignation which was soon overwhelmed by the authority of the Church. The printers made Luther's Gospel a 'safe stronghold' (as his own most famous hymn proclaimed God to be), and in 1526 another event took place, more decisive than the book-burning. In exile, William Tyndale completed the printing of his English translation of the New Testament. While living in London Barnes got hold of it, absorbed it and sold copies of it to others. Inspired by it, he eventually fled from England and became a Lutheran. He often had supper with Luther, who teased him as 'St Robert'. In 1535 he returned to England under the protection of the king, who was at that time trying to make allies in Germany. Thomas Cromwell employed him and even arranged an interview at which he tried to explain the Reformation to Henry VIII. But Henry never fully trusted him; he persisted in preaching the religion he had learned from Tyndale's New Testament and from the Lutheran lectures in Wittenberg; and in 1540, two days after Cromwell's own execution, he was burned with two other Protestants. At the stake he protested that he did not know for what heresies he had been condemned. He died, he said, a completely orthodox Christian.

William Tyndale, who had changed Barnes' life, was a man whose vocation it was to translate the Bible. As a student at Oxford and Cambridge he was disgusted by the conservatism of the theologians nicknamed the 'Trojans' but equipped himself with a knowledge of Greek. While chaplain to a Gloucestershire squire he was fired by the ambition to produce a New Testament for the English. He once shouted at a conservative with whom he had been arguing: 'If God spare my life, ere many years I will cause a boy that driveth the plough to know more of Scripture than thou dost.' He sought the patronage of the Bishop of London, but was snubbed. No doubt the bishop – Cuthbert Tunstall, who had been cautiously encouraging to Erasmus – feared that he was now dealing with another Lollard, but actually Tyndale had little admiration for the Lollard Bible; he disliked the Latinity still to be found in the fourteenth-century English and wanted his own version, based on the Greek as edited by Erasmus, to be direct and dramatic, to reach that sixteenth-century ploughboy.

Eventually Tyndale escaped to Luther's Wittenberg. He closely studied Luther's German translation of 1522 and when his own New Testament appeared it included prefaces often based on Luther's. That in itself was a fatal defect in the eyes of Thomas More, who was also indignant about particular translations. Words which More (soaked as he was in the Latin Vulgate) would have translated as church, priest, confess and do penance appeared in this new New Testament as congregation, senior, acknowledge and repent. Whatever might be thought of such innovations in an English New Testament, at least tribute might have been paid to the staggering intellectual and physical courage of Tyndale's undertaking. The printing of the first edition of 1525 in Cologne (of which only one fragment survives) was interrupted by a raid on the printers, so that Tyndale had to resume work with a fresh printer in Worms (producing an edition of three thousand of which two copies remain). It is surely to his credit that, although the authorities did their utmost to silence him, to stop his book reaching England and to punish its readers, and although he was in such a hurry, he achieved one of the most influential feats of the mind in English history by his translation. It is usually reckoned that the 1611 Authorized (or King James) Version of the English Bible did more than any other book to shape the mind of the English-speaking world, and that at least three-quarters of it was based on Tyndale. He twice revised his New Testament translation (1534-35) as he pondered the meaning of the original Greek – but not in ways which pleased his Catholic critics.

He also set out to translate the Old Testament, and com-

pleted it as far as 2 Chronicles. The first five books were
published with provocative notes in Antwerp in 1530. He had
immense handicaps in this task. He had to spend two years
learning Hebrew (a language with which he fell in love, saying
that 'the Hebrew tongue agreeth a thousand times more with
the English than with the Latin') and then lost all his notes
and money in a shipwreck. He was also distracted from his
vocation by further controversy, against his fellow-exile
George Joye as well as against the Catholic Thomas More. In
one book, of 1528, he delighted Henry VIII by urging *The
Obedience of a Christian Man*, only to infuriate him by de-
nouncing his second marriage. His Old Testament work was
incomplete when on the orders of the emperor he was burned
as a heretic at Vilvorde near Brussels in 1536. But a letter he
wrote to the prison governor asking for a Hebrew Bible,
dictionary and grammar has survived and he looked forward
to the day when his Bible would be finished and made the
basis of an official English Bible. That was the meaning of his
last prayer as given in John Foxe's *Book of Martyrs* (1563):
'Lord, open thou the King of England's eyes'.[52]

Within a year his prayer was granted. This was not surprising; seven years before, Henry had characteristically promised
his people an English Bible when they started behaving well
enough to deserve it. When Tyndale died an English version of
the whole Bible had just been printed, probably in Zurich,
and hopefully dedicated to the king. It was the work of Miles
Coverdale, a Yorkshireman and formerly an Augustinian friar
in Cambridge (and secretary to Robert Barnes). More recently
Coverdale had assisted Tyndale himself, in a shared exile.
Those parts of the Bible which Tyndale had not covered in
published work were, however, based largely on the Latin,
although helped by Luther's German. Coverdale had a good
ear for music in the English language. One proof of this is that
his translation of the psalms was incorporated into the first
Book of Common Prayer in 1549 and (despite its frequent
departures from the meaning of the Hebrew) remained in successive English prayer books until the twentieth century,

---

[52] See C. H. Williams, *William Tyndale* (London, 1969).

deeply loved. But he lacked Tyndale's mastery of Hebrew and Greek, and scholars close to Henry VIII such as Thomas Cranmer deplored this amateurishness. Less scholarly critics mocked the passage which claimed that Adam and Eve had used fig-leaves to make themselves trousers or 'breeches'. The English Bible which the king licensed for distribution in 1537 was therefore based largely on Tyndale's work; Coverdale's was used only for the books which Tyndale had not reached. This Bible was edited by John Rogers, a London parish priest who had become chaplain to the English merchants of Antwerp and who had obtained his friend Tyndale's unpublished manuscripts. The book was printed in Antwerp and was named 'Matthew's Bible' so as to conceal the identity of the editor. Rogers did not, however, deny himself the pleasure of including anti-Catholic comments. He was to become the first of the Protestant martyrs burned under Queen Mary.

Coverdale remained active, revising Matthew's Bible to become the Great Bible of 1539, splendidly printed in Paris and London and free of controversial comments. Later editions of this Great Bible, in 1540 and 1541, were 'overseen' by two conservative bishops (Tunstall and Heath) at the king's request; and 'one book of the whole Bible of the largest volume in English' was ordered to be available in every cathedral and parish church, where crowds of people gathered to hear readings from a book so long denied them. So the Holy Bible at last enjoyed Henry VIII's patronage. Thomas Cromwell was Coverdale's own patron in England, and after that minister's execution he worked quietly in Denmark and Bavaria. When Protestantism recovered the ascendancy he was called home to be Bishop of Exeter and, after a further exile on the restoration of Catholicism, enjoyed great popularity as a preacher under Elizabeth I.[53]

In his book of 1528 Tyndale had urged obedience to a Christian king – a theme frequent in English Christianity ever since King Ethelbert's baptism by St Augustine, but given a

---

[53] See J. F. Mozley, *William Tyndale* (London, 1937) and *Coverdale and His Bibles* (London, 1953), and S. L. Greenslade in *Cambridge History of the Bible*, vol. ii (Cambridge, 1963), pp.141-174.

new power. The need, he argued, was to end a situation in which 'emperors and kings are nothing nowadays but even hangmen unto the pope and bishops to kill whosoever they condemn without any more ado'. He claimed that, so far from preaching the overthrow of the government and the social order, those who wanted Christianity to be reformed on the basis of the plain, literal meaning of the Bible would be found to be the most loyal subjects of the king, rendering to Caesar the things that were Caesar's. Particularly would their enthusiasm overflow if Henry VIII gave the Bible to the people in the people's language. And the English Protestant who, more than any other, fulfilled Tyndale's prophecy was Thomas Cromwell.

Cromwell's early life is obscure, as is his personal religion; but somehow he developed the determination to construct under Henry VIII a commonwealth which would be biblical in its religion and rational in its government. Not only were the riches of the monasteries and the powers of the clergy over the laity to be ended in a revolution. Many other legacies of the Middle Ages were to be reformed away similarly — the often slack administration of the central offices of state and of the crown lands; the remaining separation of Wales from the English pattern of local government; the resistance of the men who controlled Ireland to orders from London; the 'liberties' and 'sanctuaries' which had meant that the king's justice did not run even throughout his English kingdom; the uncertainties about land ownership which had been the pretexts for much litigation and violence in the heyday of 'bastard' feudalism. Every birth in England was to be registered in the parents' parish church (this was one of the reforms which Cromwell was able to effect permanently), and until the registration of the burial that life was to be lived in peaceful work according to the commands of God and the king. The king's council was to be as benevolently active as was possible, fixing food prices, resisting any further conversion of arable land to sheep farming, encouraging exports. There was even a scheme which Cromwell accepted, but did not live to enact, for a ministry to organize employment (a Council to avoid Vagabonds), financed by an income tax. Parliament was to be an occasion not so much for the representation of local grievances as for the union of the people in the service of God as interpreted by the king.

Like his own master and teacher Wolsey, Cromwell rose to the top by sheer ability and capacity for work, and like Wolsey he was while in power the recipient of innumerable petitions for his favour (which, again like Wolsey, he liked to grant when possible). But unlike Wolsey he indulged in no personal pomp. All that was left to his royal master. His chosen instruments were words, quietly spoken in council, carefully written to his many agents, drafted and redrafted to make Acts of Parliament — words which would reshape a nation by a Reformation both religious and political.

Born about 1485, the son of a clothier in Putney who also kept an ale house, Cromwell later said that he had been a 'ruffian' in his youth. He is believed to have sought either adventure or escape from the English authorities as a mercenary soldier in Italy, but ended up as a minor merchant in Venice, Antwerp and London. He acquired some legal knowledge and built up a practice as an attorney for London merchants, but his main work in the 1520s was as Cardinal Wolsey's chief assistant, particularly in the suppression of small religious houses: a useful rehearsal for the larger drama of the 1530s. On Wolsey's fall he remained surprisingly loyal when all others fled; he cleared up his former master's affairs and did what he could to defend his interests with the king and the parliament. The king noticed Cromwell's ability more than this lingering loyalty, and had included him in his own council by the end of 1530. Once there, this former 'ruffian' was able to outstrip not only the Dukes of Norfolk and Suffolk, but also Sir Thomas More with his troublesome conscience, as well as Stephen Gardiner — a man about twelve years his junior who could well have been expected to be his political senior.

Gardiner was, like Cromwell, the son of a clothier, but his father was far more prosperous. In his youth he had mixed a salad for Erasmus while on a visit to Paris and had become a student and teacher of both civil and ecclesiastical law at Cambridge before entering Wolsey's service. He had gone to Rome to try to browbeat Pope Clement into compliance with the king's wish to get rid of Queen Catherine, and had been rewarded with the post of principal secretary to the king. The year 1531 found him Bishop of Winchester. Yet he had not been made Archbishop of Canterbury and was now politically eclipsed by Cromwell. The reason was not that Gardiner was opposed to the claim of Henry to be 'on earth supreme head of the Church of England'. In 1533 he wrote a book, *De Vera Obedientia*, to defend this title. But although Gardiner came to the same conclusion as Tyndale, it was from a very different starting point: the tradition of senior bishops serving the crown, a tradition going back to the Normans and even to the Anglo-Saxons. Although obedient, he had shown himself to be too medieval a figure, too much inclined to minimize what 'Supreme Head' might mean, too much the defender of the clergy.[54]

Radically new measures required a radically new minister – and a layman. In January 1535, therefore, Cromwell, who had already been responsible for the secular administration over a couple of years, was designated as the king's 'vicegerent in spirituals'. As Henry's deputy, his was now a legal power over the Church greater than the power which Wolsey had enjoyed as the pope's legate; and his authority symbolized the triumph of the laity by including doctrine in its scope. Letters poured out of Cromwell's office with instructions for archbishops, bishops and preachers – and with orders to sheriffs and justices of the peace to keep an eye on the clergy.

In the end religion – plus Stephen Gardiner's rivalry – was Thomas Cromwell's undoing. Jane Seymour's death in 1537 (having given birth to the future Edward VI) freed the king to marry a Continental princess. The way seemed open to making the dynasty as well as the nation thoroughly Protestant. Anne, sister of the Protestant Duke of Cleves in Germany, was selected as Henry's next bride. The way also seemed open to such despotism as was possible for a king with no large civil service, no standing army and now no real prospect of a revenue which would enable him to dispense with

---

[54] See S. E. Muller, *Stephen Gardiner and the Tudor Reaction* (London, 1926).

Parliament. There were executions of great Catholic aristocrats in England — a Percy and a Courtenay — suspected of
treason, and Parliament agreed that in future royal proclamations were to be obeyed as though they were Acts of Parliament. But Cromwell's policy to make the king and kingdom of
England Protestant now ran up against two problems: the
king's never-slumbering sexuality and his reawakened conscience as a Catholic.

Henry took an instant dislike to Anne of Cleves. Although
he went through with the marriage, he claimed that he found
himself with the new problem of being physically unable to
consummate it. Within a few days of the wedding he was
demanding another divorce. Not long before this disaster he
had already expressed the feeling that enough was enough by
way of religious reform. In June 1539 the Act of Six Articles
passed Parliament and was never repealed during the rest of
the reign. It had been agreed upon by the king and conservatives such as (among the laity) the Duke of Norfolk and
(among the clergy) Stephen Gardiner. It provided for the
burning of any heretic who denied the miracle of 'transubstantiation' in the Mass, and for the punishment of any who
asserted the necessity of giving the wine as well as the bread to
the laity. It ordered the laity still to confess their sins to priests,
and priests to remain unmarried or be hanged. Hugh Latimer
signalled the setback for Protestantism by resigning the
bishopric of Worcester.

In public Cromwell — like Cranmer, who sent his secret
wife, Margaret, away to Germany — took the blow as a loyal
subject. Privately he intrigued through a difficult winter. The
spring brought him an honour, the earldom of Essex. In May
the conservative but timid Bishop of Chichester was taken to
the Tower of London, to be examined for possible complicity
in a treasonable plot. All seemed set for another purge of the
Catholics. But the king, who had not authorized the bishop's
arrest, was now approached by the Duke of Norfolk and
Bishop Gardiner and told very different stories. Thomas
Cromwell, they argued persuasively, was himself a traitor —
and a heretic also. He was arrested in the council chamber
and the duke tore the Garter star from his neck. Parliament

(including Cranmer in the House of Lords) obligingly sentenced both him and his theological favourite, Robert Barnes, to death at the king's pleasure; and having been spared long enough to provide sordid details which could be used in divorcing Anne of Cleves, he was executed on 28 July. He was the victim of the terror which he had wielded against the enemies of the Reformation. But his fall also reflected that terror's inadequacy. He had been unable to kill off Catholicism (just as those now temporarily triumphant were to be unable to kill off Protestantism). He died, he said, 'in the Catholic faith of the Holy Church'. He would have shown more of his customary attention to detail if he had acknowledged that he died the victim of the Catholic faith's continuing hold on the hearts of the English.[55]

But because England was still so largely Catholic even in 1540, it would be wrong to end this story with the personal dramas of Protestants. We shall learn more about England in this age of the sudden storm if we look at three people whose piety, although lay, was definitely Catholic – Margery Kempe, William Caxton and Thomas More.

MARGERY KEMPE

Margery Kempe's autobiography was unknown until 1936 apart from the publication of eight pages by the printer Wynkin de Worde in 1501. When the manuscript came to light it turned out to be an early copy of what she had begun to dictate to a priest in 1436. She had had an earlier

---

[55] The best introductions are A. G. Dickens, *Thomas Cromwell and the English Reformation* (London, 1959), and B. W. Beckingsale, *Thomas Cromwell* (London, 1978). G. R. Elton has supplied more detailed studies in his trilogy: *The Tudor Revolution in Government* (Cambridge, 1953); *Policy and Police: The Enforcement of the Reformation in the Age of Thomas Cromwell* (Cambridge, 1972); *Reform and Renewal: Thomas Cromwell and the Common Weal* (Cambridge, 1973).

draft – compiled by a man who, she complained, could not write English – read back to her.[56]

She was very frank about her nervous breakdown after the birth of her first child in her twentieth year; the failure of her attempts to run a brewery and a horse-mill in order to pay for her extravagant tastes as a young married woman; her sensuality (she had fourteen children) which turned into a fixed refusal of sexual relations with her husband or anyone else (she was 'ever afraid of being ravished'). When she had to nurse her incontinent husband for several sordid years before he died, she was sure she deserved it after all the carnal delights of their marriage. She told of her journeys to learn more of religion – to Rome, Jerusalem and Compostella in Spain. More locally, she went to Norwich; there she talked with Mother Julian, who told her that 'the Holy Ghost moveth ne'er a thing against charity, for if he did he would be contrary to his own self for he is all charity'. She was herself not all charity; she sturdily spoke her mind. When the Archbishop of York, scenting heresy in her independence, told her 'I hear it said that thou art a right wicked woman', she replied: 'I also hear it said that ye are a wicked man.' When the Archbishop of Canterbury (Arundel) had kept her waiting among his servants she rebuked him for employing men who swore so much. She talked with him about his soul and hers in the garden of Lambeth Palace until the stars came out. When the monks tried to silence her as she wept 'nearly all day' in Canterbury Cathedral itself, she argued back. She was still indignant when she rejoined her husband who had retreated to their lodgings. She was a constant worshipper in her parish church of St Margaret in King's (then Bishop's) Lynn. She obtained special permission to receive the Holy Communion each Sunday. Although her parish priests cannot have welcomed her outbursts of tears when she saw a crucifix or heard a sermon about the Lord's sufferings, they were perhaps encouraged when she received a vision telling St Margaret's not to give in to pressure from its daughter-church (the chapel of St Nicholas) for the right to baptize infants and receive the fees.

[56] *The Book of Margery Kempe*, ed. W. Butler-Bowdon (London, 1936).

She was delighted when she came across a priest willing to read to her, over eight years, from the Bible and from mystics such as Rolle and Hilton. Her own book shows how carefully she listened and remembered – but, also, that she attached more significance to her frequent 'dalliance' with Christ and his mother.

The first of these conversations began typically: 'Jesus, of what shall I think?' The reply was: 'Daughter, think of my mother. . . .' She did not need to travel from Lynn to Bethlehem to be close to that family; and from her 'dalliance' with it in her prayers a homely religion grew strong. She prayed for her neighbours and gave them advice and practical help, with unceasing energy. She loved to see 'the Precious Sacrament borne about the town with lights and reverence, the people kneeling' – but would set up a different kind of cry if in the street she saw a child or horse being beaten. In her book we meet not only her invincible personality but also her conventional faith. Cross-examined at Leicester about her attitude to the Mass, she gave an outline of lay orthodoxy: 'Sirs, I believe in the Sacrament of the Altar on this wise; that whatever man hath taken the order of priesthood, be he ever so vicious a man in his living, if he say duly those words over the bread, that Our Lord Jesus Christ said when he made his Maundy among his disciples, where he sat at the Supper, I believe that it is his very flesh and his blood, and no material bread; and never may it be unsaid, be it once said.' She triumphed against many accusations that she was a Lollard, and we may suspect that she enjoyed winning the debates with men as well as the privilege of suffering with Christ. The Archbishop of York's steward once pompously rebuked her: 'Holy folk should not laugh.' 'Sir', she retorted, 'I have great cause to laugh, for the more shame I suffer, and despite, the merrier I may be in our Lord Jesus Christ'.

For all her 'nerves' and flamboyant eccentricity Margery Kempe did, it seems, win through to some of the happiness of the saints. We are told by her scribe that 'by process of time, her mind and her thought were so joined to God that she never forgot him, but continually had mind of him and beheld him in all creatures'. That does not sound like hysteria. And she won this vision of God by using what the medieval Church offered, despite all her defiance of bourgeois conventions. Her religion was based on her own parish church, she loved the Mass, she believed in it, she poured out her soul to priests, she delighted in pilgrimages, the Church's heaven came to be more real and more attractive to her than her own husband and children.

WILLIAM CAXTON

No development was more important than printing in the destruction of the faith accepted by Margery Kempe and millions like her. Printing was what enabled Martin Luther to bombard his enemies rapidly and effectively. Printed books spread Luther's doctrines through the English ports such as Lynn, as almost two centuries earlier the ships' rats had spread the Black Death – and one great difference between the new age and the age of Wyclif was that now the Church found it futile to excommunicate a heretic whose thoughts had been printed. The burning of books, even the burning of their authors, could not destroy whole editions; suppressing them by buying them up (which was the gentle Warham's policy when he had to act as Archbishop of Canterbury) merely financed new editions; and police vigilance in the ports, backed up by very severe penalties for those caught with forbidden books, could not keep England completely free of the pestilential literature. Yet William Caxton who brought printing to England seems to have accepted the faith of the medieval Church as thoroughly as Margery Kempe herself. When the churchwardens of St Margaret's, Westminster, paid for the use of four torches and the tolling of the bell at his burial in 1491 they were honouring a fellow-parishioner who had been regular at worship and who had given some of the many devotional books printed at his press for sale to help church funds.

Caxton tells us something of his own life in his history of Troy. (This was the first book he translated and the first he printed, in Bruges in 1475; it had been commissioned by Margaret, Duchess of Burgundy and sister of Edward IV, no doubt because it was believed that Britain had been founded by a refugee from Troy, one Brutus.) He had been brought up in Kent but had 'continued by the space of thirty years for the most part in the countries of Brabant, Flanders, Holland and Flanders'. He had been a businessman engaged in the export of English cloth and of anything else that would sell and had risen to be 'governor' of the English merchants at Bruges. It was when he lost that well-paid official post in 1471, and had to set up on his own, that he saw the potential in printing – an art which had been invented in the 1430s and then developed by the genius of Johann Gutenberg of Mainz. Caxton learned printing in Cologne and, having gained confidence, set up a press and a shop in Westminster in 1476.

His shop backed on the monks' chapter house in West-minster Abbey and confronted the door into the great church used by those whose work lay in the royal palace and the law courts. No site could have been more convenient for his purposes. He printed and published (and when necessary translated) books to entertain courtiers and other laymen. His *Canterbury Tales* and his *Morte d'Arthur* were only the biggest volumes in a stream of publications which appealed to memories of the Age of Chivalry and to other aristocratic (or would-be-aristocratic) tastes. The contents of these books were old-fashioned because that was what his lay patrons wanted. One of the first books which he printed in England was a col-lection of the sayings of the ancient philosophers translated by the queen's brother, Lord Rivers. But his religious pub-lications were equally old-fashioned, because that was what the Church encouraged. The first document which he printed in England was an 'indulgence' from the pope to those who contributed to a projected crusade; and his biggest book in the religious field – 600,000 words of it, which he translated from Latin and French while Richard III was king and while Edward IV's widow was hiding in sanctuary in the abbey a few yards away – was a collection of saints' lives for reading in church or privately, the *Golden Legend* ('legend' meaning simply 'reading').

He remained a businessman who knew his market, but his enthusiasm, shown in the prefaces he wrote for many of the books he issued, is such as to prevent us supposing that his kind of publishing went against the grain. It is probable that the manual labour of printing was something he only supervised; but the chivalrous and clerical culture of his time fired him with the willingness to undergo the ill-paid labours of a translator.[57]

THOMAS MORE

When Caxton died, Thomas More was aged thirteen – a page in the household of the Archbishop of Canterbury, Cardinal Morton. His adult life can be recounted as the uncomplicated story of a martyr for the Catholic Church in England; and no storyteller's art is needed to make it moving.[58] Even people who neither share his faith nor understand it readily admire the cool courage he showed at his trial and execution in 1535 'in and for the faith of the Holy Catholic Church'. He was 'the king's good servant but God's first' – those words of his on the scaffold rang through his Europe and have echoed clearly into a world with few of the landmarks he knew. He died on 6 July, the eve of the feast of the 'translation' of the body of St Thomas of Canterbury to his final shrine. When taunted at his trial that his refusal to accept Henry VIII as 'Supreme Head' of the English Church had put him in a minority against the bishops, the king's council and Parliament itself, he appealed to the Catholic consensus of a thousand years. In Westminster Hall, the scene of so much that had happened in the Middle Ages, he told his successor as chancellor: 'If I should speak of those that are already dead, of whom many be now holy saints

---

[57] See G. D. Painter, *William Caxton* (London, 1976).

[58] But tribute should be paid to the art as well as to the scholarship of R. W. Chambers, *Thomas More* (London, 1935), a biography which has this theme. See also a Roman Catholic writer's tribute to St Thomas: E. E. Reynolds, *The Field is Won* (London, 1968).

in heaven, I am very sure that it is the greater part of them that, all the while they lived, thought in this case the way that I think now; and therefore am I not bounden, my Lord, to conform my conscience to the council of one realm against the General Council of Christendom. For of the foresaid holy bishops I have, for every bishop of yours, above one hundred; and for one council or Parliament of yours (God knoweth what manner of one), I have all the councils made these thousand years. And for this one kingdom, I have all other Christian realms.'

Somehow More found time to be a prolific controversialist in defence of the faith of the Catholic Church.[59] He stated (and no one denied) that he had edited the material which various 'makers' had assembled so that Henry VIII could win honour for his book against Luther. He replied to Simon Fish's anticlerical pamphlet with a *Supplication of Souls* urging the claims of the dead in purgatory to have their souls remembered by the pious. He wrote other, far larger, more scurrilous and more dreary books against Luther, Tyndale and the other heretics who had wickedly disturbed the peace of Christendom; he was specially licensed to read their works by Cuthbert Turnstall, then Bishop of London, in 1528. In these replies he was the lawyer appealing to a jury — playing to the gallery with homely humour, blackening his opponents' reputations, twisting their arguments so that they made nonsense, defending his own side whether or not it was fully defensible. While chancellor he prided himself on being the enemy of heretics as well as of murderers and thieves; he said so on the epitaph which he wrote when he expected to be buried in Chelsea Old Church. And being the enemy of heretics meant, in some cases, doing all that a lay judge could do to make sure they were burned. This frantic activity resulted from his indignation against the Protestantism of the 1520s, but his personal religion was not a late development. As a young man he had made his home for 'three years or more' among the strict Carthusian monks, wondering all the time whether or not it

[59] See R. Pineas, *Thomas More and Tudor Polemics* (Bloomington, Ind., 1968).

was his vocation to be a priest. In the end he had decided that he did not have a vocation to remain unmarried, although his family lived a semi-monastic life as they grew up. He was a model Catholic layman, attending Mass daily, singing in his parish church's choir (even while Lord Chancellor), using a block of wood as a pillow, wearing a hair shirt.

Yet More's martyrdom was of a kind different from the other executions of those who refused to swear the oath about the royal supremacy in 1535.

John Fisher died as an old, weary and sick bishop, who was probably not sorry when the pope's defiant gesture in making him a cardinal precipitated his death. It was said that he looked like a skeleton when he went to his execution. He had heard the confessions of Henry VII and had preached at his funeral. He had taught the faith of the Church for so many years during and since the days when he had dominated Cambridge that he had no mind to dissimulate when the loathsome Solicitor-General, Richard Rich, came to his prison. Rich claimed that the king had sent him to ask him as a priest about the theological and ethical correctness of the new title; and with his reply 'that the king was not, nor could be, by the Law of God, Supreme Head on earth of the Church of England' Fisher signed – and knew that he was signing – his own death warrant.[60] More, in contrast, was far more subtle in refusing to incriminate himself. When at his trial Rich reported a roughly similar conversation which he had had with him, More accused his accuser of perjury and tore his character into ribbons. Richard Rich had tried to trick the cleverest lawyer of the day.

Thomas More was with his daughter, the beloved 'Meg', as they watched the priors of three Carthusian monasteries being dragged in their habits on wattle hurdles to excrutiatingly painful deaths. He told her to note that they were as cheerful as bridegrooms, because they were being taken to heaven. He had, he added, been so worldly that he did not deserve the same reward. And in a sense what he said was true. The three priors, John Houghton, Robert Lawrence and Augustine

---

[60] See E. Surtz, *The Works and Days of John Fisher* (London, 1967).

Webster, were contemplative monks with simple convictions, remote from the world's intrigues, pure in their silence and austerity.[61] So were the other Carthusian monks who were chained to posts and left to starve to death in the Tower of London while More was a prisoner there. The only human kindness they experienced as they died was shown by More's adopted daughter Margaret Giggs, who, disguised as a milk-maid, made some courageous visits to put meat into their mouths and to wash the filth off their bodies.

More's life, when he had decided not to join the Carthus-ians, took him far from their great simplicity of faith and life. He freely acknowledged that for much of his life he had thought the pope's authority to be of human origin, 'for the more quietness of the ecclesiastical body'. He knew perfectly well how unspiritual the popes of his time were, and had urged King Henry to tone down his praise of the papacy in his book against Luther. He once confessed that he had not seriously studied the papacy's theological claims until 1524; but after his one youthful fling as a Member of Parliament opposing Henry VII in 1504, he knew all the arguments for obeying the king – and accepted almost all of them. He had been Henry VIII's courtier from 1517 to 1532, often discussing the classics or the stars or theology or politics with his master; frequently summoned to the royal supper table for light conversation; en-trusted with many important missions. Indeed, he accepted the great post of chancellor from Henry at a time when he knew that the king was resolved to marry again and would not be able to keep for ever his promise not to involve him in this 'great matter'. He kept that post through two and a half years, and revealed that he had many sleepless nights before at last deciding to defy his king at one point. There was, it is clear, a long, secret battle in his conscience before he was able to tell William Roper, as they rowed him from his home in Chelsea to the crucial examination in Lambeth Palace about his attitude to the royal supremacy: 'I thank our Lord, the field is won.'

---

[61] See David and Gervase Matthew, *The Reformation and the Con-templative Life* (London, 1934).

What makes Thomas More worthy to stand at the end of the line of the saints of England up to the Reformation is that he was acutely aware of the defects left in Church and State after the Christian centuries. He was not a simple martyr.

He was always the friend of Erasmus and was for many years his most reliable supporter. It was in his house that, returning bitterly disillusioned from the Rome of Pope Julius II in the summer of 1509, Erasmus wrote *Moriae Encomium*, 'the Praise of Folly', with all its satire on monks and theologians; and it was he who wrote to warn Erasmus that a copy of *Julius Exclusus*, the more severe lampoon on the worldly pope, had been found in the scholar's own handwriting. His own first book was an admiring translation of a short *Life* of the Florentine nobleman, Pico della Mirandola, whose beliefs had been more Platonist than Catholic. He did not write much in his twenties or thirties, despite his intimate association with scholars such as Grocyn, Linacre and Lily who were bringing to England a love of Greek literature in its original language; but this silence as an author was due to his busy involvement in legal and other work in the City of London. It is clear from the records that he was a lawyer thoroughly trusted by the city merchants, as his father was before him.

It is also clear from his *Utopia*, which he began to write in 1515 in the intervals of negotiations on behalf of the City of London with the merchants of Flanders, that he nursed radical thoughts. He had no respect for rich abbies; although there were 'gorgeous' churches and monks in Utopia, the monks there had no wealth. Nor did he have any respect for money-making landlords; in Utopia there was no private property. No money was used within the country, gold being thought suitable to make chains. Nostalgia for the Age of Chivalry — the widespread emotion which had brought fame to Malory and profit to Caxton — More treated with contemptuous silence. He did not even have much respect left for the grasping colleagues with whom he had worked; in Utopia there were no lawyers and very few merchants, because such men were not needed by the Utopians as they moved about their prosperous family farms or spacious cities in uniforms of undyed cloth like Franciscan friars' habits. Added later, the first book of *Utopia* showed what were the ideals with which More now entered the king's service after many heart-searchings. It was written around an indignant picture of the miseries of the English poor. Although he had accepted the role of a subordinate to Wolsey he hated the cardinal's arrogant magnificence as much as he hated the wars he launched, and when he replaced Wolsey as chancellor he openly expressed that hatred to Parliament. Compliments to the cardinal are also on record from the period of Wolsey's power. They were no doubt a courtier's flattery, justified in More's conscience only by the thought of the justice over which the cardinal presided and by the wish to get more actively involved in that justice. A philosopher entering the service of a king whom he still trusted, More aspired to bring justice to the English poor – and wealth to their country by peaceful industry and trade.

When he wrote *Utopia*, he wanted to hold up a mirror to a nation 'where they speak still of the commonwealth, but every man procureth his own private gain'. So he had to use discretion. That was why the book took the form of a conversation with a Portuguese explorer in a garden at Antwerp, remained in Latin until 1551, and was presented as an entertainment almost in the same class as Amerigo Vespucci's recent account of his transatlantic discoveries. The ambiguity of the dialogue, the appeal in Latin to scholars only (More declared that it would be better to burn the book than to translate it), and the flippancy ('many things be in the Utopian weal public, which in our cities I may rather wish for than hope after') – all these devices provided a protective smokescreen which was effective then and has been effective since. C. S. Lewis wrote: 'All seem to be agreed that it is a great book, but hardly any two agree as to its real significance; we approach it through a cloud of contradictory eulogies. . . . If it were intended as a serious treatise it would be very confused indeed.'[62] Lewis reckoned *Utopia* 'a holiday work, a spontaneous overflow of intellectual high spirits'; but it is also

---

[62] C. S. Lewis, *English Literature in the Sixteenth Century* (Oxford, 1954), pp.167-9.

possible, and more convincing, to regard More's intention as fundamentally serious, the overflow of his ideals now that he was for a few months released from the daily pressure of law and business in London.[63]

He did not judge the social evils of his time by the traditional teaching of the medieval Church. In the imaginary island which he created to be a contrast with Tudor England there were no guilds of tradesmen or merchants any more than there were orders of knighthood, although such groups had been among the medieval Church's chief instruments in regulating society. Only the monarchy and the family were left standing (but the prince could be deposed for tyranny). Most of the inhabitants of the island were not even Christians. What regulated Utopia was reason – specially the reasoning that 'there is a certain godly power unknown, everlasting, incomprehensible, inexplicable, far above the capacity and reach of man's wit'. In Utopia this led to practices, such as euthanasia and divorce, of which More no doubt disapproved as a good Catholic; whether as a Catholic he would have felt obliged to condemn the strict family planning practised in Utopia is more difficult to say. But his serious purpose, amid a certain amount of not always serious provocation, was to stimulate Christians into thinking out what was reasonable, not what was traditional, for Christendom. And when he appealed to 'reason' More had in mind the Sermon on the Mount, not the cynicism of power politics as expounded in Italy by his contemporary, Niccòlo Machiavelli.

More did not keep the ideals expressed or implied in *Utopia* untarnished. As Speaker of the House of Commons in Wolsey's Parliament of 1523 he found himself pleading for taxes. His treatment of heretics while chancellor did not completely accord with the Utopians' hatred of violence in religious disputes – although even in Utopia there was no toleration for those who denied the existence of God or the immortality of the soul, while the punishment for a moral offence such as

---

[63] See R. Ames, *Citizen Thomas More and His Utopia* (Princeton, N.J., 1949), and J. H. Hexter, *The Vision of Politics on the Eve of the Reformation* (London, 1973).

adultery was first enslavement (there were many slaves) and, after a second offence, death. But during his imprisonment in the Tower of London he wrote short books, letters and prayers; and in them compromise was forgotten and the violence of the polemical style he had used against the Protestants dropped away.

He wrote a *Dialogue of Comfort against Tribulation*, again diplomatically distancing the scene from England; this time two Hungarian Christians were strengthening themselves from the Bible against 'the terror of shameful and painful death' at the hands of the Turks. He wrote in Latin an exposition of Christ's passion in the medieval style, halted when his writing materials were taken away from him. He then wrote letters to his family with charcoal from his fire: letters as tender and as noble as can be found in the literature of true heroism. By constant meditation on Christ's agony in Gethsemane and sufferings on Calvary, he made his soul ready for the end which was (he said several times) the entry into being 'merry in heaven'. He was, as he knew, now in a realm purer than religious controversy. When a group of rich clergymen had offered him a large sum after his resignation as chancellor as a reward for his anti-Protestant books, he had refused the money, declaring that people would be better off reading books such as Hilton's *Ladder of Perfection* or the more recent *Imitation of Christ*. But unexpectedly this lawyer and courtier, this friend of Erasmus and author of *Utopia*, was high on the ladder of Christlike perfection while preparing to mount the scaffold as a martyr for that in which he really believed.

More's prison writings, and above all his conduct at his trial and execution, may therefore be said to be the climax of the story of Christian England to the Reformation. And he has been remembered — by those who have revered him as a Catholic martyr; by those who have more highly valued his *Utopia*; by those who have been impressed most by the fact that the head which conceived *Utopia* was placed voluntarily on the executioner's block for the sake of an ideal not in *Utopia*. He was respected as a courageous Christian gentleman even at the height of Protestant patriotism. Three pages almost certainly in Shakespeare's handwriting form part of a sympathetic play, *Sir Thomas More*. As translated into English by Ralph Robinson in 1551, More wrote that the Utopians 'suppose the dead to be present among them when they talk of them, though to the dull and feeble eyesight of mortal men they be invisible. . . . Therefore they go more courageously to their business. . . .'

PART TWO: FURTHER READING
(in addition to the books in the footnotes)

4. Freedom under the King

BARLOW, F., *The English Church, 1066-1154*, London, 1979.

BROOKE, Z. N., *The English Church and the Papacy from the Conquest to the Reign of John*, London, 1968.

CANTOR, N. F., *Church, Kingship and Lay Investiture in England, 1089-1135*, Princeton, N.J., 1958.

DOUGLAS, C., *William the Conqueror*, London, 1964.
The Norman Achievement, 1050-1100, London, 1969.
The Norman Fate, 1100-1154, London, 1976.

LE PATOUREL, J., *The Norman Empire*, Oxford, 1976.

POOLE, A. L., *From Domesday Book to Magna Carta*, Oxford, 1951.

SOUTHERN, R. W., *The Making of the Middle Ages*, London, 1953.

WARREN, W. L., *King John*, London, 1961.

5 The Age of Faith

BATSFORD, H., and FRY, C., *The Cathedrals of England* (architectural), revised, London, 1960.

BOASE, T. S. R., *English Art, 1100-1216*, Oxford, 1953.

BRENTANO, R., *Two Churches: England and Italy in the Thirteenth Century*, Princeton, N.J., 1968.

BROOKE, R. B., *The Coming of the Friars*, London, 1975.

CLAPHAM, A. W., *English Romanesque Architecture after the Conquest*, Oxford, 1934.

COLVIN, H. M., *The White Canons in England*, Oxford, 1951.

COOK, G. H., *Medieval Chantries and Chantry Chapels* (architectural), London, 1947.
The English Cathedral through the Centuries (architectural), London, 1957.

EDWARDS, K., *The English Secular Cathedrals in the Middle Ages* (their life), Manchester, 1949.

GIBBS, M., and LANG, J., *Bishops and Reform, 1215-72*, Oxford, 1935.

HILL, B., *English Cistercian Monasteries and their Patrons in the Twelfth Century*, Urbana, Ill., 1968.

HINNESBUSCH, W. A., *The Early English Friars Preachers*, Rome, 1951.

338 *Further Reading*

MOORMAN, J. R. H., *Church Life in England in the Thirteenth Century*, Cambridge, 1945.
A History of the Franciscan Order, Oxford, 1968.
MORRIS, R., *Cathedrals and Abbeys of England and Wales*, London, 1979.
ROTH, F., *The English Austin Friars*, 2 vols., New York, 1961-66.
SOUTHERN, R. W., *Western Society and the Church in the Middle Ages*, London, 1970.
WOOD, S., *English Monasteries and their Patrons in the Thirteenth Century*, Oxford, 1955.
WOOD-LEGH, K. L., *Perpetual Chantries in Britain*, Cambridge, 1965.

6 *Rebels and Pilgrims*

BENNET, H. S., *Chaucer and the Fifteenth Century*, Oxford, 1947.
BROWN, C. (ed.), *Religious Lyrics of the Fourteenth Century*, revised, Oxford, 1952.
HILTON, R., *Bond Men Made Free: Medieval Peasant Movements and the English Uprising of 1381*, London, 1973.
HUSSEY, S. S., *Chaucer: An Introduction*, London, 1971.
KEEN, M. H., *England in the Later Middle Ages*, London, 1973.
KNOWLES, D., *The English Mystical Tradition*, London 1961.
LAWLOR, J., *Piers Plowman: An Essay in Criticism*, London, 1962.
McFARLANE, K. B., *John Wyclif and the Beginnings of English Nonconformity*, London, 1952.
McKISACK, M., *The Fourteenth Century*, Oxford, 1959.
MATTHEW, G., *The Court of Richard II*, London, 1968.
OWST, G. R., *Literature and Pulpit in Medieval England*, revised, Cambridge, 1961.
PANTIN, W. A., *The English Church in the Fourteenth Century*, Cambridge, 1955.
PEARSALL, D., *Piers Plowman by William Langland*, London, 1979.
SALTER, E., *Piers Plowman: An Introduction*, Oxford, 1969.
SISAM, K. (Ed.), *Fourteenth Century Verse and Prose*, Oxford, 1921.
TRISTRAM, E. W., *English Wall Painting of the Fourteenth Century*, London, 1955.
VASTA, E. (ed.), *Interpretations of Piers Plowman*, Notre Dame, Ind., 1968.
WOOD-LEGH, K. L., *Church Life in England under Edward III*, Cambridge, 1934.
ZIEGLER, P., *The Black Death*, London, 1969.

7 The Sudden Storm

ASTON, M. E., *Thomas Arundel*, Oxford, 1967.

BENNET, H. S., *English Books and Readers, 1475-1557*, Cambridge, 1952.

BLECH, J. W., *Preaching in England in the Late Fifteenth and Six- teenth Centuries*, Oxford, 1964.

CHRIMES, S. B., *Henry VII*, London, 1972.

DU BOULAY, F. R. H., *An Age of Ambition: English Society in the Later Middle Ages*, London, 1970.

ELTON, G. R., *Reform and Reformation: England, 1509-58*, London, 1977.

HAIGH, C., *The Last Days of the Lancashire Monasteries and the Pilgrimage of Grace*, Manchester, 1964.

HOSKINS, W. G., *The Age of Plunder: King Henry's England, 1500-47*, London, 1976.

JACOB, E. F., *The Fifteenth Century*, revised, Oxford, 1969.

MACKIE, J. D., *The Earlier Tudors, 1485-1558*, Oxford, 1952.

McCONICA, J. K., *English Humanists and Reformation Politics*, Oxford, 1965.

PORTER, H. C., *Reformation and Reaction in Tudor Cambridge*, Cambridge, 1958.

ROSS, C., *Edward IV*, London, 1974.

RUPP, E. G., *Studies in the Making of the English Protestant Tra- dition*, Cambridge, 1947.

SMITH, L. B., *Tudor Prelates and Politics*, Princeton, N.J., 1953.

STOREY, R. L., *Diocesan Administration in Fifteenth .Century England*, York, 1959.

General

BETJEMAN, J. (ed.), *Collins Guide to English Parish Churches*, London, 1958.

BLAKE, N. F. (ed.), *Middle English Religious Prose*, London, 1972.

BUTLER, L. H., and WILSON, C. G., *Medieval Monasteries of England*, London, 1979.

DAVIES, R. T. (ed.), *Medieval English Lyrics*, London, 1963.

DICKINSON, J. C., *The Later Middle Ages*, London, 1979.

FINUCARE, R., *Miracles and Pilgrims*, London, 1977.

GRAY, D., *Themes and Images in the Medieval English Religious Lyric*, London, 1972.

HARRISON, F. L., *Music in Medieval Britain*, London, 1958.

KNOWLES, D., *The Religious Orders in England*, 3 vols., Cambridge, 1948-59.

LAURENCE, C. H. (ed.), *The English Church and the Papacy in the Middle Ages*, London, 1965.

MYERS, A. R. (ed.), *English Historical Documents, 1327-1485*, London, 1969.

ORME, N., *English Schools in the Middle Ages*, London, 1973.

POSTAN, M. M., *The Medieval Economy and Society*, London, 1972.

REYNOLDS, S., *English Medieval Towns*, Oxford, 1977.

RICKERT, M., *Painting in Britain: The Middle Ages*, London, 1964.

RODES, R. E., *Ecclesiastical Administration in Medieval England*, Notre Dame, Ind., 1977.

STONE, B., *Medieval English Verse* (translated in Penguin Classics), London, 1971.

SUMPTION, J., *Pilgrimage: An Image of Medieval Religion*, London, 1974.

ULLMANN, W., *A Short History of the Papacy in the Middle Ages*, revised, London, 1974.

WEBB, G., *Architecture in Britain: The Middle Ages*, London, 1956.

WOODFORDE, C., *English Stained and Painted Glass*, Oxford, 1954.

WOOLF, R., *The English Religious Lyric in the Middle Ages*, Oxford, 1968.

The English Mystery Plays, London, 1972.

Outline of Events

937	King Athelstan's victory at Brunanburh
937	King Edgar's coronation at Bath by St Dunstan
1012	Martyrdom of St Alphege
1014	Wulfstan's sermon in York
1035	Death of King Cnut
1065	Death of St Edward the Confessor
1066	William the Conqueror's victory near Hastings
1070	Lanfranc Archbishop of Canterbury
1093	St Anselm Archbishop of Canterbury; Durham Cathedral begun
1147	St Ailred Abbot of Rievaulx
1170	Martyrdom of Archbishop (St) Thomas Becket
1174	Fire leads to rebuilding of Canterbury Cathedral
1186	St Hugh of Avalon Bishop of Lincoln
1214	Oxford University chartered
1215	*Magna Carta*; Lateran Council's reforms
1220	Salisbury Cathedral begun
1221	Dominicans reach England
1224	Franciscans reach England
1235	Robert Grosseteste Bishop of Lincoln
c. 1240	West front of Wells Cathedral
c. 1260	Five Sisters window in York Minster
1269	Westminster Abbey rebuilt by Henry III
c. 1280	Angel Choir of Lincoln Cathedral
1292	Death of Roger Bacon
1327	Death of Edward II leads to Perpendicular choir at Gloucester
1343	Richard Rolle completes *The Fire of Love*
1348	Black Death reaches England
1351	Statute of *Provisors*, followed by *Praemunire*
1363	William of Wykeham Edward III's chief minister
1373	'Showings' to Dame Julian of Norwich
c. 1375	*Gawain* poet at work
1377	Coronation of Richard II
1381	Peasants' Revolt
1384	Death of John Wyclif
1386	Geoffrey Chaucer begins *Canterbury Tales*
c. 1390	William Langland completes *Piers Plowman*
1401	Statute for burning Lollards

1415 Henry V's victory at Agincourt
1441 Henry VI founds King's College, Cambridge
1461 Death of Bishop Reginald Pecock
1483 Edward IV buried in St George's Chapel, Windsor
1485 Henry VII's victory at Bosworth; Caxton's edition
        of Malory
1514 Thomas Wolsey Henry VIII's chief minister
1525 William Tyndale's New Testament in English
1531 Martyrdom of Thomas Bilney
1533 Thomas Cranmer Archbishop of Canterbury
1534 Henry VIII legally Supreme Head of Church
1535 Martyrdom of Sir (St) Thomas More
1536 Suppression of monasteries begins
1537 Matthew's Bible in English authorized
1540 Execution of Thomas Cromwell

INDEX